The Science of Making Friends

Helping Socially Challenged Teens and Young Adults

Elizabeth A. Laugeson, PsyD

Foreword by John Elder Robison

JB JOSSEY-BASS™

A Wiley Brand

Cover design by JPuda
Cover image: © Laurence Mouton/Getty

Published by Jossey-Bass
A Wiley Brand
One Montgomery Street, Suite 1200, San Francisco, CA 94104-4594—www.josseybass.com

Jossey-Bass books and products are available through most bookstores. To contact Jossey-Bass directly call our Customer Care Department within the U.S. at 800-956-7739, outside the U.S. at 317-572-3986, or fax 317-572-4002.

Wiley publishes in a variety of print and electronic formats and by print-on-demand. Some material included with standard print versions of this book may not be included in e-books or in print-on-demand. If this book refers to media such as a CD or DVD that is not included in the version you purchased, you may download this material at http://booksupport.wiley.com. For more information about Wiley products, visit www.wiley.com.

Library of Congress Cataloging-in-Publication Data has been applied for.

ISBN (paperback): 978-1-118-12721-6
ISBN (ebk): 978-1-118-41895-6
ISBN (ebk): 978-1-118-41650-1

Printed in the United States of America

FIRST EDITION
PB Printing   10 9 8 7

CONTENTS

PART THREE

THE SCIENCE OF HANDLING PEER CONFLICT
AND REJECTION: HELPFUL STRATEGIES

DVD CONTENTS

The DVD features video demonstrations of many of the rules and skills covered in the book. Throughout the book you'll find references to videos marked with a "play" icon ▶ (shown to the right). These videos are also available at www.wiley.com/go/makingfriends. The password is the last five digits of this book's ISBN, which are 27216.

*This book is dedicated to all of the parents who
work tirelessly to support their children*

FOREWORD

ARE YOU A PARENT OF A CHILD on the autism spectrum, or do you have a kid with ADHD, anxiety, or depression? Does your child struggle to make and keep friends? You've come to the right place. This book—*The Science of Making Friends*—describes one of the first evidence-based systems for helping teens and young adults achieve that all-important goal.

The words *evidence based* are very important. They mean that the creators of the therapy have tested it against other therapies and verified that it is effective and delivers lasting benefits. In the world of therapy, evidence-based practices are the gold standard. An evidence-based therapy for making friends is the mental health equivalent of a drug that's shown to be effective. It's the best therapy we know how to deliver.

As a person who grew up with undiagnosed autism, I know how important social skills are for people who are neurologically different. I know firsthand the pain of loneliness and the sense of failure unwanted social isolation brings. The sting of childhood rejection followed me long into adulthood, and I'd do anything to save today's kids some of what I went through.

As a parent of a young adult with autism, I also know how powerful the effect of parental coaching can be. Like me, my son is on the autism spectrum but with recognition of his challenges and social skills coaching he grew up to be far less isolated and more socially successful than I did.

When I raised my son—as I describe in my memoir *Raising Cubby*—I flew by the seat of my pants. I watched him struggle and fail, pondered his actions, and gave the best advice I could based on my limited life experience. That's all most people could hope to do, until now.

Dr. Liz Laugeson has devoted her career to studying the behaviors that lead to social failure and finding ways to teach alternate ways of acting. Most important, she has kept records of her work, and she's learned what works and what doesn't.

She leads a team of researchers and therapists at UCLA's Semel Institute, where they have developed and proven the benefit of an intervention known as PEERS, which stands for Program for the Education and Enrichment of Relational Skills. It's one of the first programs of its kind and the first to be backed by solid evidence of its effectiveness.

The PEERS program was originally designed to be delivered by two therapists. One would meet with the kids, the other with the parents. Right now, Dr. Laugeson and her staff are training teams to do PEERS all over the world, but there are still many families in need who are not near a trained PEERS team, hence, this book.

In it, you will find all the core concepts of PEERS with advice on how to work through the elements with your teen or young adult. If you're like me, you may even find the lessons of PEERS relevant in your own life or those of your partner.

If you follow the guidelines, I guarantee you will see greater social success. And that is one of the best predictors of happiness and good life outcome. I can't stress strongly enough what it's meant to me.

John Elder Robison
Author, *Look Me in the Eye: My Life with Asperger's,*
Be Different, and *Raising Cubby*
Member, Interagency Autism Coordinating Committee,
US Department of Health and Human Services

PREFACE

THIS BOOK IS THE CULMINATION of years of research in social skills training for teens and young adults with social challenges conducted at the UCLA PEERS Clinic. Many of our clients come to our clinic with a diagnosis of autism spectrum disorder (ASD). Others have been diagnosed with attention-deficit/hyperactivity disorder (ADHD), depression, anxiety, or any other number of disorders that cause social difficulties. Some have no diagnosis at all but struggle with knowing how to make and keep friends. All find themselves at sea socially and need a little help navigating their way. The strategies presented in the following chapters are based on a decade of research in the skills necessary to make and keep friends. The UCLA PEERS Clinic has helped hundreds of teens find and keep friends and become socially adept at doing so. The PEERS model is unique from other programs in that it involves parents in the curriculum and is the only existing research-based model of its kind for teaching friendship skills to teens and young adults.

Through rigorous scientific investigation, we have identified the essential elements needed for developing and maintaining meaningful relationships and have organized these essential social behaviors into easy-to-understand concrete rules and steps. We have broken down complex social behaviors to make them simple for any teen or young adult to follow. Yet we have also taken into consideration the special needs of some of the young people we work with. Those with ASD and ADHD, for example, sometimes have required that steps be smaller, more digestible, and methodical. We also know, for example, that some individuals on the autism spectrum have a tendency to think in concrete and literal ways. The use of figurative language such as metaphors and analogies is often lost on them. Likewise, abstract thinking about social behaviors may be equally confusing. Rather than trying to remedy this deficit by attempting to teach teens and young adults with ASD how to think like typically developing people, we embrace their unique thinking style and use it to create a program that can help a vast array of people with social skills challenges. We are particularly indebted to the teens and young adults with ASD whom we've encountered; thinking about their needs and unique perspectives provided the program with an elegant solution to teaching social skills challenges—breaking down complex social behaviors into rules and steps. The result is a researched-based model for teaching social skills to teens and young adults.

In the following pages you will see how we take what appear to be abstract social behaviors, such as starting or entering conversations, and break those behaviors down into their smaller, individual parts. By reducing complex social behavior into smaller, more manageable segments, we're able to decode the social world for individuals who have social challenges, making it more likely that they will be able to successfully navigate this world and thereby develop more meaningful relationships.

DOWNLOAD THE APP!
The FriendMaker app (available for iPhone and iPad) helps teens and young adults navigate social situations, practicing the skills taught in this book in real time. To download the app, open iTunes on your computer or the App Store on your device and search for **FriendMaker**. You can download from there.

ACKNOWLEDGMENTS

SOMEONE ONCE SAID *mentors are everyday heroes.* To my mentor, Andrew Leuchter, I would like thank you for being *my* hero. This work would not have been possible if it were not for your mentorship, and without your support and guidance, this book would never have been written and the research on which it is founded would never have been conducted. Thank you for being my hero and the kind of person I aspire to be.

This work would also not have been possible without the love and support of my family and friends. To my husband, Lance Orozco, I am forever indebted. You are my greatest source of support, my biggest fan, and the kindest and most thoughtful person I know. To my mother, Janet Tate, I am forever your student. You have taught me by example what it is to be a strong woman, and I carry your voice with me always. To my colleagues, Fred Frankel, Mary O'Connor, and Blair Paley, I am forever grateful. You have shown me the world of social skills research and have transformed my life in the most meaningful way. To my dear friends, Jennifer Wilkerson, Carrie Raia, and Dan Oakley, I am forever your friend. You have taught me what true friendship means, and I am a better person for knowing each of you.

No list of gratitude would be complete without acknowledging the incredible contributions of my wonderful team. The work on which this book is founded is a collaborative effort on the part of two dedicated and talented labs. To my amazing research and clinical teams at UCLA (Team PEERS) and The Help Group (Team Alliance), I would like to thank you for your tireless efforts and unparalleled dedication. Most especially to

Shannon Bates, Lara Tucci, Ruth Ellingsen, Yasamine Bolourian, Jessica Hopkins, Jennifer Sanderson, and Ashley Dillon—I am eternally grateful for your commitment and enthusiasm to our work and the warmth and compassion you show to our families.

To my amazing team of actors—Yasamine Bolourian, Mary Goodarzi, Lara Tucci, Alex Friedman, and Ben Schwartzman, who moonlight as autism researchers when they are not conducting fabulous role-play demonstrations of social skills—I commend you on your wonderful acting abilities in the accompanying DVD and thank you for your willingness to embarrass yourselves a little in the interest of social skills!

To my friends and colleagues at UCLA and The Help Group, I thank you for your endless support and encouragement of this work. Most especially to Barbara Firestone, Peter Whybrow, Jim McCracken, and Philip Levin for their loyal and steadfast support of our research efforts. To my dear friends and colleagues Vicky Goodman and Sally Weil at The Friends of the Semel Institute, Vera and Dana Guerin with the Shapell and Guerin Family Foundation, and the Organization for Autism Research—I thank you for making possible the research on which this book is founded.

To my talented editorial team—Margie McAneny, Pat Stacey, and Tracy Gallagher—I thank you for your patience and persistence in helping me find my voice. To Melissa Wasserman, Lyndsay Brooks, Meagan Cronin, Rohini Bagrodia, and Jason Tinero—who masquerade as graduate students when they're not busy copyediting—thank you for helping me dot my i's and cross my t's.

Finally, to the inspirational families we have had the great privilege of working with, thank you for guiding this work and reminding us what is important in life. You never cease to amaze me, supply me with endless amounts of laughter, and inspire me to always do better and work harder. Thank you for touching my heart and making this work more meaningful than I could ever have imagined.

ABOUT THE AUTHOR

Elizabeth A. Laugeson, PsyD, is a licensed clinical psychologist and an assistant clinical professor in the Department of Psychiatry and Biobehavioral Sciences at the UCLA Semel Institute for Neuroscience and Human Behavior. Laugeson is the founder and director of the UCLA PEERS Clinic, which is an outpatient hospital-based program providing parent-assisted social skills training for youth with autism spectrum disorder (ASD), attention-deficit/hyperactivity disorder (ADHD), depression, anxiety, and other social impairments. She is also the director of The Help Group—UCLA Autism Research Alliance, which is a collaborative research initiative dedicated to developing and expanding applied clinical research in the treatment of children and adolescents with ASD.

Laugeson has been a principal investigator and collaborator on a number of research studies investigating social skills training for youth from preschool to early adulthood and is the co-developer of an evidence-based, parent-assisted manual on social skills intervention for teens and young adults known as the Program for the Education and Enrichment of Relational Skills (PEERS®), which has been translated and disseminated in over a dozen countries to date.

Laugeson received her doctorate in psychology from Pepperdine University in 2004 and completed a predoctoral psychology internship and a postdoctoral research fellowship at UCLA in 2004 and 2007, respectively. She has presented her research at conferences throughout the world, and her work has been featured on national and international media outlets such as *People Magazine, Los Angeles Times, New York*

Times, Washington Post, USA Today, CBS, NBC, and Channel 4 in the United Kingdom.

In this book, Laugeson shares her research-supported strategies for helping adolescents and young adults with social challenges learn to make and keep friends.

The Science of Making Friends

PART

1

Getting Ready

1

Why Teach Social Skills to Teens and Young Adults?

HAVE YOU EVER HEARD OF SOCIAL SKILLS described as an art form? Some would say there's an art to being social and making friends—an innate quality that you're either born with or you're not. Take conversational skills for example. Sometimes referred to as the *gift of gab,* many believe you're either good at making small talk or you're not. Although it may be true that some have a natural knack for the conversational arts, it's not necessarily true that all social skills are hardwired or fixed. What if conversational skills, and more broadly social skills, were not an art but a science?

Our research in social skills training for teens and young adults with social difficulties is based on this premise. We believe that social skills can be taught, much in the way we might teach math or science. By breaking down complex, seemingly sophisticated social skills into concrete rules and steps of social behavior, we can demystify and to some extent decode the "art form" that is social skills.

Purpose of This Book

This book will give parents a step-by-step guide for helping teens and young adults struggling with social skills learn how to make and keep friends. The strategies outlined were developed at the University of California, Los Angeles (UCLA) PEERS (Program for the Education and Enrichment of Relational Skills) Clinic, our hospital-based program that provides parent-assisted social skills training for young people with autism spectrum disorder (ASD), attention-deficit/hyperactivity disorder (ADHD), depression, anxiety, and other social impairments. Although the skills we've developed were largely created through our work with teens and young adults with ASD, the tips and strategies can be used by anyone.

> *This book will give parents a step-by-step guide for helping teens and young adults struggling with social skills learn how to make and keep friends.*

Through the use of concrete rules and steps of social behavior, you will become knowledgeable in the skills necessary to help your child develop and maintain friendships, expand social opportunities, and handle peer conflict and rejection.

Rules and Steps of Social Behavior

Many of the teens and young adults whom we work with at the UCLA PEERS Clinic, particularly those diagnosed with ASD, are fond of rules. In fact, what often happens when you break a rule in front of your child? If your child is like others in our program, he or she probably notices rule violations and may even feel compelled to point them out. We call this social error *policing*. Although we don't advocate the tendency to point out rule violations or police others, we do recognize that teens and young adults with social challenges often have a penchant for rules and may be likely to follow them. Consequently, we've developed a program that teaches social skills using concrete rules and steps of social behavior. The vast majority of the teens and young adults we've worked with appreciate our use of rules and steps of social behavior because it clears away the gray fog of the social world, making social behavior more black and white and easier to see. You might consider how your own child responds to rules and think about how he or she will react to this approach.

To better understand the importance of rules and steps in teaching social skills, consider for a moment why people with social challenges, such as those who have ASD and other syndromes, are fond of rules. One reason is that rules are *predictable*. For example, we've noted that a lot of the socially challenged clients we see at the UCLA PEERS Clinic have strong inclination toward math, science, engineering, or computer technology, particularly those who come to us diagnosed with ASD. Perhaps these preferences relate to *predictability*. Numbers, algorithms, and formulas are predictable; you know what to expect. But in the social world, where human emotion, response, and humor exist, behaviors are not so predictable; you don't always know what to expect. Decoding social behaviors into concrete rules and steps will help to demystify the social world for those with social difficulties, neurological issues, and sensitivities that often accompany ASD or other conditions or emotional patterns. This is what makes the PEERS approach and this book unique.

> *Decoding social behaviors into concrete rules and steps will help to demystify the social world.*

Ecologically Valid Social Skills

Another aspect of the PEERS approach that is unique compared to other models is our use of ecologically valid social skills. Although the term *ecologically valid* sounds quite technical and scientific, what it essentially means is that we're teaching social behaviors that are naturally used by teens and young adults who are socially successful. In other words, we're not teaching what we think young people *should* do in social situations but what actually *works* in reality. Although well intentioned, parents and professionals sometimes make the mistake of trying to teach social skills to teens and young adults by offering advice about what we think young people should do in certain social situations but, as you will soon discover, the problem with this approach is that the advice given is often wrong. The goal of this book is to help you avoid those common pitfalls of giving misinformed advice and equip you with ecologically valid rules and steps of social behavior that will allow you to help your child make and keep friends through the use of acceptable real-world social skills discovered through science.

Evidence-Based Approach

What also makes this book different from typical how-to guides about social skills is that the skills offered here reflect behaviors that research has shown to be effective. This is why we call the book *The Science of Making Friends*. Through rigorous scientific study, we have uncovered the tools needed to teach critical friendship skills to teens and young adults with social challenges. Not only are the strategies contained in this book based on ecologically valid social skills but the method described here has also been shown to be effective through scientific investigation. Our research through the UCLA PEERS Clinic, in conjunction with other PEERS research programs throughout the world, has demonstrated improvement in friendships and overall social skills for teens and young adults with social challenges through multiple clinical trials, making the PEERS method the only evidence-based social skills program of its kind.

Scientific Evidence for the UCLA PEERS Model

Our research with PEERS, conducted at the UCLA Semel Institute for Neuroscience and Human Behavior, has primarily focused on teens and young adults with ASD, although the benefit of the program has also been examined for teens with ADHD, fetal alcohol spectrum disorders (FASD), as well as teens and adults with intellectual disabilities. Because social problems are a hallmark feature of ASD, we base many of our rules of social behavior on the common social errors exhibited by those with ASD, in combination with the appropriate social behaviors used by socially successful teens and adults.

Findings from our research conducted in the community and school settings primarily come from parents, teachers, and youth, using standardized measures of social functioning. Improvements in social functioning following PEERS typically include the following:

- Improved overall social skills in
  - Cooperation
  - Assertion
  - Responsibility
- Decreased problematic social behaviors in
  - Self-control
  - Externalizing behavior
- Improved social responsiveness in
  - Social communication
  - Social awareness
  - Social motivation
  - Social cognition
  - Decreased autistic symptoms
- Decreased social anxiety
- Increased frequency of peer interactions and get-togethers
- Decreased loneliness
- Improved empathy
- Improved friendship quality
- Improved knowledge of adolescent or young adult social skills

Unlike most social skills interventions cited in the research literature, our research team has conducted extensive follow-up research and investigated the sustainability of these improvements over time to make sure that what we're teaching is continuing to work for those going through our program. A long-term, follow-up study conducted with families one to five years after receiving the PEERS treatment revealed that improvements in social skills, social responsiveness, frequency of peer interactions, and social skills knowledge were maintained over time and in some cases improved even further. These findings are very encouraging when you consider that the social trajectory for many young people with social

> *A long-term follow-up study conducted with families one to five years after receiving the PEERS treatment revealed that improvements were maintained over time and in some cases improved even further.*

challenges such as those diagnosed with ASD sadly tends to worsen with age and entering adulthood.

It's probably worthy of note that the previously mentioned studies not only comprise the largest number of participants reported in the social skills treatment literature for older adolescents and young adults with ASD, but the improvements are also far greater than what is typically reported in the autism research literature. Most social skills treatment studies for young people with ASD tend to show minimal or modest improvements, often with a very small group of people, and with improvements rarely sustained or reported over time. Conversely, our research using the PEERS model has shown much greater improvements in social skills among larger groups of people, with improvements generally maintained over time and improved even further in some cases.

Although the exact cause of these improvements cannot be pinpointed with a perfect degree of certainty, we believe that the true power of the PEERS model can be attributed to the high degree of involvement of parents and teachers in the treatment. Our belief is that by teaching parents and teachers to be social coaches to teens and young adults with social difficulties, we're far more likely to generalize good social skills to multiple settings including home, school, and the community. Furthermore, these improvements are more likely to be maintained over time, as our research suggests, because involving parents and teachers as social coaches ensures that treatment never ends.

Reason to Use the PEERS Method

Teens and adults with social difficulties, such as those with ASD, ADHD, or other challenges, frequently struggle with friendships. They're often isolated and withdrawn, perhaps choosing not to socialize with others, or if they do wish to socialize, they may be rejected by their peers. To make matters worse, isolation and rejection may lead to other mental health problems such as depression or anxiety. Not surprisingly, parents are often desperate to help their children improve their social skills, yet may struggle with knowing what advice and support to give.

Although many programs exist to assist younger children in improving their social skills, very few programs target older adolescents and young adults with social challenges. Among the few programs that do exist, the vast majority do not have scientific evidence to support their claims of improving social skills, nor do they provide parent assistance. To date, the only known research-supported social skills program available for teens and young adults with ASD and other social challenges is PEERS.

PEERS is the research platform on which the rules and steps of social behavior will be described and taught in this book. Typically facilitated by mental health professionals and educators, PEERS is widely available as a treatment manual, with PEERS treatment groups offered in community mental health agencies, clinics, hospitals, and schools throughout the world. The training is typically provided in a group or classroom setting, where parents and teens or young adults attend separate co-occurring group sessions with the goal of teaching friendship skills using parent-supported social coaching.

> *PEERS is the research platform on which the rules and steps of social behavior will be described and taught in this book.*

Although PEERS has been widely disseminated through published treatment manuals, professional training seminars, and the development of countless programs in the international community, the reality is that access to this scientifically supported treatment is not available to all families, nor was the manual written specifically for families. That's the reason for this book: to provide information about the skills taught in PEERS for families.

Tips for Parents: How to Use This Book

This book is organized into three main parts. Part 1 includes the current introduction you are reading, which is intended to give you an overview of our approach and the scientific rationale on which this book is based. Part 2 includes strategies for developing and maintaining relationships. This part includes information about how to find good friends; how to have good conversations; how to start, enter, and exit conversations; how to use electronic communication appropriately; how to be a good sport; and how to have successful get-togethers with friends. Part 3 includes strategies for handling peer conflict and rejection. This part includes information about how to handle arguments, verbal teasing, cyber bullying, rumors and gossip, physical bullying, and how to change a bad reputation. An epilogue also includes general conclusions and thoughts about moving forward.

Within parts 2 and 3, each chapter outlines a different ecologically valid social skill, presented using concrete rules and steps of social behavior. Chapters are broken down into separate sections as described in the following.

Narrative Lessons for Parents

The first section of each chapter contains a narrative lesson for parents. This section outlines critical skills needed for your teen or young adult to make and keep friends. You will notice that the parent narrative sections are longer or more detailed than other sections because we expect parents to act as social coaches to teens and young adults as part of this approach. In our clinical experience, being a social coach requires a great deal of information on your part so these sections will naturally be longer. Each relevant chapter will also offer advice on how to provide social coaching to your teen or young adult using the material outlined in this book. Although the narrative lessons were written for parents, interested teens and young adults are also welcome to read this section, too.

Success Stories

At the end of each parent section, you will find a brief success story relating to the skills taught in that chapter. These inspirational stories highlight the experiences of families who've gone through PEERS, often in their own words. Although these stories and the people they chronicle are real, we have changed the names and identifying information of these families to protect their anonymity—although all have given their permission for us to tell their unique stories.

Chapter Summaries for Teens and Young Adults

The next section, which can be easily located by its shaded box, includes a chapter summary for teens and young adults. This section is intended to be read by your teen or young adult, although you should also have a look. Chapter summaries are meant to help you convey the information contained in this book without having to lecture to your child. Some teens and young adults will find it off-putting to have their parents explain the material directly to them. In that case, he or she should feel free to read the chapter summaries independently from you, leaving room for discussion later. Although the chapter summaries provide an overview of the narrative lessons, using more kid-friendly language, this section also includes social vignettes and transcripts from DVD demonstrations that you will need to be familiar with when discussing the skills with your teen or young adult. So don't skip over this section without giving it a look.

DVD Demonstrations and Social Vignettes

As a companion to this book, you have a DVD of role-play demonstrations of appropriate and inappropriate social behavior. If your child is at all like our teens and young adults who attend the UCLA PEERS Clinic, he or she may benefit greatly from seeing video models of behaviors that work or don't work with their peers. Similarly he or she may be unwittingly turning off other people merely because of a few quirky habits or gestures. Through our research with PEERS, we have learned that showing teen and young adult models of some of the more common appropriate and inappropriate social behaviors has helped many to become more socially polished, accelerating their progress in learning to be more effective listeners and friends. Video demonstrations are intended to be shared with interested members of your family, most importantly with your teen or young adult. Transcripts of these DVD demonstrations can be found in the chapter summaries for teens and young adults in the social vignette section. When DVD demonstrations are unavailable, alternative social stories are provided in the social vignette section.

Perspective-Taking Questions

DVD demonstrations and social vignettes are intended to be viewed or read in conjunction with corresponding perspective-taking questions, located immediately after each social vignette section in the chapter summaries for teens and young adults. Perspective-taking questions are also presented on the DVD following each video demonstration. These questions will help you facilitate a discussion with your teen or young adult about appropriate and inappropriate social behavior and also assist your child with reading social cues and putting him- or herself in someone else's shoes.

Chapter Exercises for Teens and Young Adults

Each chapter includes chapter exercises for teens and young adults to promote use of these skills in more natural settings. Like all teen and young adult content, this section can be easily located by its shaded box. Chapter exercises are intended to be completed by you and your teen or young adult with the relevant amount of coaching provided by you. You will want to carefully read this section in order to help encourage the practice of these skills in the real world. In our clinical experience, if your teen or young adult doesn't practice these skills, the program and your efforts will be less effective.

Mobile Application for Smartphones

In addition to the material presented in this book and companion DVD, you and your teen or young adult may also want to access the mobile application for smartphones developed to accompany this book. The FriendMaker mobile app is intended to act as a virtual coach in the absence of live social coaching. The mobile app includes a summary of strategies from relevant social skills highlighted in this book, along with embedded video demonstrations of appropriate and inappropriate social behavior and perspective-taking discussions. We have found that many teens and young adults prefer this method of virtual social coaching in real-life social settings because it's less conspicuous and more natural than live social coaching. Suggestions for incorporating the use of the FriendMaker mobile app in everyday practice of the skills provided in this book are offered in the chapter exercises for teens and young adults when relevant.

Social Coaching Tip: Although you will have many tools at your disposal as part of this model, reading this book alone will not be the magic ingredient to helping your child. Assuming your teen or young adult is motivated to learn the skills we have to offer, in order to receive the full benefit of this book, your role will be to do the following with your child:

- Share the rules and steps summarized in the chapter summaries for teens and young adults located in the shaded boxes of this book.
- Read the social vignettes and watch the DVD demonstrations of appropriate and inappropriate social behavior with your teen or young adult.
- Discuss the social vignettes and DVD demonstrations with your teen or young adult using the perspective-taking questions.
- Encourage your teen or young adult to practice these skills through the completion of chapter exercises located in the shaded boxes of this book.
- Provide social coaching about the rules and steps of social behavior during chapter exercises and teachable moments.
- Assist your teen or young adult in finding a source of friends as described in chapter 2.

Social Coaching Tip: Although you may be excited to get started, it's possible that you may find your teen or young adult is unwilling to learn more about these skills or practice what we're offering. Although it may be tempting to try to force this information on your child, knowing that these skills may be just what he or she needs, the sad truth is that if your teen or young adult doesn't want to learn or practice these skills, they aren't likely to work. Although it's naturally frustrating and even heartbreaking to want to help your child but be met with resistance, you may still want to familiarize yourself with the skills provided in this book, saving the tools for a rainy day when they might be of use. The reality is that most parents provide social coaching to their kids, often on a daily basis, whether their child wants it or not. So even if your teen or young adult claims to be disinterested, familiarizing yourself with rules and steps of social behavior identified in this book may still provide you with a powerful tool to help your child.

> *Even if your teen or young adult claims to be disinterested, familiarizing yourself with rules and steps of social behavior identified in this book may still provide you with a powerful tool to help your child when he or she least expects it.*

Importance of Social Motivation

Before we begin to explore how to help your teen or young adult develop the critical skills needed for making and keeping friends, we need to consider the level of social motivation of your child. It's important that we be honest and acknowledge that there are some people who actually choose to be left alone. Perhaps your child is one of them. Although some who choose to isolate actually do want to learn to make and keep friends, others may be satisfied with their lives and don't really see the benefits of friendship. These teens and adults may be very self-directed and self-oriented and appear to be happy on their own. Yet parents of these teens and adults are often at their wits' end worrying that their child will never marry, never find a suitable job in the workforce, and never enjoy all of the breadth that a healthy social life offers. They long for their child to branch out and get involved with their peers, but their kids insist they don't want to.

At the UCLA PEERS Clinic, where we run our social skills groups, we see many families facing this challenge: parents who want their child to be more socially adept and engaged and teens and young adults who are perfectly content with their current social situation. As clinicians, it's our job to determine who will benefit from treatment in our program and also who will not. One of the deciding factors determining who is included in our social skills groups is based on social motivation. If a teen or young adult says that he or she is content being socially isolated, having no friends or social contact outside of family, yet expresses an interest in learning and practicing the skills we offer in PEERS, then we have room to work. However, if the teen or young adult isn't interested in learning or practicing the skills we offer, then our efforts will be useless. When considering whether your child will benefit from the skills in this book, you'll need to think about whether he or she actually wants to have friends. By familiarizing yourself with the skills suggested here and providing good social coaching to your child during teachable moments, even if your child seems uninterested in these skills, there is still hope for helping your son or daughter, perhaps when he or she least expects it.

> *When considering whether your child will benefit from the skills in this book, you'll need to think about whether he or she actually wants to have friends.*

For many young people struggling with social challenges, it's not so much an issue of not *wanting* to have friends but not *knowing how* to have friends. This book is focused on the how-to of making and keeping friends. For socially motivated teens and young adults, the skills described here will help many to begin to venture forth into the world of friendship, even the die-hard loners.

Introducing This Book to Teens and Young Adults

Read the following shaded section with your child to provide him or her with an overview of this book. If after reading this section, your teen or young adult wishes to read more, have him or her proceed to the other shaded sections of this book, including chapter summaries and chapter exercises, and make yourself available for discussion. For those parents of teens and young adults uninterested in reading more, feel free to read on yourself. Remember that you're likely the most important social coach in your child's life and any additional knowledge you gain will only benefit the social life of your son or daughter.

PURPOSE OF THIS BOOK
Chapter Summary for Teens and Young Adults

> The following information is intended to be read by teens and young adults with their parents in order to understand the purpose of this book.

Through our work at the UCLA PEERS Clinic, we help teens and young adults make and enjoy lasting friendships. Doing this work is more rewarding than we could ever have imagined because we understand how important it is to have friends. We, too, make friends and work hard to maintain healthy relationships, so we're hoping that you'll let us join you on a journey to having more fun and lasting friendships. If your goal is to make and maintain meaningful relationships or you simply

(continued)

have an interest in learning more about how friendships develop, then you're in the right place.

So how does this work? We call this book *The Science of Making Friends.* We chose the word *science* for a reason. What makes this book unique from other books about friendships is that the tips and strategies we offer come directly from scientific research about what works and what doesn't work in social situations. We call the strategies we teach *ecologically valid,* which is a fancy way of saying that they work in the real world. They work because they're actually used by socially successful teens and young adults in real-life situations. What might surprise you is that the strategies you'll be learning may be different from what you've been told to do before. That's because we're not going to be suggesting what some people *think* teens and young adults should do in social situations but what *actually works.* You won't be surprised to hear that adults sometimes recommend doing things to make friends that completely fail, maybe leaving you feeling frustrated or confused. The truth is that adults sometimes give advice with good intentions but may not actually know the right thing to do. We're going to fix this problem by giving you and your parent the right tools you'll need for making and keeping friends, relying on science to make sure we get it right.

To help you practice these new strategies, your parent will be reading additional information on how to be a good social coach to you during real-life practice and to answer any questions you may have about what you're learning. To make it easier to understand what these strategies are supposed to look like, we'll break everything down into concrete rules and steps of what works socially, taking the mystery out of the social world, which we all know can be confusing and frustrating. We've also provided you with a DVD of video demonstrations highlighting many of these rules and steps of what works socially, along with perspective-taking questions that will help you get why these rules apply. Although these video demonstrations are meant to highlight the rules and steps for making and keeping friends, they're also often humorous and fun to watch, like watching a YouTube video or a funny commercial. That was intentional, so enjoy.

In addition to this book and the DVD, you'll also have access to a mobile application for smartphones, outlining the rules and steps of what to do and what not to do in social situations. The FriendMaker mobile app includes quick summaries of the strategies you'll be reading about and embedded video demonstrations from your companion DVD. The mobile app is meant to be used as a virtual coach for you to use in real-world situations when you're looking for a little social coaching or a refresher about the rules and steps of what works socially for teens and young adults.

The strategies that we'll talk about in the DVD and the app include things such as how to find good friends; how to have good conversations and meet new people; how to organize successful get-togethers with friends; and how to handle things like bullying, teasing, and other social problems. We won't make believe that making and keeping friends is easy but we will provide you with exact rules and steps that you can follow to make this process easier. We won't sugarcoat the realities of things like bullying or teasing, and we won't pretend that these harsh realities don't exist. Instead, we'll give you the tools you need to handle these situations more effectively, allowing you to achieve the social success you deserve.

One last point, although this book and the research it's based on focus on individuals with social differences, you don't need to have significant social challenges to benefit from these tools. Fortunately, as you will soon discover, the skills you're about to learn will apply to anyone interested in making and keeping friends!

The Science of Developing and Maintaining Friendships

2

Finding and Choosing Good Friends

SOCIAL FUNCTIONING IS AN AREA of tremendous gratification and often frustration for nearly everyone; it represents an area of constant trial and error. We are all learning to be better friends, better partners, and better people, no matter what our age, challenges, and gifts. Entering the world of others is of course classic fodder for adolescent anguish, even for the most adept social players. In fact, navigating the social world can be so fraught with challenges that studies show nearly one-third of all adolescents struggle with friendships. Although not all of these teens have any particular documented challenges, approximately 30 percent of teens find it difficult to develop and maintain meaningful

Approximately 30 percent of teens find it difficult to develop and maintain meaningful friendships often because of two social phenomena: peer rejection or social neglect.

friendships often because of two social phenomena: peer rejection or social neglect.

Although the majority of teens in middle school or high school are able to develop and maintain meaningful friendships and experience a healthy amount of peer acceptance, research suggests that about a third of teens are not so fortunate. Within that unfortunate third lay a large number of teens struggling with social challenges, shyness, anxiety, behavioral problems, and neurodevelopmental issues, all of which can stand in the way of a robust social life. That means if your teen or young adult is struggling socially, he or she is not alone, sharing social difficulties with the rest of the third of the population. This also means that there is room for improvement—which is what PEERS was designed to address.

Peer Rejection and Social Neglect

Let's look more closely at what kinds of situations your teen or young adult is encountering. It might be useful to consider what your child's true challenges are. If we consider the different categories of peer acceptance during adolescence, as shown in figure 2.1, we see that there are generally four types. The majority of teens, approximately 55 percent, experience what we might call *average acceptance*, meaning that an average number of peers know them and like them. Then there are those teens who are well known and often well liked, also referred to as the *popular kids*, making up about 15 percent of adolescents in middle school and high school. Although not all popular kids are well liked, they are generally accepted by their peers. Finally, there are two major groups of adolescents who struggle with their social lives. Research suggests that approximately 15 percent of teens are *peer rejected*, meaning that they're excluded and possibly even disliked by the larger peer group. The other major group of adolescents struggling with their social world includes those who are *socially neglected*, making up the final 15 percent of the pie. These teens are also set apart from the larger peer group, not because they're intentionally excluded by others but because they rarely even attempt to engage their peers. If you're concerned about your child's ability to make and keep friends, with nearly one-third of young people struggling socially, chances are that your teen or young adult is likely struggling with peer rejection or social neglect.

Figure 2.1. *Categories of Peer Acceptance*

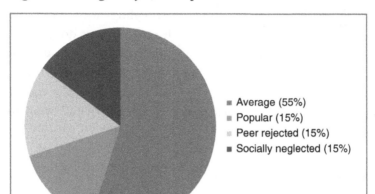

Average (55%)
Popular (15%)
Peer rejected (15%)
Socially neglected (15%)

Peer Rejection

Research suggests that roughly 15 percent of teens fall into the *peer-rejected* category of peer acceptance. When peer rejection is the culprit, the social barrier comes in the form of intentional exclusion from the peer group, which not only occurs in adolescence but may also continue into adulthood. Peer-rejected teens and young adults are those who are actively seeking out their peers and trying to make friends but are actively rejected. Rejection may occur for multiple reasons. Perhaps they appear socially awkward or "weird" as judged by their peers or are considered social outcasts because of their obvious differences. They may be seen as intrusive and interfering during social interactions, possibly barging into conversations or talking about their own interests with little regard for their conversational partner. They may have behavior and emotion regulation problems, their actions appearing impulsive and uninhibited, as if they didn't think before acting. Or they may be hyperverbose, talking incessantly with little notice of the interests of others. Peer-rejected teens and adults also include those who see themselves as class clowns: constantly trying to make jokes, only no one else is laughing. Or if others are laughing, heartbreakingly, they're laughing *at* them, rather than *with* them. Teens and young adults exhibiting these behaviors are often branded with a bad reputation. Yet, although reputations can be branding, they need not be permanent. PEERS has

> *Peer-rejected teens and young adults are those who are actively seeking out their peers and trying to make friends but are actively rejected.*

helped teens and young adults struggling with peer rejection learn to tone it down, pay attention to social cues, and blend in and make room for their peers. The exercises at the end of each chapter in this book were designed to teach your child strategies for minimizing such behaviors.

Social Neglect

The approximately 15 percent of remaining teens struggling socially are called *socially neglected*. For these teens, social impairment comes in the form of withdrawal and social isolation and may persist beyond adolescence and into adulthood. Socially neglected teens and adults are those who tend to fall between the cracks, often unnoticed by their peers and even their teachers or supervisors. Seen as shy or withdrawn, they rarely approach others or speak up during conversations. Often described as timid or introverted, they sometimes even experience depression or anxiety. Because they rarely engage others, unlike those who are peer rejected, those who are socially neglected don't necessarily struggle with a bad rep-

> *Socially neglected teens and adults are those who tend to fall between the cracks, often unnoticed by their peers and even their teachers or supervisors. Seen as shy or withdrawn, they rarely approach others or speak up during conversations.*

utation. In fact, they may not have a reputation at all. They're the forgotten ones, the ones who keep to themselves, don't bother others, and typically go unnoticed. Yet, just like peer-rejected teens and young adults, they struggle to make and keep friends, only the social drama for them happens internally rather than externally.

As a parent and ultimately your child's social coach, it will be helpful to consider where your teen or young adult falls on the social continuum of peer acceptance. Concrete clues for unraveling this mystery will be provided later but be aware that identifying how your teen or young adult is perceived and treated by others will be a critical element to helping him or her find a source of good friends.

Finding a Source of Good Friends

We often mistakenly think that all a person needs to be socially successful are good social skills but another important component of a healthy social life is having a source of good friends. It's not only essential that we have the skills to know how to behave socially, but we must also have access to people with shared mutual interests if we are to be socially successful. If the recipe for social success is measured by the development and maintenance of close and meaningful relationships, then we will need to combine these two critical ingredients.

> It's not only essential that we have the skills to know how to behave socially, but we must also have access to people with shared mutual interests if we are to be socially successful.

Many social skills groups in the community attempt to help kids with social challenges by bringing these kids together in the hopes that friendships will develop in the group. We call these programs *friendship-matching groups*. These programs are essentially like dating services for friends, where kids turn up and parents hope there will be a match or a good fit. The problem with these types of programs is that they're not only failing to teach the critical skills needed for making and keeping friends but they also fail to teach kids how and where to find their own source of friends. This failure will quickly become apparent when the friendship matching group ends and the teen or adult no longer has access to this source of friends.

The first step in PEERS is not finding a friend or matching friends; rather, it has to do with stepping back a bit and observing the social milieu. We do this by becoming aware of the social surroundings in which we exist and seeing what's out there socially. Then we look for an appropriate pool of companions for our teens and young adults.

The Social Landscape of Adolescence and Adulthood

Within every social milieu, at all developmental levels, there are multiple levels of peer affiliations. At the smallest level of peer affiliation is the clique. This typically includes a few close friends, often identified as best friends. At the middle level of peer affiliation is the social group. This may include dozens of peers, all sharing some common interest. These social groups are often identified with a name or label, which defines their common interest. For example, one familiar social group in adolescence and young adulthood includes the jocks, who of course share a common interest in sports. Equally abundant are the gamers, who share a common interest in video games. Research shows that many socially accepted teens and young adults belong to more than one social group, floating naturally between different friendship networks and often finding their best friends from among these social groups. At the largest level of peer affiliation is the larger peer group. This group typically includes teens or young adults around the same age, made up of individuals from different cliques or social groups but who do not necessarily share common interests or socialize with one another. For adolescents, the larger peer group may include the entire student body of a school. For young adults, this may include all the students in their college setting or all the employees at their place of work.

The Importance of Social Groups

Although several levels of peer affiliation are present throughout adolescence and even to some extent in later adulthood, the social group—the middle level that includes dozens of peers with common interests—is never more important than in middle school through early adulthood. It's this middle level of peer affiliation that typically defines the social world of young people, often determining their reputation and defining whom they will become friends with. Yet for adolescents and young adults with social challenges, affiliation with a social group is not necessarily something they've given much thought about. The problem with this oversight is that not identifying with a particular social group makes it difficult to find a source of friends, which leads to diffi-

> *Best friendships and cliques often develop out of social groups, perhaps because friendships are based on common interests and common interests are at the very core of social groups.*

culty developing close and meaningful relationships. Best friendships and cliques often develop out of social groups, perhaps because friendships are based on common interests and common interests are at the very core of social groups.

Consider your past and current friends for a moment. It's likely that you share common interests with these people, which probably determine what you talk about and what you do together as friends. These common interests become integral to close friendships because without them, you would have little to say and little to do. Through our work with families through the UCLA PEERS Clinic, we've seen time and again that successfully identifying a social group is the first step toward building friendships. Yet many teens and adults with social difficulties don't intuitively know to seek out appropriate social groups. Although they often know these groups exist, and they are even able to identify and list dozens of social groups existing in their surroundings, they don't generally know the function of these groups.

So why is affiliation with a social group critical to social success? Social groups are not only essential to helping find a source of friends with similar interests and hobbies but they also provide protection from individual bullying and victimization. Who do bullies like to pick on: people who are by themselves or with a group? You've probably noticed that people who are by themselves, who appear unprotected and without support, are the ones often targeted by bullies. This is because when you're alone, you look like an easy target, with no one there to stick up for you or have your back so to speak. Consequently, teens and young adults with social challenges become easy targets for bullying and peer victimization, partly because they're often isolated and outside of these social groups.

> Social groups are not only essential to helping find a source of friends with similar interests and hobbies but they also provide protection from individual bullying and victimization.

It's important to understand that between-group rivalry is not uncommon among social groups. Consider the jocks and the nerds, for example, who have shared an age-old history of rivalry and dislike. Countless films and TV shows have characterized this conflict. Although it's not particularly pleasant to talk about between-group rivalry, its existence is part of the natural social landscape. This is not so different from rivalries between sports teams, for instance, perhaps even promoting bonding and in-group solidarity between members of the same social group. Yet, even when rivalries exist, we've often observed that when teens and young adults find their natural place in an accepting social group, they often enjoy the secondary benefits of not being so easily bullied or victimized. The bottom line is that social groups provide protection in numbers and a source of good friends.

Identifying the Right Social Group

Although many teens and young adults with social challenges fail to naturally find a social group for themselves, this doesn't mean they can't find an accepting social group if they were to try. But in order to do so, they have to take the first step. This involves identifying the right social group. Interestingly, in our work with teens and young adults with social skills challenges, we are constantly impressed with their ability to correctly categorize and name the dozens of social groups existing within their social milieu. They are easily able to identify the popular kids, jocks, cheerleaders, geeks, nerds, gamers, skaters, and so on. Table 2.1 in the chapter summary for teens and young adults includes a list of common social groups generated by teens and young adults at the UCLA PEERS Clinic. Whereas all of these groups aren't necessarily appropriate choices, such as the stoners and gang bangers, these are social groups sometimes found in the social world of teens and young adults. Just as this list isn't an endorsement of any particular social group, it's also not exhaustive but simply includes the most commonly referenced social groups identified by teens and young adults in our program.

Although teens and young adults with social difficulties are commonly able to generate long lists of social groups existing in their social world, they're rarely able to answer one very basic question: "What's the purpose of these groups?" The reality is that social groups are essential toward finding a potential source of friends, a way of feeling connected to something larger than yourself, which is an important part of adolescence and adulthood. But not just any social group will do. Choosing the right social group will depend on your child or young adult's interests, likes, and hobbies because members of social groups always share some common interest. For example, gamers have video games in common, enjoying and playing them often. Computer geeks and techies have computers and technology in common, sharing enjoyment and knowledge of computers and technology.

> *Social groups are essential toward finding a potential source of friends, a way of feeling connected to something larger than yourself, which is an important part of adolescence and adulthood.*

In our clinical experience, once a solid understanding about the link between common interests and social groups has been established and the importance of these social groups in providing a source of friends has been embraced, many socially motivated teens and adults with social challenges, especially those diagnosed with ASD, will naturally gravitate toward gamers, computer geeks, techies, science geeks, comic book geeks, and anime geeks, given their inclination toward video games, computers, technology, science, comic books, and anime, respectively.

Although finding the right social group is a personal choice and will vary according to interests and hobbies, it's important to understand the cultural meaning and evolving characteristics of social groups. For instance, not long ago the term *geek* was considered a derogatory term, synonymous with the term *nerd*. Yet, the label of *geek* has evolved greatly since the new millennium. At present, *geek* refers to someone who has great interest and exceptional skill in a certain area. For example, *video game geeks*, more commonly referred to as *gamers*, enjoy video games, are very good at playing video games, and are proud to call themselves *gamers*. Computer geeks are very interested in computers, are very good with computers, and are proud to call themselves *computer geeks* or *techies*. Science geeks enjoy science, have a great knowledge of science, and are proud to call themselves *science geeks*. Likewise, comic book geeks and anime geeks are really interested in comics and anime, have exceptional knowledge of comics and anime, and are proud to call themselves *comic book geeks* or *anime geeks*.

Since about 2000, the term *geek* (and to some extent the term *nerd*) has been embraced and empowered by those who identify with it. In fact, it's become cool to be a geek in recent years because it means that you're really interested in something and you're really good at it. Pop culture references such as *geek chic* or the *geek squad* are complimentary in nature, whereas the slang term *geeking out* is often used to describe an interesting and lively conversation between people with similar interests. Although most teens and young adults know that the term *geek* is no longer considered derogatory, in our clinical work with PEERS, we occasionally need to destigmatize and normalize the term *geek* because many of the teens and young adults we've worked with have found a source of friends among these social groups. As your child's social coach, you may need to do the same.

Understanding and Determining Your Child's Reputation

Whether the right social group for your child includes geeks or not, it's important to understand that your teen or young adult's social group will be determined by his or her interests and reputation. We've discussed the importance of common interests, but what about your child's reputation? By definition, a reputation is the general estimation in which a person is held by others and often involves certain characteristic traits attributed to that person, whether good or bad. Many young people experiencing peer rejection have bad reputations among their peers. These reputations often precede them, with people sometimes knowing details about them before ever meeting them. The painful truth about having a bad reputation is that it's less likely others will want to be friends with you if they know or care about your reputation. This is because you get your reputation based on whom you hang out with, so if someone has a bad reputation, chances are that fewer people will want to be friends with that person. Even the most subordinate social group on the social hierarchy will shy away from someone with a bad reputation. This creates quite a conundrum for teens and young adults with social challenges who are struggling with a bad reputation. Where are these kids going to find a social group or any source of friends if they have a bad reputation? Fortunately, there is hope in overcoming a bad reputation, and in our experience working with

> *Your teen or young adult's social group will be determined by his or her interests and reputation.*

families through the UCLA PEERS Clinic, those teens and young adults who are motivated to change have had success in making friends and forging past their bad reputations.

For teens with social challenges attempting to combat and overcome a bad reputation, two things need to happen: they need to follow the steps toward changing their bad reputation in their current social environment (see chapter 14) and they need to find another source of friends outside of their current social environment where no one knows or cares about their reputation. This might involve joining an extracurricular activity or social hobby in the community, away from peers familiar with the teen or young adult's reputation. For example, a teen who loves video games but has a bad reputation at school should avoid trying to make friends with the gamers at school until his reputation dies down (see chapter 14); in the meantime, he might join a gaming club in the community where no one knows or cares about his reputation.

One of the most valuable roles you play in assisting your teen or young adult in making and keeping friends is helping him or her find a source of friends. Identifying your child's interests is often the easy part but knowing what your child's reputation is may be more difficult if you're not part of the social milieu. Chances are if you're reading this book, your child isn't fending off text messages on a minute-by-minute basis (and as we know, many teens and young adults are not). Still, if you're struggling to uncover the status of your child's current reputation, the following questions may provide you with a focus for uncovering the signs. Although it's naturally painful to realize that your child may have a bad reputation, remember that he or she can always find a different group of friends and still succeed socially. If you've ever gone to a high school reunion, for example, you may recall reuniting with people from adolescence whom you never dreamed would grow up to be sophisticated, charming, successful people. In any case, here are some questions to help you determine your child's current social standing among his or her peers:

- Do peers share their contact information, such as screen names, e-mail addresses, and phone numbers with him or her?
- Do peers ask for his or her contact information?
- Do peers text message, instant message, e-mail, or call him or her just to talk?

- When he or she text messages, instant messages, e-mails, or calls peers, do they respond?
- Is he or she invited to get-togethers and parties by peers?
- When he or she invites peers to get-togethers and parties, are these invitations accepted?
- Does he or she sit alone at lunch or during break times?
- Does he or she belong to any extracurricular activities or social hobbies and does he or she spend time with peers from these groups outside of the organized activity?
- Do others send him or her friend requests on social networking sites such as Facebook?
- When he or she tries to friend request others on social networking sites, are these requests accepted?

One of the most valuable roles you play in assisting your teen or young adult in making and keeping friends is helping him or her find a source of friends.

These are just a few questions you can ask to gather information about your child's reputation. A negative response to one of these questions is not a guarantee that your teen or young adult has a bad reputation. Even several negative responses to these questions don't guarantee a bad reputation. Some socially neglected teens or young adults may not even be making attempts to engage their peers; others may be committing some type of social error in these situations that's leading to individual rejection but not wholly a bad reputation. Whatever the case may be, it will be helpful to get a better sense of the reputation of your child in his or her current social environment before attempting to encourage your teen or young adult to engage a particular social group. Impressions from teachers and other school members may also be helpful for parents of teens. For parents of young adults, it may be more difficult to find a third party privy to important and telling impressions. Nevertheless, identifying the status of your child's reputation will be an important element to determining where he or she will find a potential source of friends.

If you suspect that your teen or young adult has a bad reputation in his or her current social environment, it will be critical to find an alternative source of friends. This will likely involve identifying extracurricular activities, social activities, clubs, or sports in the community away from the rejecting peer group while their reputation dies down in the unaccepting environment. Of utmost importance, these activities should always be based on shared common interests with individuals around the same age and developmental level.

> *If you suspect that your teen or young adult has a bad reputation in his or her current social environment, it will be critical to find an alternative source of friends.*

Finding Friends through Social Groups

Assuming that your child doesn't have a bad reputation with his or her peers, once you've worked with your child to identify an appropriate social group, it will be important to help your teen or young adult identify members of that social group and find ways in which to interact with them. So how do you know which social group a person belongs to? The answer is rather simple. You need to pay attention to the following:

- Their interests
- Their appearance
- Whom they hang out with
- Where they hang out
- Which extracurricular and social activities they belong to

Fortunately, the clues for identifying which social group someone belongs to are very much on the surface and easy to identify if you know what you're looking for. Take the jocks, for example, because they're easy to spot. You can easily tell if someone is a jock because of his or her interests: jocks tend to talk about sports and play sports. You can tell by their appearance: jocks often wear athletic gear like jerseys, sweats, tennis shoes, letterman jackets; they may carry around their sports equipment; and they're usually in good physical shape and often have an athletic build. You can tell by whom they spend time with: jocks typically hang out with other jocks or cheerleaders, often during lunch and free times like most social groups. You can tell by where they hang out: jocks are often near locker rooms, gyms, and other athletic areas. You can tell by which extracurricular and social activities they belong to: jocks are members of various sports teams; they don't simply organize or assist at the sporting events but actually play the sport; and although being a manager or an assistant on a sports team is an important role, these roles don't make you a jock—you actually have to play the sport on a given team to make that distinction. Teens and young adults who make this mistake often fall into the category of *sports fan*. Fortunately, there are lots of sports fans, and they're also easy to spot, usually wearing their sports gear from their favorite teams and attending sporting events.

So that's one example of how to identify a fairly familiar social group by using concrete, observable information. Now let's consider some other social groups, perhaps more likely to be appropriate for your child. Although there are dozens of social groups from which your teen or young adult may identify, we will limit our discussion to the social groups most commonly identified through the UCLA PEERS Clinic.

Let's imagine your child has a strong interest in video games. We know that friendships are based on common interests, so a good source of friends for your teen or young adult will be other people around the same age who also like video games. We call this particular social group the *gamers* but how will your child find them? Just like the jocks, gamers are also easy to spot but we need to know what to look for. Their interest in video games means that gamers are often talking about video games, wearing T-shirts with gaming logos, carrying around their portable gaming devices, and playing video games before and after classes and during free times such as lunch. When they're not at each other's homes playing video games, they hang out at gaming stores and arcades with friends and enroll in gaming clubs at school and in the community.

Now imagine your child has a strong interest in computers and technology. If your child were on the lookout for *computer geeks* or *techies*, how would he or she find them? Computer geeks and techies love to talk about computers and technology, so you will often find them talking about these topics with one another. They're often found carrying around technological devices, computers, and laptop bags, and will often wear T-shirts with computer- or technology-related logos. They hang out with other computer geeks and techies, often in computer labs or places where they have access to technology. They're enrolled in computer clubs and computer classes, are involved in technology-based activities, and often study computer science in college.

If your child were on the hunt for *science geeks*, how would he or she find them? Science geeks like talking about science, so of course you will often find them talking with other students, teachers, or professors about science-related topics. They're often fond of science fiction and may spend a great deal of time talking about science fiction movies, TV shows, and books. They may be found carrying around science books, texts, or magazines; and they'll sometimes be found wearing T-shirts with science fiction themes or science-related logos, often from science museums or expos. They hang out with other science geeks, sometimes near the science lab at school; they go to science fiction movies with their friends, enroll in science clubs, participate in science fairs, attend science camp, join other science-related activities such as robotics clubs; and not surprisingly, they tend to study some form of science in college. Some science geeks with a particular bent for science fiction might also engage in live action role-playing (LARP) games, also known as larping, in which the participants physically act out scenes with characters from fictitious settings. Only a small subgroup of science geeks may consider themselves larpers, but the majority of larpers would probably consider themselves science fiction geeks.

Finally, if your child were seeking *comic book geeks* or *anime* (a form of Japanese animation) *geeks*, where would he or she find them? Comic book and anime geeks love to read comic books and anime magazines. They talk about comic books or anime with their friends. They wear T-shirts with comic book or anime characters, carry around magazines, and sometimes even draw the characters, often littering notebooks and other personal items with these figures. They hang out with other comic book geeks or anime geeks, talk about the characters, and sometimes engage in heated debates about anime, manga, and *otaku* (a Japanese term for people with obsessive interests in anime, manga, or certain video games). They read comic books or anime magazines in their free time, watch comic book or anime television series, and go to films about comic book heroes or anime characters. They often enroll in comic book clubs or anime clubs, take art classes to learn how to draw the characters, attend comic book conventions such as Comic-Con, and sometimes they even repeat dialogue or act out scenarios from their comics, also referred to as *cosplay*, or costume play. Cosplay is a type of performance art in which players wear costumes of favorite characters (usually from anime and manga) and try to act out the mannerisms of their characters. Just as with science geeks and larpers, not all comic book or anime geeks are cosplayers but the majority of cosplayers are probably anime or comic book geeks.

Finding Friends through Extracurricular Activities and Social Hobbies

It's important for you to help your teen or young adult obtain regular access to members of these social groups. One simple way of doing this is by helping your teen or young adult enroll in extracurricular activities or social hobbies based on his or her interests. Enrollment and participation in extracurricular activities is the most common method for developing new friendships with people from related social groups. For example, jocks play on sports teams and often meet other jocks through membership on these teams. Computer geeks and techies often belong to computer clubs or take computer classes and often meet other computer geeks and techies through these activities.

> *Enrollment and participation in extracurricular activities is the most common method for developing new friendships with people from related social groups.*

When teens and young adults with social challenges are left to their own devices, very few choose to enroll in social activities, usually because they don't think to join or don't know how to join. The result is that many end up isolated and rarely engaged in organized sports, clubs, or extracurricular activities. Instead, they may choose to stay in their room, playing on their computer or playing video games—isolative behavior that makes it very difficult to develop friendships. Some teens and young adults we've worked with through the UCLA PEERS Clinic have also been drawn into an online life in which they replace real-life friends with online friends through guilds and clans, which are organized groups of players who regularly play together in multiplayer computer or video games called *massively multiplayer online games (MMOs)*. In some cases, these teens and young adults have even created a second life using an *avatar*, which is a graphic representation of a user, much like an alter ego or a character. Using their avatar, they interact in a virtual world, socializing with other avatars using voice and text chat and perhaps participating in individual or group activities. Having a virtual second life may be intoxicating to many youth with social skills difficulties because it affords an opportunity to act out social scenarios without the pressure of unpredictable real-world social challenges. Yet, the reality is that these avatars are not in fact real, and *online friends* are not a true replacement for real-life friends.

Although the existence of a second life or an avatar can be disconcerting and even frustrating for some parents, it's important to consider the positive social motivation driving a second life. In our experience, teens and young adults with social difficulties who choose to engage in these online activities often do so because they desperately want to have friends. The good news is that with that positive level of social motivation, in combination with learning appropriate social skills and good social coaching from parents, teens and young adults who once may have been obsessed with their second life are able to find a source of real-world friends. One important way to make sure this objective is accomplished is through enrollment in extracurricular activities and group social hobbies focused on your teen or young adult's interests.

Many teens and young adults who come to our program are already enrolled in extracurricular activities. However, they tend to be enrolled in individual activities such as music lessons or tutoring. Although there is nothing inherently wrong with these activities, they're not always a good source of friends. For example, individual music lessons are very nice if you have an interest in playing a musical instrument but they are generally not a good source of friends because they're usually conducted one-on-one with a music teacher. This isn't to say that this activity should be given up. Instead, helping your child find additional activities where he or she might find a source of friends with similar interests should be the goal. In the case of music, perhaps joining the school band or school orchestra, joining a musical ensemble group in the community, or attending band camp might be good options.

Tutoring, although extracurricular in that it involves an activity outside of the classroom, isn't generally a good source of friends. Similar to individual music lessons, tutoring is often conducted one-on-one with an adult tutor and doesn't usually afford access to potential friends. Tutoring groups are also rarely a good source of friends, even when they include same-aged peers, because the young people attending tutoring groups are there to learn and not socialize, and needing help with academics isn't a common

> *Extracurricular and social activities should be based on the interest of your teen or young adult because friendships are based on common interests.*

interest. Remember, when your child's goal is to find a source of potential friends, extracurricular and social activities should be based on the interest of your teen or young adult because friendships are based on common interests.

In our experience working with families of youth with social difficulties, parents will sometimes think they know what the best activity is for their child; however, this decision must always involve the teen or young adult if it's going to be beneficial. Most important, the activity *must* be based on the interest of the teen or young adult. This is because the goal of these activities is to provide access to potential friends with common interests. If friendships are based on common interests, then it will be essential to find an activity focused on the interests of your child, where he

> *It should never be a question of do they want to join a social activity; it will be a question of which social activity they want to join.*

or she will find others with these same interests. Finally, if the goal is to make and keep friends, then it should never be a question of *do* they want to join a social activity; it will be a question of *which* social activity they want to join.

It's ultimately your responsibility as a parent and social coach to assist your child with finding these sources of friends. If you're unsure whether clubs or activities exist at your child's school, you might look on the school website or call the school and request a list of clubs. For those not enrolled in school or teens and young adults struggling with a bad reputation at school, you can help your child pursue activities and hobbies in the community. Web searches can be helpful in identifying community-based groups, and asking other parents, clinicians, and teachers is also a good resource.

Finally, when considering which extracurricular activity or group social hobby to help your child join, it's best if the social activity chosen meets at least once a week to give your teen or young adult frequent access to these potential friends. Anything that meets less than twice a month will make it difficult to form close friendships. You will also want to help your child find a social activity that includes same-aged peers, who are around the same developmental and intellectual level and are likely to be accepting. If you suspect others enrolled in the activity will be rejecting, it may be best to find another source of friends.

Assessing Peer Acceptance

Once your teen or young adult has identified an appropriate social group and has enrolled in extracurricular or social activities related to his or her interests, it will be important to help assess whether he or she feels accepted by the peers in the group. In other words, you'll need to consider whether this is a good source of potential friends for your child. Group acceptance can take a couple of weeks or even months to establish, so you may need to be patient. Although social acceptance and rejection may seem subtle, involving social cues that are often difficult for teens and young adults with social challenges to interpret, the reality is that acceptance and rejection can actually be examined by looking at very concrete behaviors. So how can you tell when your teen or young adult is accepted by others? The answer is actually rather simple, although for parents beginning this journey, the process can be very painful to analyze. When making the following assessment, it's important to remember that this information is a critical step toward growth. Through the UCLA PEERS Clinic, we have worked with many teens and young adults experiencing tremendous peer rejection. Though perhaps not initially accepted by their peers, the majority of these teens and young adults eventually find an accepting social group. It takes patience and persistence. So, take a deep breath and ask yourself to make an honest assessment of the following behavioral signs that your child is being accepted.

When teens or young adults are accepted, an individual or a group of people

- Seek them out to do things individually or in the group
- Talk to them and respond to their attempts to talk
- Give them their contact information
- Ask for their contact information
- Text message, instant message, e-mail, or call them just to talk
- Respond to their text messages, instant messages, e-mails, or phone calls

- Invite them to do things
- Accept their invitations to do things
- Add them to their social networking pages
- Say nice things to them and give them compliments

If these are the signs of acceptance, how can you tell when your child is not accepted by a group? Chances are that you know. Again, the answer is actually simple and relies on behavioral signs. When teens and young adults are not accepted, an individual or a group of people

- Don't seek them out to do things in the group
- Ignore them and don't respond to their attempts to talk
- Don't give them their contact information
- Don't ask them for their contact information
- Don't text message, instant message, e-mail, or call them
- Don't accept or return their calls and messages
- Don't invite them to do things
- Don't accept their invitations to do things
- Put off their invitations to do things by saying things like, "Yeah, let's do that sometime" but never follow through
- Ignore their friend requests on social networking sites
- Laugh at or make fun of them

If through your assessment of your teen or young adult's friendships (or attempts at friendships) you suspect your child is not accepted by his or her peers, you're not alone. Although it can be very painful and upsetting to recognize that your child is being rejected by his or her peers, there is hope. We have worked with countless families facing similar circumstances through the UCLA PEERS Clinic, the majority of whom made great strides in making and keeping friends. So try not to worry too much, have faith, and focus on the skills outlined in this book.

Friendship Is a Choice

One important first step in managing peer rejection is to help your teen or young adult avoid forcing unwanted friendships. Many teens and young adults seeking help through the UCLA PEERS Clinic have a long history of trying to force friendships with people who aren't interested. If your child has that tendency, too, one way of handling this is to explain that *friendship is a choice*. We don't need to be friends with everyone, and everyone doesn't need to be friends with us. Just because we want to be friends with someone doesn't mean we get to and just because someone wants to be friends with us doesn't mean we have to.

> *Friendship is a choice. We don't need to be friends with everyone, and everyone doesn't need to be friends with us. Just because we want to be friends with someone doesn't mean we get to and just because someone wants to be friends with us doesn't mean we have to.*

Social Coaching Tip: This important buzz phrase, *friendship is a choice,* is one you'll want to keep in your back pocket to use when things get tough. What do you say if someone rejects your child's invitations to do things? *Friendship is a choice.* What do you say if a get-together goes badly? *Friendship is a choice.* What do you say if your child's "friend" constantly says mean and hurtful things? *Friendship is a choice.* There are good choices and bad choices in friendships. Understanding the characteristics of a good friendship will be another important step for developing and maintaining healthy relationships, so use the shaded box that begins on page 38 to begin a dialogue with your teen or young adult about the idea that *friendship is a choice.*

Success Story: Fred Finds a Source of Friends

In our experience working with families through the UCLA PEERS Clinic, some parents feel skeptical about whether their teen or young adult will be able to find the right social group. Many have a long history of peer rejection and some parents have begun to lose hope.

Consider the story of Fred, a seventeen-year-old high school student with a previous diagnosis of ASD with social anxiety and depression. Fred's parents contacted the UCLA PEERS Clinic seeking help for Fred, who at the time had only two friends, both of whom he'd known since childhood and attended different schools. Fred was quiet and shy, rarely speaking unless spoken to, and often slow to respond. He often held his head down, letting his long hair cover his eyes like a mask, and rarely engaged in conversation unless forced. Fred had a great love of drawing and was a talented artist, spending countless hours drawing comic book characters from his anime magazines. His parents reported that the only thing that seemed to light Fred up was talking about anime and his drawings.

Similar to other parents in PEERS, Fred's parents expressed some concern that they might be setting him up for failure by placing him in our program. Expecting him to do what he hadn't been able to in his seventeen years seemed like too much to ask. They knew he wanted to make friends, but they just couldn't see him pushing past his anxiety and reserve. After weeks of assurances and gentle nudges from our team, Fred's parents helped him enroll in two extracurricular activities. The first was an anime club at his school. The second was an art class for teens in the community. The anime club was active and lively and a bit off-putting for quiet Fred, although he was able to make one friend in his three short weeks in the club. The art class in the community was another story. There Fred met a number of boys his age who also shared his love of drawing. Even better, the class was an introduction to comic book drawing, and even though Fred was advanced for the class, he found others who shared his enthusiasm for anime. According to Fred, "Going to that class helped me find friends. It didn't feel so hard because we had stuff to talk about, . . . usually I don't know what to say . . . but this was easy. We just talked about manga and *Vagabond*. It was cool. I liked it."

If you're feeling like Fred's parents, worrying that you may be expecting too much of your teen or young adult, try to put your concerns aside. If it helps, focus on the research. Remember that in multiple research studies, the PEERS method has been shown to be effective in helping teens and young adults learn to make and keep friends. And remember Fred's story—a young man now, who five years after completing our program has graduated from college, has a number of close friends, and even is in his first romantic relationship.

CHARACTERISTICS OF GOOD FRIENDSHIPS
for Teens, Young Adults, and Parents

> *The following information is intended to be read by teens and young adults with their parents in order to understand the qualities associated with good friendships.*

Now that you've decided that you're interested in learning to make and keep friends, it's important to think about what makes a good friend. At the UCLA PEERS Clinic we often explain to teens and young adults that *friendship is a choice*. It's one of our guiding principles. It means that you don't have to be friends with everyone, and everyone doesn't have to be friends with you. So if friendship is a choice, then there are obviously going to be good choices and bad choices. One way you can consider whether you're making good choices or bad choices is to become familiar with the characteristics of good friendships. But what makes a good friend? The answer will be different depending on who you ask, but the nine characteristics described in the following have been identified as important to teens and young adults seeking friends. Feel free to use them as guiding sign posts as you navigate your way through your friendships.

Sharing of Common Interests

Most friendships are based on common interests. In order to develop a friendship, it's important to have similar interests, likes, and hobbies. These interests are the lifeblood of your friendship, providing you with things to talk about and things to do with your friends.

Caring

Any decent friendship involves some degree of caring. Good friendships are based on fondness, warmth, affection, and mutual caring, as well as feeling and showing compassion, concern, and empathy through difficult times. Without the shared experience of caring, there would be little point to the friendship.

Support

Another important characteristic of a good friendship is support for one another. This may involve providing help and assistance when needed, giving encouragement and reassurance when times

(continued)

are hard, or simply offering an empathic ear when it's needed. Support is often the demonstration of caring in a friendship.

Mutual Understanding

Good friendships also include some form of mutual understanding. This is the sense that your friend gets you. This may simply mean that your friend understands your likes and dislikes, or it could mean that he or she understands (or may even anticipate) your thoughts and feelings, sometimes with very little effort. The degree to which a friend is capable of this type of understanding will vary like all of these characteristics. Some people may struggle more with understanding their friends, finding it difficult to take on the perspectives of others. Yet, most good friendships include some degree of mutual understanding.

Commitment and Loyalty

Close and enduring friendships are usually based on commitment and loyalty. Commitment is almost like a silent promise or pledge to your friend that you'll be there for each other, even in tough times. Loyalty is the execution of that commitment, the actions that signify your support and allegiance to your friendship.

Honesty and Trust

Good friendships must also include some level of honesty and trust. Truthfulness and sincerity are aspects of honesty required in a true friendship. Honesty is how we gain trust. Without honesty, there's little trust or security in the friendship. Trust is necessary to sustain the friendship and gives you the assurance that your friend will support you and have your back if needed.

Equality

Shared friendships are equal and reciprocal in nature. In the case of an equal friendship, no one person dominates the other; the needs of both friends are equally important and the enjoyment is reciprocal and shared. Friendships low in equality are volatile and subject to ruptures when one person's needs are not being fulfilled.

Ability to Self-disclose

Another characteristic important to close friendships is the ability to feel comfortable sharing your private thoughts, feelings, and history. The degree to which you feel comfortable self-disclosing or sharing secrets will be different from person to person, and the extent to which it's appropriate to share will depend on the closeness of the friendship. Whatever the degree of disclosure, even casual friends are generally able to share at least some of their thoughts and feelings with one another.

Conflict Resolution

Perhaps one measure of the strength of a friendship is the ability to resolve arguments and conflicts without hurting the friendship. The reality is that even close friends may argue or disagree from time to time. The ability to resolve conflict in friendships is often determined by other characteristics such as caring, commitment, and trust. You must care for the person whose friendship you are trying to save; you must also be committed to this friendship to even want to save it; and you must trust your friend enough to be willing to try to resolve the conflict and allow yourself to be vulnerable.

Identifying the characteristics of a good friendship is important to the process of making and keeping friends. When you remind yourself that friendship is a choice, you unburden yourself from unhealthy relationships. Although not all friendships will include all nine of these characteristics, the closer and healthier the friendship is, the more characteristics it will likely have.

(*continued*)

Keeping in mind that our list represents the gold standard for friendship, you must expect that your relationships will have different degrees of these qualities. For example, acquaintances (those whom you only know slightly) are likely to have fewer of these characteristics. Casual friendships (those that may involve socializing but not closeness) may have only a few of these characteristics. Regular friendships (those that involve regular socializing and a slight degree of closeness) will have many of these characteristics whereas close friendships or best friendships (those that involve frequent socializing and a high degree of closeness) will have most if not all of these characteristics. If throughout reading this book you or your parent feel like you're not sure if you're making good choices in friends, you may want to review this section again.

FINDING AND CHOOSING GOOD FRIENDS
Chapter Summary for Teens and Young Adults

> The following information is intended to be read by teens and young adults and contains a brief summary of the chapter.

Each chapter of this book highlights important social skills needed for making and keeping friends. Parents are encouraged to read the whole book, and although teens and young adults should feel free to do the same, chapter summaries (like this one) and chapter exercises have been developed to give you a snapshot of the rules and steps of what works socially and provide you with concrete ways to practice the skills with your parents and others.

This chapter is focused on finding and choosing good friends. Ironically, the first step toward finding lasting friends is getting to know yourself. So what are you interested in? When you begin to consider what you're interested in, you'll be well on your way to identifying a potential group of friends. The reason that identifying your interests is so important is that friendships are based on common interests. It's your common interests that give you things to talk about and things to do with your friends. If you don't have things in common with your friends, it may be harder to socialize and get close.

So where do you find other people you share things in common with? This is where the importance of social groups comes into play. In every social setting there are groups of people who socialize in different ways and for different reasons. There are cliques, which may include a few close friends or best friends. There are social groups, which may include dozens of peers, all sharing some common interest, such as the *jocks*, for example, who share an interest in playing sports, or the *computer geeks*, who share an interest in computers. Then there is the larger peer group, which may include the entire student body of a school or all the employees in a workplace. If your goal is to make and keep friends, social groups are particularly important in helping find a potential source of friends.

When you're trying to make friends it's helpful to think about which social group you might fit in with. This will be determined by what you're interested in and even what you're good at. For example, if you're really interested in video games and are pretty good at playing them, then trying to become friends with the *gamers* would be a good option. If you're really interested in computers or technology and are relatively knowledgeable in this area, then trying to hang out with the computer geeks or *techies* would be a good choice. If you're really interested in science and know a lot about it, then trying to make friends with the *science geeks* would be a good plan. Or if you love comic books, then hanging out with the *comic book geeks* would be a good idea. The key here is that when choosing

(continued)

a social group to hang out with, it may not be enough to just be interested in the same topic—you may actually need to have some knowledge or skill in this area. For example, some people are really interested in sports and even know infinite amounts of sports trivia, but if they don't actually play an organized sport or aren't on a sports team, they don't get to be jocks. Instead, it's more likely they're *sports fans* and would do well to try to find other sports fans who also enjoy talking about sports rather than playing them.

Table 2.1 provides a list of different social groups found in many schools and communities. This list was generated by teens

Table 2.1. *Different Social Groups Identified by Teens and Young Adults*

Jocks	Nerds	Stoners, burners, druggies
Cheerleaders	Computer geeks, techies	Rockers
Popular kids	Gamers, video game geeks	Hip hop group
Student council	Science geeks	Gang bangers, taggers
Drama club	Comic book geeks, anime geeks	Artists
Choir, chorus, glee club	Math geeks, mathletes	Musicians (rock bands)
Greeks (college only)	Band geeks	Skaters
Groups by major (college only)	Chess club	Surfers
Partiers	Goths, emos	Hippies, granolas
Preppies	Scene kids	ROTC, military groups
Brains, smart kids	Hipsters	Ethnic, cultural, religious groups

and young adults attending the UCLA PEERS Clinic, where we conduct our research on teaching young people how to make and keep friends. Although all of these social groups are not necessarily good choices, such as stoners and gang bangers, these are social groups sometimes found in the social world of teens and young adults like you. Again, we're not going to make believe that bad choices don't exist; instead, we're going to help you to find good choices for social groups based on your likes and interests.

Now that we've identified some different social groups, it's helpful to consider why these groups are so important. For starters, social groups give you a source of friends whom you share things in common with. Another reason social groups are so important is that they protect you from individual bullying. Think about it. Who do bullies like to pick on: people who are by themselves or in a group? You've probably noticed that people who are by themselves are usually the ones who get targeted by bullies. This is because when you're alone, you look like an easy target, with no one there to stick up for you or have your back. This can be scary and intimidating, but fortunately we have strategies for finding your appropriate social group, so you don't have to be alone and unprotected.

Although having a social group is helpful in finding a source of friends with similar interests and likes, and may even protect you from individual teasing and bullying, it's important to understand that between-group rivalry is common among social groups. For example, in some schools the jocks and the nerds are known to dislike one another. Although it's not particularly pleasant to know that rivalries exist between groups, this conflict is part of reality. What makes these rivalries less concerning is that they often promote bonding between members of the same social group. This isn't so different from sports fans who while rooting for their team might bond over disliking a rival team. The

(*continued*)

bottom line is that this rivalry isn't a big deal and the benefits of having a social group outweigh everything else.

Now that you're familiar with the importance of social groups and how to identify which group may be best for you based on your interests, we need to consider how you can tell which social group someone belongs to and where you might find members of these groups. Ways to identify which social group someone belongs to include considering their interests, their appearance, whom they hang out with, where they hang out, and which extracurricular and social activities they belong to. For example, let's imagine you have a strong interest in video games and are really good at playing them. In this case, the gamers might be a good social group for you to try to join and make friends with. Fortunately, gamers are really easy to spot if you know what you're looking for—you just need to be aware of the signs. So what are the signs that someone is a gamer? Their interest in video games means that they're often talking about video games, wearing T-shirts with gaming logos, carrying portable gaming devices, and playing video games before and after classes and during free time at school or work. They often hang out at gaming stores and arcades and enroll in gaming clubs at school and in the community. So if you were interested in becoming friends with the gamers or simply meeting people who like video games, you might try identifying some of these individuals at your school or work by paying attention to the signs. Then identify extracurricular activities and social clubs focused on video games, such as gaming clubs, and enroll in and attend these activities.

The next step in finding and choosing good friends is to consider whether you're accepted by the people you're trying to be friends with. Sometimes it can be difficult to know if you're accepted by others. Fortunately, there are concrete signs that you can look for that will give you clues about whether you're accepted or not accepted by the social group you've identified. Table 2.2 shows some signs that highlight some of these clues.

Table 2.2. *Signs of Acceptance and Lack of Acceptance from Social Groups*

Signs You Are Accepted	Signs You Are Not Accepted
They seek you out to do things individually or in the group.	They do not seek you out to do things.
They talk to you and respond to your attempts to talk.	They ignore you and do not respond to your attempts to talk.
They give you their contact information.	They do not give you their contact information.
They ask for your contact information.	They do not ask for your contact information.
They text message, instant message, e-mail, or call you just to talk.	They do not text message, instant message, e-mail, or call you.
They respond to your text messages, instant messages, e-mails, or phone calls.	They do not accept or return your calls or messages.
They invite you to do things.	They do not invite you to do things.
They accept your invitations to do things.	They do not accept your invitations or put off your invitations to do things.
They add you to their social networking pages.	They ignore your friend requests on social networking sites.
They say nice things to you and give you compliments.	They laugh at or make fun of you.

Now that you've seen a snapshot of some of the key elements to finding and choosing good friends, it will be important for you and your parents to complete the chapter exercises together in order to put this information into practice. Without completing these exercises, it will be difficult to meet your goal of making and keeping friends. Remember that the skills being offered in this book come directly from a program known as PEERS. This program has been shown through many

(continued)

research studies to be effective in helping teens and young adults like you learn to make and keep friends. The skills you are learning from this book and the corresponding chapter exercises come directly from this scientifically supported program. If you follow along with these guidelines and practice the rules and steps of social behavior as advised in the chapter exercises, you will have a better shot of benefitting from this program, like so many others before you.

CHAPTER EXERCISES
for Teens, Young Adults, and Parents

In each chapter of this book, you'll find suggestions for exercises to bring to life the information you are gaining. Completing these exercises is critical to benefitting from this book. Without using and practicing the skills within these pages, there is only knowledge but no action. If your goal is to make and keep friends, then completing these exercises is an essential ingredient to the recipe.

It's recommended that you and your parent complete the first five chapters of this book before you begin to attempt to make new friends with people from new social groups or extracurricular activities. You may want to rely on existing friends or old friends as you practice the strategies related to conversational skills described in chapters 3 to 5. If you don't have any good options among existing friends, proceed slowly with any new potential friends until you and your parent have read and completed the chapter exercises in the first five chapters.

Teens and young adults should complete the following exercises with parents:

- Brainstorm the different social groups that exist in your social surroundings (see table 2.1 for examples of common social groups).
- Identify what your interests and talents are (for example, computers, technology, video games, and so on).
- Make a list of the different social groups that share similar interests with you (for example, computer geeks, techies, gamers, and so on), and then consider how you might identify members of these social groups based on the following:
  - Their interests
  - Their appearance
  - Whom they hang out with
  - Where they hang out
  - Which extracurricular and social activities they belong to
- Make a list of extracurricular activities and social clubs where you might find people around your age who have the same interests as you (for example, computer clubs, gaming clubs, and so on).
- Work with your parent to find these extracurricular activities and social clubs in your school or community and begin the process of enrolling. Try to find activities that accomplish the following:
  - Are based on your interests
  - Include same-aged peers who are likely to be accepting
  - Are located in a place where you don't have a bad reputation
  - Meet regularly (preferably at least once a week)
- Think about whether you have ever tried to make friends with people from these social groups or extracurricular activities and identify how you can tell if you've been accepted or not accepted by them (see table 2.2 for signs of acceptance and lack of acceptance from social groups).

(continued)

- If it feels like you're not being accepted by others, remember that you're not alone. Many teens and young adults who have gone through PEERS started in similar circumstances but were eventually successful at making and keeping friends.
- While you work on learning these skills and becoming more aware of things like social acceptance, be careful not to force friendships. Remember that friendship is a choice. We don't get to be friends with everyone, and everyone doesn't get to be friends with us. If we're not accepted by one group, we can always find another group. So hang in there and remember that your parents are here to help and we're just getting started!

3

Good Conversations

The Basics

HAVING GOOD CONVERSATIONAL SKILLS IS ONE OF the essential ingredients to developing and maintaining meaningful relationships in adolescence and adulthood. However, difficulty having good conversations as a teen or adult can create a significant social barrier. So why are conversational skills so important once we reach adolescence? One reason relates to the social demands placed on each of us during this period of transition. Consider the usual social interactions of younger children. How do young children interact and socialize with one another? Generally, interaction is initiated and sustained through play. Consequently, play skills, good sportsmanship, and knowing how to enter play appropriately are essential social skills needed to succeed in early childhood. However, when children grow into adolescence, the need for play skills becomes less relevant and is replaced with another critical social skill. Typically, interaction is initiated and sustained through conversations. Friendships and romantic relationships are formed and maintained around meaningful communication with others. Thus, having good conversational skills becomes critical to social success on reaching adolescence and remains so throughout life.

> *Having good conversational skills becomes critical to social success on reaching adolescence and remains so throughout life.*

In our clinical experience working with families through the UCLA PEERS Clinic, many teens and young adults with social challenges struggle with social communication, committing social faux pas such as hogging conversations or perseverating on topics of personal interest—creating a social barrier for making and keeping friends. However, this barrier isn't necessarily immovable or permanent. Understanding the common social errors committed during conversations and replacing those errors with appropriate rules of conversation may eliminate some or most of these obstacles. So if your child also struggles with conversations, like so many others, don't despair. As long as your teen or young adult is motivated to learn and practice the rules of good conversations described in this chapter, much can be achieved.

Perspective Taking in Conversations

Some teens and young adults with social challenges have a tendency to focus on topics of personal interest in conversations, often with what appears to be very little notice of their conversational partner. For those with autism spectrum disorder (ASD), this might include perseverating on topics of special interest, sometimes called *obsessions* or *restricted interests,* with little notice or regard for their partner's interest in the subject. Contrary to how this interaction may make the other person feel, this tendency to dominate the conversation or even to monologue or lecture is not necessarily done out of complete indifference or apathy toward the other person. More likely the person committing this social error is unaware of how his or her actions are making the other person feel.

Does your teen or young adult have a tendency to make this social error? Have you ever wondered why he or she does this? Lack of awareness of how your child's behaviors affect others may be due to an impairment in social cognition, which is the ability to attribute the mental states of others—to understand or intuit their thoughts, feelings, wishes, desires, or intentions. Social cognition is essentially the ability to take on another person's perspective, to put yourself in someone else's shoes, and imagine how he or she might think, feel, or react in a given social situation. Is this something your teen or young adult struggles with? If so, you're not alone. Difficulty with this type of perspective taking is a common characteristic of those with social challenges, and although social cognition is not necessarily innate or hardwired for some, there is some research evidence to suggest that perspective taking can be taught to a certain extent. In our work through the UCLA PEERS Clinic, we've developed a method of helping teens and young adults with social difficulties learn to take on the perspectives of others. This approach has been modified for this book so that you and your child might also benefit from these strategies.

Throughout the next several chapters, you and your child will be presented with various social vignettes, representing appropriate and inappropriate social behavior. In some cases there will be video demonstrations of these skills and social errors provided on the accompanying DVD. It's important for you and your child to read the social vignettes and watch the DVD demonstrations while considering what these interactions might be like using the perspective-taking questions offered at the end of each example. These social vignettes and video demonstrations will help you and your teen or young adult consider the experiences of others: a critical step toward friendship development and maintenance.

> *It's important for you and your child to read the social vignettes and watch the DVD demonstrations while considering what these interactions might be like using the perspective-taking questions offered at the end of each example.*

Perspective-taking questions will often follow a very specific pattern in order to help you and your child internalize and habitualize the thought processes associated with understanding the perspective of others. The three most commonly used perspective-taking questions are as follows:

- What was that interaction like for the other person?
- What did they think of me?
- Are they going to want to talk to me again?

The perspective-taking questions provided in this book will always relate to some specific rule or step of social behavior associated with making and keeping friends. In this chapter, this involves the rules for good conversations, which are based not only on what we want to do but also what we want to avoid doing. The former refers to ecologically valid social skills, or what people who are socially accepted naturally do in conversations. The latter refers to the common social errors committed by some individuals with social communication problems. Both are based on what science tells us works and doesn't work.

The rules for good conversations are presented in the following and in many cases include examples using social vignettes, DVD demonstrations, and perspective-taking questions, which can be found in the chapter summary for teens and young adults at the end of this chapter. Be sure to review these examples with your child and have a discussion about each using the perspective-taking questions.

Rules of Good Conversations

Trade Information

Video

The fundamental practice of having a good conversation involves informational exchange. We call this social behavior *trading information*. Trading information involves at least two partners exchanging information back and forth about one another. I tell you something about me. You tell me something about you. I ask something about you. You ask something about me, and so on. We can liken this conversational exchange to a game of tennis or ping pong, where the ball goes back and forth over the net, just as a conversation should go back and forth between partners. If the ball stays on one side of the court too long, we're no longer playing the game; just as if the conversation stays on one partner too long, we're no longer having a conversation.

Social coaching tip: The chapter summary for teens and young adults includes an appropriate example of trading information. Read the social vignette and view the DVD demonstration of trading information with your child, then follow up with a discussion using the perspective-taking questions. Presenting the rules of conversations in this way will help you convey the significance of this rule to your teen or young adult.

Find Common Interests

The goal of any good conversation is to trade information and find common interests. Common interests are important in social communication because they provide common ground on which to keep a conversation interesting and stimulating. Common interests are also important because they're typically the foundation of friendships. Think about who you are (or have been) friends with. You probably share common interests, the things you probably talk about and do together. We seek common ground because it gives us a foundation on which to build a conversation and even a friendship.

Social coaching tip: Because the most fundamental rule of good conversations is to trade information and find common interests, it will be essential for you to stress this point with your teen or young adult. Any deviation from this goal (or committing of social errors such as those described in the following) should be addressed by you with the simple question, "What is our goal in a conversation?" Of course, the answer is to trade information and find common interests. When deviations from this goal are committed by your teen or young adult, you will want to follow up with social coaching questions related to whatever social error was committed, followed by perspective-taking questions such as the ones outlined in this book. Helpful perspective-taking questions include, "What was that conversation like for the other person?" and "What do you think that person thought of you?" and "Do you think that person will want to talk to you again?" This social coaching should of course be conducted in private, when your child's peers are not present.

> The most fundamental rule of good conversations is to trade information and find common interests.

Social coaching tip: Once common interests are found, a key follow-up social coaching question for you to ask is, "What could you do with that information if you were ever to hang out?" As the social coach, it's your job to help connect the dots for your child along the way, and in this case, have your teen or young adult begin to generate ideas for how he or she might use common interests to develop ideas of things to do with friends. In order for your child to have successful conversations, ultimately leading to friendships, decoding these important social communication goals and identifying the linkages will be the key to helping your child unlock the mystery of conversational skills.

> Once common interests are found, a key follow-up social coaching question for you to ask is, "What could you do with that information if you were ever to hang out?"

Here are some examples:

- If your teen or young adult discovers a common interest in video games with a friend, they might play video games, talk about video games, go to a gaming store or arcade, or surf the Internet for video games they'd like to play.
- If they discover a common interest in computers, they might play with their computers, talk about computers, go to a computer store or a computer expo, or surf the Internet for computers they'd like to purchase.
- If their common interest is science, they might go to a science museum or science expo, talk about science, go to a science fiction movie, look at science-related YouTube videos online, or watch the Science Channel or Discovery Channel.
- If their common interest is comic books and anime, they could share their comic books and anime with one another, talk about comic books and anime, watch a TV show or movie related to comic books or anime, go to a comic book store, or attend a comic book convention.

Ask the Person about Him- or Herself

So now that you know the goal of a conversation, how do you actually trade information and find common interests? Trading information typically involves a process of asking the person you're talking to about him- or herself and sharing related information about you. Teens and young adults have a long list of conversational topics often covered but general questions such as "What have you been up to lately?" or "What did you do over the weekend?" or "What are you doing this weekend?" can provide useful information about a person's likes, interests, and hobbies.

Common conversational topics among teens and young adults often relate to school or work gossip; problems with friends, family, school, or work; weekend activities including dating, parties, and get-togethers; professional and school sports; movies and TV shows; video games and computer games; comic books and anime; music and concerts; fashion, clothes, hair, and makeup; and so on. Although some teens and young adults with social challenges will have a natural inclination toward talking about their own interests, the fact is most are generally capable of talking about topics apart from their most specialized interests. It's just that many don't think to do this and subsequently make the mistake of persevering or talking incessantly about what primarily interests them. Yet, if their goal is to make and keep friends, correcting this social error by trading information and finding common interests will be more motivating than what they're accustomed to doing.

Social coaching tip: If your teen or young adult has restricted or special interests, it's your responsibility as your child's social coach to assist him or her in practicing talking about topics outside of these special interests. Sharing the list of conversational topics in table 3.1 with your teen or young adult and practicing trading information about some of these topics will be a good start. You will quickly find that he or she does in fact have other interests aside from those perseverated on. For example, movies and TV shows are very common topics of interest for most young people, even for those with specialized interests.

> It's your responsibility as your child's social coach to assist him or her in practicing talking about topics outside of special interests.

Table 3.1. *Common Conversational Topics among Teens and Young Adults*

School and work gossip	Video games and computer games	Classes
Problems with friends	Computers and technology	Exams
Problems with family	Comic books and anime	Teachers and professors
Problems with school and work	Movies	School major and minor
Dating	TV shows	Sports
Parties and get-togethers	YouTube and viral videos	Cars, motorcycles, and bikes
Weekend activities	Internet websites	Celebrities
Extracurricular activities	Music and concerts	Fashion and clothes
Social clubs and activities	Books	Shopping
Hobbies and interests	News and media	Makeup and hairstyling

Answer Your Own Questions

Once you've determined the interests and likes of your conversational partner, it's important to share something related about yourself. Although some conversational partners will ask similar questions to learn more about your interests, you shouldn't wait for the person to ask. If they don't ask, you could end up having a one-sided conversation, only focusing on the other person. Instead, you can answer your own questions while trading information. For example, if your teen or young adult asked a friend what she'd been up to lately, and she responded that she's been going to a lot of movies recently, your child might answer his or her own question by mentioning seeing one of the movies talked about. This technique keeps the conversation going back and forth so your teen or young adult is trading information and finding common interests. In this example, your child's common interest with his or her friend was that they'd seen the same movie, which would likely lead to further discussion and perhaps even a get-together to the movies as their friendship develops.

> *Once you've determined the interests and likes of your conversational partner, it's important to share something related about yourself.*

Social coaching tip: The chapter summary for teens and young adults provides an example of trading information and answering your own question. Read the social vignette with your child, then follow up with a discussion using the perspective-taking questions.

Share Relevant Information

Another important rule of having good conversations is to share relevant information. So what makes information relevant in a conversation? If your child has a special interest in ancient Chinese symbols, for example, this information is relevant to him or her. However, if your child's conversational partner is not interested in Chinese symbols, then the information becomes less relevant. You will need to help your teen or young adult understand that if his or her ultimate goal is to develop and maintain meaningful relationships, then the goal in a conversation must be to trade information and find common interests. In this conversational example, that does not include Chinese symbols. Yet, through trading information back and forth with his or her conversational partner, your child may eventually discover a mutual interest in video games. This information is now relevant because it's a common interest that your teen or young adult shares with his or her partner.

Ask Follow-up Questions

Some teens and young adults with social challenges have a tendency to switch topics frequently in conversations. They'll sometimes jump from one topic to the next, with little or no connection from one topic to the next. This form of abrupt topic switching can be rather jarring and confusing to their conversational partners. Perhaps your teen or young adult has a tendency to topic switch, too. If so, as your child leaps from one topic to the next, where does he or she often leap to? If your child has restricted interests, like so many others, he or she probably tends to leap back to these special interests. Although it's difficult to know for certain the thought process associated with topic switching and topic leaping, if your teen or young adult has a tendency to leap back to his or her special interests in conversations, it's possible he or she is doing this because it's a topic of comfort and ease. Perhaps when your child becomes lost in a conversation and is unsure where to go, he or she chooses to leap back to what is known best. Whatever the case may be, topic switching is a common social error committed by teens and young adults with social difficulties that should be avoided. A helpful replacement behavior for this mistake is the use of follow-up questions.

> Topic switching is a common social error committed by teens and young adults with social difficulties that should be avoided. A helpful replacement behavior for this mistake is the use of follow-up questions.

Follow-up questions are the questions we use to naturally keep the conversation going on a given topic while we're trading information. For example, if your child were to ask a friend what she did over the weekend, the friend might mention that she caught up on some TV watching. Your child might then ask some follow-up questions about the shows watched, perhaps leading to the discovery of a common interest.

Social coaching tip: Because asking follow-up questions can be difficult for some teens and young adults with social difficulties, a useful coaching tip is to have your child pick various topics and practice asking follow-up questions on a regular basis until his or her skills improve. It's helpful to frequently switch the topics during these practice exercises to refine the skills. You might begin with a topic of common interest but then switch to topics your child is less familiar with because we still need to know how to trade information politely even about topics we know or care little about. Start with the list of common conversation topics for teens and young adults in table 3.1. You might introduce this exercise by saying, "I want you to ask me about movies I like and then ask me five follow-up questions." Although this method may seem somewhat artificial at first, it will be a good foundation on which to build and improve your child's ability to ask follow-up questions in normal conversations.

Social coaching tip: The chapter summary for teens and young adults provides a social vignette with an example of asking follow-up questions while trading information. Read the social vignette with your child, then follow up with a discussion using the perspective-taking questions.

Ask Open-Ended Questions

Another common social error committed by teens and young adults with social challenges is the failure to elicit extended responses from conversational partners. One possible reason for this conversational shortcoming may be the tendency to ask repeated closed-ended questions. Closed-ended questions are those that limit the possible responses of the person talking (usually in the form of yes or no responses or multiple choice answers), making it less likely to draw out more detailed responses. For example, "What's your favorite video game" or "Which *Star Wars* movies have you seen?" would be examples of closed-ended questions. Although closed-ended questions are not inherently bad in and of themselves, when repeatedly used in a conversation, they tend to sound like an interview. However, open-ended questions are not constrained by defined response limits. They allow for spontaneous and unrestricted replies that may lead to more extended responses and further conversation. For example, "What kind of video games do you like?" or "What kind of movies do you like?" or

"What do you like to do on the weekends?" would be examples of more open-ended questions. Questions beginning with, "What kind of . . ." are generally open-ended and lead to further discussion. More general questions such as, "What have you been up to lately?" or "What are you doing this weekend?" are also good examples of open-ended questions that may lead to further conversation.

> *Open-ended questions are not constrained by defined response limits. They allow for spontaneous and unrestricted replies that may lead to more extended responses and further conversation.*

Given the fact that teens and young adults with certain social challenges may have a tendency to become overly rigid with these social rules, we would not want to confuse them by suggesting that they should never ask closed-ended questions. Instead, you'll want to convey to your child that closed-ended questions are fine when used in combination with open-ended questions.

Social coaching tip: A good coaching tip to help your child use more open-ended questions is to present examples of closed-ended questions and have your teen or young adult generate several alternative open-ended questions. For example, you might say, "If the closed-ended question were, 'What is your favorite video game?' what would some open-ended questions be?" Your child might then generate some examples of related open-ended questions, such as, "What kind of video games do you play?" or "What kind of multiplayer games do you like?" or "What kind of RPGs (role-playing games) do you like?"

Check Your Humor

Although humor is often seen as an allurement for friendship, when used inappropriately, humor is one of the fastest ways to push people away. It's a harsh reality for parents to face, but it's important to consider that although you may find your child's humor charming and delightful, sadly, others may not. Therefore, your child may need to be cautious with his or her use of humor and check his or her humor at all times. Checking your humor essentially means that your teen or young adult needs to pay attention to the feedback he or she gets after telling a joke or attempting to say something funny. For example, when your

> *Although humor is often seen as an allurement for friendship, when used inappropriately, humor is one of the fastest ways to push people away.*

child tells a joke, are the listeners laughing? And if they are laughing, are they laughing *at* your child, laughing *with* your child, or simply giving your child a courtesy laugh?

Certain subsets of teens and young adults with social challenges have a tendency to use humor inappropriately, and therefore as a social coach, helping your child to check his or her humor will be imperative. Teens and young adults who struggle with appropriate use of humor often fancy themselves comedians or class clowns, engaging in silly, odd, or immature joke telling that no one else seems to understand. They may repeat dialogue from movies or TV shows out of context, confusing the listener who doesn't understand the meaning of the joke. They may repeat the same jokes over and over, not realizing that jokes don't tend to be funny once you've already heard them. These are the teens and young adults who seem to be constantly seeking a laugh, but when they get one, may not realize that people are actually laughing *at* them, not *with* them. For these teens and young adults, learning to use humor appropriately will be of paramount importance.

Unbeknownst to many teens and young adults with social difficulties, their inappropriate use of humor may be creating a social barrier between them and their peers, making it difficult to make and keep friends. Their failure to recognize this rejection may cause them to be further rejected and may even result in a bad reputation among their peers. Because teens and young adults that regularly engage in inappropriate use of humor are often seen as "strange" or "weird" by their peers, checking humor will be a critical component to making and keeping friends.

As a parent, it's naturally painful to imagine other teens or adults laughing at your child, but the sad reality is that for some young people struggling to make and keep friends, this experience is very real and may even happen quite frequently. Perhaps this is true for your teen or young adult. If so, the realization can be heartbreaking. Although it's understandable that you may be reluctant to draw attention to a form of rejection that your child may be completely unaware of, as has been the case for many families we've worked with, you will be doing your child a disservice if you don't help check his or her humor.

So what are the behavioral signs for checking humor? When people are laughing with you, they often smile, shake their head up and down, or perhaps make comments such as, "That was funny" or "Good one," without a sarcastic tone. When people are giving you a courtesy laugh, they may give a polite laugh and a smile, but this doesn't mean they think your joke was funny. When people are laughing at you, they may roll their eyes, make a face, point at you, look at someone else and laugh, or make sarcastic comments such as, "Yeah, you're really funny" or "Yeah, that was hilarious." Remember that with your help, your teen or young adult has a shot at moving past these negative interactions and finding more successful ways of connecting with others.

You will have to judge whether your teen or young adult is using humor in a way that's creating a social barrier toward making and keeping friends. When uncertain, a good rule of thumb for your child is to be a little more serious when first getting to know someone. Remember that when used inappropriately, humor can be one of the fastest ways to push people away. So suggest to your teen or young adult that he or she give new friends and acquaintances time to get used to his or her sense of humor.

Social coaching tip: As your teen or young adult's social coach, it's critical that you help check his or her humor if relevant. If you notice that in response to joke telling, people are either not laughing, giving a courtesy laugh, or laughing at him or her, you may want to help your child reconsider his or her use of humor. Although this can sometimes be a painful reality check for your child, you're actually doing him or her a favor by pointing out potential pitfalls that may be preventing friendships. Helping your teen or young adult check humor involves having regular discussions about his or her use of humor and may also include privately pointing out inappropriate uses of humor during teachable moments. In our work with families facing the challenge of giving subtle feedback during these moments, many parents have found it helpful to use short verbal cues, such as quietly saying, "humor check" when others wouldn't overhear or even giving discreet hand gestures that might alert their child to their social faux pas. Whatever is decided, you'll need to negotiate this feedback with your teen or young adult to avoid embarrassment and hurt feelings.

Social coaching tip: Because many teens and young adults use humor as a way to try to connect with others, you'll need to help your child figure out another way to connect if humor isn't working. Remind your child that trading information and finding common interests is one of the best ways to form connections with others and is a far less risky behavior. Assure your child that he or she isn't going to lose the ability to connect with others. Instead, by using the tools for having good conversations, making connections will be something your child will do more naturally and successfully.

Listen

Some teens and young adults with social challenges struggle with listening skills. The problem with this is that when people don't listen it makes it seem like they're uninterested and indifferent to the person they're talking to. However, when people listen and demonstrate this by asking follow-up questions or sharing related information, it shows that they are interested and care about the information shared. Sometimes in conversations, people will appear to be listening when they're actually just waiting for the other person to stop talking so they can say something else. Although simply pausing long enough to let the other person talk is an important aspect of having good conversations, people still need to show their partner that they're listening through verbal and nonverbal forms of communication. So how can your teen or young adult show that he or she is listening? On the verbal side, trading information, finding common interests, and asking follow-up questions are good methods for demonstrating the act of listening. On the nonverbal side, smiling or laughing when appropriate, having good eye contact, and shaking his or her head up and down (showing agreement) or side to side (showing mutual disapproval) are good methods for showing interest and listening. Commenting on what the other person says and remembering details of conversations at a later time are also good ways for your teen or young adult to show that he or she has been listening.

When people listen and demonstrate this by asking follow-up questions or sharing related information, it shows that they are interested and care about the information shared.

Use Good Eye Contact

Video

On how many occasions have parents uttered the words, "Look at me" or "Look at them" or "Look me in the eye"? For parents of teens and young adults diagnosed with ASD, these requests may be too numerous to count. Perhaps you too have spoken these commands countless times. You likely do this because you know that your child's failure to make good eye contact means that he or she may appear disinterested in others, as if in another world. As your child's social coach, you'll need to be ready to coach your teen or young adult on good use of eye contact during teachable moments, being sensitive not to provide embarrassing feedback in front of others.

> *Your child's failure to make good eye contact means that he or she may appear disinterested in others, as if in another world.*

Although using good eye contact obviously includes not looking away from your conversational partner for long periods of time, it also excludes staring at your partner without ever looking away. Interestingly, some teens and young adults we've worked with through the UCLA PEERS Clinic have overlearned the act of eye contact by the time they reach us. For years they've been hounded by family members, therapists, and teachers to "look me in the eyes." Although these coaching efforts obviously come with good intentions, occasionally the end result may be a teen or young adult who overuses eye contact. Can you imagine what this might look like? Picture a young teen who stares you in the face, rarely blinks, and never looks away. How might it feel to be watched so intensely—your conversational partner never looking away, never blinking, and never taking his or her eyes off of you? Many describe the act of being watched so intensely as creepy or weird, perhaps even intrusive or predatory. The experience of being stared at tends to conjure up feelings of discomfort, uneasiness, and even anxiety or fear.

To help remedy this problem in your child, you'll need to coach him or her on good use of eye contact during teachable moments when others won't overhear. So what does good eye contact look like? Generally when people converse naturally, they make eye contact with their partner for several seconds and then periodically look away. The period of time someone looks away is brief, perhaps only a second or two, but it's the looking away that tells our conversational partner that we're safe, that we're not a predator.

Social coaching tip: When sharing this information with your child, a good coaching tip is to present the rule that we need to use good eye contact when conversing, which includes making eye contact with our conversational partner, but not staring too much. To help convey this point, it is also helpful for you and your teen or young adult to read the social vignette in the chapter summary for teens and young adults and view the DVD demonstrations of the two corresponding social errors (too little eye contact and too much eye contact), followed by a discussion using the perspective-taking questions.

Use Good Body Boundaries

Video

Another common social error sometimes committed by teens and young adults with social challenges relates to bad body boundaries. The act of standing too close or too far away can quickly create an awkward social dynamic. Consider what it feels like to have someone stand too close during a conversation. At best, you may think the person is weird or odd. At worst, you may think the person is creepy or predatory. The experience of having someone invade your personal space can be incredibly uncomfortable and disconcerting—often generating the feeling of wanting to flee. Perhaps your child has the tendency to stand too close during conversations, unaware of the discomfort it may cause others. Although likely an unintentional social faux pas, if your child's goal is to make and keep friends, then disobeying the rules of body boundaries and invading someone's personal space is not a good start. Don't feel discouraged though. In our experience through the UCLA PEERS Clinic, adjusting body boundaries is one of the simpler coaching jobs our parents have. You'll just have to be sure to stay on your toes and jump in during teachable moments.

Also related to poor body boundaries are those who overindulge the use of personal space and stand too far away from their partner when attempting to converse. Imagine the person who is trying to have a conversation with you from across the room. What does that experience feel like? Many say that it's awkward and strange to have a conversation involving more than a couple of exchanges from a distance. Even worse, when others are present and might overhear the conversation, the experience can be rather embarrassing. Placed in this situation, imagine what you might think of people committing this odd social error. You might think they're strange or weird or you might find them embarrassing. Whatever the case, it's unlikely that the act of talking to someone from across a room or engaging others in conversation from a large distance will win any social points. Perhaps your child makes this social error. If that's true, then it will be important for you to coach your child on the use of good body boundaries when conversing with others.

So what constitutes good body boundaries? A good rule of thumb in conversations is to stand about an arm's length away from the person you're talking to. The distance of about three feet (approximately one meter) is generally considered to be a comfortable distance when talking with others. Although it's important for you to present this concrete rule to your child, take this advice learned from personal experience: be sure to clarify with your child that although an arm's length away is the acceptable distance, that doesn't mean he or she should go up and measure the distance with an arm before talking to someone! Although a funny mental image, a more appropriate tactic would be to calculate the distance with friends and family during practice conversations (like those described in the chapter exercises). All other conversations should only include ballpark estimates of the measurement.

> A good rule of thumb in conversations is to stand about an arm's length away from the person you're talking to.

Social coaching tip: To help convey the social rule about body boundaries, you should read the social vignette in the chapter summary for teens and young adults with your child and then view the DVD demonstrations of these two social errors (standing too close and standing too far away), followed by a discussion using the perspective-taking questions. You should also be prepared to step in during teachable moments and offer social coaching when your teen or young adult violates rules about body boundaries. Like coaching on any of these skills, be sure to provide feedback in a subtle way that doesn't cause embarrassment or hurt feelings and has been negotiated beforehand.

Video

Use Good Volume Control

Have you ever had a conversation with someone who spoke too loudly? Recollect how the interaction made you feel. Perhaps you were startled at first, then maybe a little embarrassed by the thought that others might be listening. What did you think of the speaker who did this? Perhaps you thought he or she was odd or weird or maybe you even wondered if he or she had hearing difficulties. Whatever the case, you probably didn't find the experience terribly pleasant, which may account for your memory of the event. Now consider the reverse. Have you ever had a conversation with someone who spoke too quietly? Again, think of the encounter and recall how the interaction made you feel. You might have felt confused, struggling to understand what the person said. You might have been frustrated, working hard to decode the conversation. What did you think of the speaker? You might have thought he or she was shy or timid or perhaps you thought he or she seemed sad or depressed. Whatever you thought, the conversation probably felt like a lot of work and wasn't particularly enjoyable. Simple social behaviors such as volume control have the capacity to greatly affect our interactions with others, even getting in the way of our ability to make and keep friends.

The tendency to speak either too loudly or too quietly is not uncommon among teens and young adults with social challenges. Anecdotally, in our work with teens and young adults through the UCLA PEERS Clinic, those who commit the social error of speaking too loudly are more likely to fall into the peer-rejected category described in chapter 2—often seen as obnoxious or annoying by their peers. Those youth who make the mistake of speaking too quietly may be more likely to fall into the socially neglected category—often seen as shy and withdrawn by their peers. Another important rule for you to share with your teen or young adult is to use good volume control when talking to others.

> *The tendency to speak either too loudly or too quietly is not uncommon among teens and young adults with social challenges.*

Social coaching tip: Although sharing this important rule with your teen or young adult is a first step, you'll likely have to provide additional coaching during teachable moments to help highlight the point. It's difficult to provide an exact measurement of what constitutes good volume control because of changes in context, so direct coaching during teachable moments will probably be needed to get this point across. Additionally, reading the social vignette in the chapter summary for teens and young adults and viewing the DVD demonstrations of these two social errors (talking too loudly and talking too quietly), followed by a discussion using the perspective-taking questions, may also help to convey this social rule to your child.

Don't Be a Conversation Hog

One of the more common social errors committed by those with social challenges is the tendency to monopolize and dominate conversations. These tend to be the teens and young adults who focus on their own personal interests when conversing, often with little regard for the other person's interest in the topic. For example, they may go on and on espousing their views on RPGs (role-playing games), MMOs, (massively multiplayer online games), or FPSs (first-person shooter games), but the listener doesn't know the first thing about video games. Or perhaps they may give a lecture on their theory of robotics, including a lengthy discussion about the importance of homogeneous transformations, kinematics, and trajectory generation, covering all sorts of terms and concepts their listener may have never heard before.

We call this social error being a *conversation hog*. Aside from the fact that this experience is uninteresting and boring for the listener, the act of conversation hogging is the equivalent of a one-way conversation. Remember that your fundamental goal in having a conversation is to trade information and find common interests. In a two-person exchange, this involves having a two-way conversation. Yet, if your child is being a conversation hog, the end result is a one-way conversation. In this case, the conversation will be all about your teen or young adult, and he or she will probably fail to find common interests with the other person.

The act of conversation hogging is akin to the act of ball hogging, a term likely to be familiar to anyone who has ever played on a schoolyard playground. Imagine the child at recess who when playing with his peers refuses to share or pass the ball. He selfishly hogs the ball to himself for his own amusement, oblivious to the reactions of his teammates. Consider how the teammates feel about this interaction. They're likely to feel annoyed and frustrated, perhaps even angry at not having the chance to play. How will they feel about the boy hogging the ball? They're likely to find him annoying, rude, selfish, and aggravating. Worse still, they're not likely to want to play with him again.

Just like the kid who hogged the ball in the schoolyard game, not allowing others to have their turn at play, conversation hogs monopolize the talking in conversations, not allowing others to have their turn at speaking. Similar to schoolyard playmates, the partners of conversation hogs are likely to feel annoyed, frustrated, bored, and possibly even angry at not having a chance to speak. They're also likely to think the person hogging the conversation is selfish, rude, annoying, and aggravating. Even worse, they're unlikely to want to become friends with that person or even talk to him or her again. Other peers may also begin to notice this tendency to hog conversations, possibly resulting in peer rejection and even a bad reputation for the person committing the social error. Although it may seem difficult to alter this bad social habit, in our experience through the UCLA PEERS Clinic, socially motivated teens and young adults who are interested in making and keeping friends will quickly learn the importance of trading information and finding common interests as a replacement for conversation hogging. For many of these young people, it's not that they're unable to talk about things apart from what interests them; they just don't always think to talk about other things. By giving your teen or young adult the goal to find common interests, you will ultimately help change the direction of your child's conversational patterns.

Social coaching tip: Given the propensity of teens and young adults with social challenges to engage in conversation hogging, it will be critical to underscore the importance of avoiding this common social error. If your child has a tendency to conversation hog, you might unobtrusively point out this social error as it occurs during teachable moments, being sensitive not to embarrass your child in front of his or her peers. Reading the social vignette in the chapter summary for teens and young adults and viewing the DVD

> *Given the propensity of teens and young adults with social challenges to engage in conversation hogging, it will be critical to underscore the importance of avoiding this common social error.*

demonstration of being a conversation hog with your child, followed by a discussion using the perspective-taking questions, will also be essential to conveying this vital social rule.

Don't Be an Interviewer

Video

Another common social error often committed by teens and young adults with social difficulties is the tendency to repeatedly ask questions without providing reciprocal responses. For example, asking someone what kind of video games he or she likes and asking follow-up questions related to this topic is fine, but if you fail to answer your own questions and share relevant information about yourself (in this case, information related to video games), then you fail to trade information and find common interests. Remember that your child's goal in a conversation is to trade information and find common interests. Yet, it's impossible to find common interests if your child doesn't share information about him- or herself. Simply asking the other person questions without providing reciprocal information is another type of one-way conversation. Unlike conversation hogging, which was all about your child, when your child is being an interviewer, it's all about the other person. The problem with this type of one-way conversation is that you fail to find the common links that form the foundation of a friendship, the things that make it fun for you to talk to one another and give you things to do together.

> Another common social error often committed by teens and young adults with social difficulties is the tendency to repeatedly ask questions without providing reciprocal responses.

Social coaching tip: Just as with conversation hogging, if your child has a tendency to be an interviewer, you will need to discreetly point out instances of interviewing as they occur naturally during teachable moments, being sensitive not to embarrass your child in front of others. Reading the social vignette in the chapter summary for teens and young adults and viewing the DVD demonstration of being an interviewer with your child, followed by a discussion using the perspective-taking questions, will also be important to conveying this point.

Don't Be Repetitive

As previously mentioned, a common social error committed by people with social challenges is becoming hyperfocused on topics of personal interest, also referred to as restricted interests or obsessions. Teens and young adults diagnosed with ASD have a particular tendency to focus on these narrow interests in conversations, often having difficulty shifting to other topics regardless of the interests of the person he or she is talking to. The technical term for this behavior is called *perseveration* but in PEERS we call this social error *being repetitive in conversations.*

The problem with being repetitive in conversations is that the topic eventually gets old for the people you're talking to, even if you share a common interest in the subject. For example, through the course of trading information, your child may discover that the person he or she is talking to shares a mutual interest in the game *World of Warcraft*, a massively multiplayer online role-playing game (MMORPG). Whereas your child and his or her friend may initially enjoy talking about *World of Warcraft*, if every time your child saw this friend all he or she wanted to talk about is this particular game, eventually the friend would get bored. Although this repetitiveness may be fun for your child, it's less likely to be fun for his or her partner, who might prefer to talk about a variety of topics—as is usual for teens and young adults. So just because your child's goal in conversations is to find common interests doesn't mean that once found, that's all your child should talk about.

> The problem with being repetitive in conversations is that the topic eventually gets old for the people you're talking to, even if you share a common interest in the subject.

If you're a parent of a teen or young adult with restricted interests (sometimes described as obsessions), rest assured that when tempered with flexibility of conversational topics, these passionate interests may actually lead to friendships and even ultimately to successful careers. Consider the computer geek who grew up to be a successful computer programmer, the math geek who grew up to be a prosperous engineer, or the gamer who grew up to be a flourishing video game designer. With every great passion, there is the potential for great success. Yet, if these special interests become too obsessive, they may create a barrier to developing and maintaining friendships, so your child may need your help in establishing some ground rules.

Social coaching tip: In order to make way for these future successes and avoid potential social barriers, it will be important for you to provide feedback when topics become perseverative, or repetitive. Your child's tendency to be repetitive will require a good deal of perspective taking and a fair amount of coaching by you during teachable moments. Once your teen or young adult is familiar with the social rule to not be repetitive, violations of this rule might be gently pointed out by you in the moment in the absence of peers. For example, you might simply say, "Let's not be repetitive" or "Are we being repetitive?" or "What could be the problem with being repetitive?" As your teen or young adult becomes more familiar with this social error, you might simply say, "What's your goal in a conversation?" or "Are you trading information?" or "What social error could you be making?" Like coaching on any of these skills, these teachable moments might also include a brief discussion using your three perspective-taking questions:

- What was that interaction like for the other person?
- What did they think of you?
- Are they going to want to talk to you again?

Social coaching tip: Another social coaching tip that's been useful for parents in PEERS has been to establish time limits with teens and young adults about how much time can be spent talking about or engaging in a particular restricted interest while socializing with friends, at least until they become more comfortable with different topics of conversation. For example, a parent of a teen obsessed with video games, concerned that his son might perseverate on this topic at an upcoming get-together, might enforce the rule that only 50 percent of the time can be spent playing or talking about video games. The teen might even break the news to his guests, blaming his parent for the rule, and thereby reducing any potential conflict or boredom arising from a hyperfocus on special interests.

Video

Don't Police

Some teens and young adults with social challenges have a tendency to think in concrete and literal terms—often strictly adhering to rules and regulations. The social world, which is often thought of as unpredictable and confusing, is a mystery to them. Sticking closely to rules and sets of law is a safe way to survive in this unpredictable and ever-changing world. If your child is like others and has a tendency to be rule-driven, he or she might also feel compelled to point out the rule violations of others, regardless of how embarrassing or impolite his or her comments might be perceived. In PEERS we call this social error *policing.* We use the term *policing* because the act of pointing out rule violations has the appearance of someone designated to uphold the law.

Very often teens and young adults with social difficulties who choose to point out rule violations do so because it seems correct and factual to note these violations, much like a police officer would give a citation for breaking a law. The problem with policing when you're not in fact a police officer is that the person on the receiving end often experiences the observation as a criticism or reproach. So if your goal is to make and keep friends, then policing is not an effective strategy.

Social coaching tip: Just as with the other rules of social behavior, once your child is familiar with the social rule that he or she is not to police others, it will be important to gently point out violations of this rule in the moment but away from peers. If your child is socially motivated and has expressed an interest in making and keeping friends, then he or she will want to follow this rule. Coincidentally, the social coaching you'll provide during teachable moments is actually a form of policing (which your child may be quick to point out). However, as long as you have an agreement with your teen or young adult that he or she wants to learn how to make and keep friends, and is willing for you to help with this process, then you're safe from breaking your own rule! Finally, reading the social vignette in the chapter summary for teens and young adults and viewing the DVD demonstration of policing with your child, followed by a discussion using the perspective-taking questions, will also be helpful in passing along this important social rule.

Don't Tease   Video

Teasing is a common social behavior often seen between socially successful teens and young adults. Teens and young adults with social challenges will sometimes observe socially accepted peers engaging in this behavior with their friends and think this is a way to make friends and be cool. Boys and men in particular are known to engage in *bantering* (a form of teasing) with good friends. Banter involves the exchange of playful and friendly teasing comments between friends. Although banter isn't typically conveyed or received with malicious intent, it's still risky behavior nonetheless. The problem with friendly banter is that it has a tendency to escalate and lead to hurt feelings. One relatively innocent jab may lead to a counter jab, with the responder feeling the need to outdo the original teaser. This may result in a back-and-forth game of high-stakes teasing, each player attempting to up the ante. The result may be that one or both of the players becomes offended or upset, leading to conflict. Knowing when to fold or back down from this game of banter before conflict arises requires that the players know how to read their opponent. Picking up on such subtle social cues isn't typically the forte of teens and young adults with social difficulties.

Social coaching tip: When advising your teen or young adult about how to navigate the world of friendly banter, it's best to present this important point: if your goal is to make and keep friends, then teasing or bantering with others is risky. When your child teases or even banters with others, he or she risks offending them, hurting their feelings or making them angry. As your child's social coach, it's important for you to normalize this social behavior by acknowledging that many people do in fact tease and banter with their friends, but add that if your child's ultimate goal is to make and keep friends, then the risk outweighs the benefits. In our experience, most socially motivated teens and young adults will appreciate this guideline and follow the rule. Reading the social vignette in the chapter summary for teens and young adults and viewing the DVD demonstration of teasing with your child, followed by a discussion using the perspective-taking questions, will also be helpful in conveying this rule.

> *If your goal is to make and keep friends, then teasing or bantering with others is risky.*

Don't Get Too Personal at First

Video

A final social error related to conversational skills involves the tendency to get too personal too quickly or share too much information (sometimes referred to as *TMI*). When we're first getting to know someone, it's important not to get too personal too quickly. Asking personal questions or sharing too much personal information before you know someone well can risk scaring that person off. Occasionally, teens and young adults who have a history of peer rejection will make this mistake. They may get so excited that they're connecting with someone and potentially developing a friendship that they metaphorically go "all in" and put all their cards on the table—revealing personal details about themselves or asking personal questions of the other person. This social error is something akin to a young child making a new friend on the playground and immediately asking to be best friends. Although innocent and well intentioned, this overzealous behavior in adolescence and adulthood can frighten off potential friends.

> When we're first getting to know someone, it's important not to get too personal too quickly.

A more common reason for this mistake among teens and young adults with social challenges may involve trouble judging what's too personal versus not too personal in conversations. Gauging what types of conversational topics are appropriate from one situation to the next takes some social savvy. Interpreting the subtle social cues that tell you if you've gone too far also takes some social skills. Because it's difficult to provide concrete rules or measurements of what's too personal from one situation to the next, particularly because these judgments are often based on context and degree of acquaintance, it will be essential for you to provide social coaching around this particular rule.

Social coaching tip: Once your teen or young adult has been exposed to the rule to not get too personal at first, any violations of this rule should be pointed out and discussed privately during teachable moments. You might ask simple questions like, "Is that too much information?" or eventually shortening this question to the popular acronym, "TMI?" These discussions should also include a review of the three routine perspective-taking questions. Reading the social vignette in the chapter summary for teens and young adults and viewing the DVD demonstration of getting too personal at first, followed by a discussion using the perspective-taking questions, will also be helpful in demonstrating this social rule.

Success Story: Lance Learns to Trade Information

Although conversational skills are often thought of as an art form—some type of hardwired skill that you're either born with or you're not—using ecologically valid social skills in conjunction with rules about common social errors, the PEERS method seeks to turn this art into a science. The good news is that if your teen or young adult is motivated to use the rules for good conversations and you're willing and able to provide good social coaching, much can be accomplished.

Consider the case of Lance, a sixteen-year-old boy diagnosed with ASD and ADHD who came to PEERS with his mother because he wanted to make friends. Lance was a self-reported class clown, who loved to tell jokes and was desperate for attention. Lance had no friends but everyone in his high school knew him. His reputation preceded him. In addition to his attempts at being a class clown, Lance also had a tendency to perseverate about politics, getting into heated and passionate debates with his peers—whether they were interested in debating or not. Most of his jokes revolved around politics, with the meaning often lost on his peers. When on a political rant, Lance could go on and on for several minutes without ever letting another person speak. When first arriving at the UCLA PEERS Clinic, Lance's mother was skeptical that he would be able to change his behavior. She thought these tendencies were beyond his control. Yet, when the rules of good conversations were presented to Lance, reinforced through social coaching and perspective-taking discussions with his mom, Lance slowly began to change his habits. In describing how the change came about, Lance commented, "I never knew I was supposed to trade information. I didn't know that if I wanted a friend I had to find common interests. I thought if I was funny people would like me 'cuz that's what guys do. . . . I was pretty bummed out when you told me I couldn't tell jokes. That was my thing, . . . but then I met these guys on the debate team and they're pretty cool, . . . we have fun."

Lance's story is not so different from what many PEERS families experience after going through the program. So if you're feeling skeptical or you find yourself feeling discouraged, remember Lance's story and keep moving forward.

RULES OF GOOD CONVERSATIONS
Chapter Summary for Teens and Young Adults

> *The following information is intended to be read by teens and young adults and contains a brief summary of the chapter.*

This chapter focuses on the rules of good conversations. One of the most important skills you need to make and keep friends is being able to carry on a good conversation with others. If this is something you've found hard to do in the past, don't worry: you're not alone and help is on the way. Because we know that having good conversations can be difficult, we've come up with very simple rules for how to do it. These rules are listed in the following and include what to do and what not to do. To help you understand what this should or shouldn't look like, we've put together some pretty funny video demonstrations on the accompanying DVD. Take a moment to go over these rules of conversations with your parent and watch the related videos. If you can't watch the videos, a transcript of each video demonstration is provided in this section. Your parent will go over a few questions after each example to help you understand what these conversations might be like for other people. It only takes a few moments to watch these videos and talk about what you've seen, so sit back and enjoy this glimpse into the rules of good conversations.

Video

Trade Information

- Good conversations go back and forth equally between partners. Your friend shares something about him- or herself, then you share something related, and so on.

Social Vignette: Trading Information

The following social vignette is a transcript of the video demonstration from the accompanying DVD of trading information.

Alex and Ben: (facing each other, making eye contact, standing about an arm's length away)

Alex: "Hey, Ben, how's it going?"
Ben: "Good, how are you?"
Alex: "I'm good. Did you catch the game last night?"
Ben: "Yeah, that game was awesome."
Alex: "Unbelievable, right?"
Ben: "Yeah, the buzzer beater."
Alex: "Ugh, it was crazy. I was actually there."
Ben: "No way? You went to the game?"
Alex: "Uh huh . . ."
Ben: "Do you have season tickets?"
Alex: "Uh, no, but a friend took me."
Ben: "Ah, that's awesome."
Alex: "Yeah, so do you watch any other sports?"
Ben: "Well, I watch baseball."
Alex: "Ah, cool. Do you play also?"
Ben: "I used to play. I used to play in high school."
Alex: "Ah. Yeah, I played, too, but I don't really . . . I'd like to play more."
Ben: "Oh, well, a couple of buddies of mine, we get together on Saturdays and we play. Maybe you should come?"
Alex: "Where do you play?"
Ben: "We play at the park."
Alex: "Oh, yeah, maybe I'll come. Definitely."
Ben: "Yeah, that would be great."

Perspective-Taking Questions

- What was that interaction like for both people?
  Answers: Pleasant, enjoyable, interesting, fun
- What do you think they thought of each other?
  Answers: Nice, pleasant, friendly, interesting, easy to talk to
- Are they going to want to talk to each other again?
  Answer: Yes

(*continued*)

Find Common Interests

- The goal of a conversation is to find common interests because these interests are usually the foundation of a friendship.

Ask the Person about Him- or Herself

- Ask the person about his or her likes, interests, and hobbies, with the goal of finding common interests.

Answer Your Own Questions

- Don't wait for the person to ask questions about you. Be prepared to share related information about yourself.

Social Vignette: Answer Your Own Questions

The following social vignette is an example of answering your own question.

Jennifer: "Hey, Carrie. I haven't seen you in a while. What have you been up to lately?"

Carrie: "Oh, not much. Just hanging out. I went to the movies this weekend."

Jennifer: "Oh yeah? So what did you see?"

Carrie: "I saw that new romantic comedy we were talking about the other day."

Jennifer: "How cool! So what did you think?"

Carrie: "It was pretty good. Better than I expected."

Jennifer: (answers her own question) "I'm actually going to see it this weekend. I can't wait!"

Perspective-Taking Questions

- What was that interaction like for both people?
  Answers: Pleasant, enjoyable
- What do you think they thought of each other?
  Answers: Nice, friendly, interesting, fun

- Are they going to want to talk to each other again?
  Answer: Yes

Share Relevant Information

- Talk about topics of interest to everyone in the conversation.

Ask Follow-up Questions

- Try to stay on a topic for a while before moving on to something new, especially if that topic is a common interest.

Social Vignette: Ask Follow-up Questions

The following social vignette is an example of asking follow-up questions.

Carrie: "So, what did you do over the weekend, Jennifer?"
Jennifer: "I just laid low and caught up on some TV shows."
Carrie: (asks a follow-up question) "Oh, yeah, what did you watch?"
Jennifer: "I watched an entire season of that sitcom you told me about!"
Carrie: "I love that show!" (asks another follow-up question) "Which season did you watch?"
Jennifer: "The second season. It was so great!"
Carrie: "That's so cool!" (asks another follow-up question) "So what was your favorite episode?"

Perspective-Taking Questions

- What was that interaction like for both people?
  Answers: Pleasant, enjoyable, fun
- What do you think they thought of each other?
  Answers: Nice, friendly, interesting, fun, easy to talk to
- Are they going to want to talk to each other again?
  Answer: Yes

(continued)

Ask Open-Ended Questions

- Try to ask questions that bring out extended and lengthier responses instead of asking questions that only require a brief preset reply, like yes or no.

Listen

- Listen and try to remember what the person has to say.
- Not listening will make it appear as if you're not interested or you don't care.

Video

Use Good Eye Contact

- Don't look away too much because this will make you look like you're not interested.
- Don't stare too much because this can feel creepy and uncomfortable for the person you're staring at.

Social Vignette: Too Little Eye Contact

The following social vignette is a transcript of the video demonstration from the accompanying DVD of too little eye contact.

Mary: (making eye contact) "Hey, Yasamine!"

Yasamine: (looking to the left) "Hey, Mary, how's it going?"

Mary: (looking over shoulder where Yasamine is staring) "I'm good. How are you?"

Yasamine: (still staring to the left) "I'm good; what did you do this weekend?"

Mary: (confused) "Um, I went hiking."

Yasamine: (looking around) "Oh, that's cool, I like to hike."

Mary: (confused, looking over shoulder where Yasamine is staring) "Yeah, I like hiking, too."

Yasamine: (still staring to the left) "Who did you go with?"

Mary: (confused) "I went with my sister."

Yasamine: (looking around) "Oh, that's cool."

Mary: (trying to make eye contact) "Uh huh."

Yasamine: (still staring to the left) "I like to hike on a trail kind of by the beach."

Mary: (confused, looking over shoulder where Yasamine is staring) "Yeah, the beach is a cool place to hike."

Perspective-Taking Questions

- What was that interaction like for Mary?
  Answers: Confusing (not sure if Yasamine was interested), awkward, weird
- What do you think Mary thought of Yasamine?
  Answers: Disinterested, weird, strange
- Is Mary going to want to talk to Yasamine again?
  Answer: Probably not, too weird, didn't seem interested

Social Vignette: Too Much Eye Contact

The following social vignette is a transcript of the video demonstration from the accompanying DVD of too much eye contact.

Yasamine: (staring) "Hey, Mary, how's it going?"

Mary: (confused) "I'm good, how are you doing, Yasamine?"

Yasamine: (staring) "I'm good; what'd you do this weekend?"

Mary: (uncomfortable, looking away) "Um, I went hiking."

Yasamine: (staring) "That's cool! Who'd you go with?"

Mary: (shrugging shoulders) "Um, my sister."

Yasamine: (staring) "Nice, what trail did you go to?"

Mary: (uncomfortable, looking down) "It was, uh, right by my house."

Yasamine: (staring) "Nice, I like to go hiking, too."

Mary: (shrugging shoulders) "Yeah . . . cool."

Yasamine: (staring) "There's a trail by my house that I like to take."

(*continued*)

Mary: (uncomfortable, looking away) "Uh huh."
Yasamine: (staring) "It's really fun."
Mary: (quietly) "That sounds good."

Perspective-Taking Questions

- What was that interaction like for Mary?
  Answers: Uncomfortable, awkward, creepy, weird
- What do you think Mary thought of Yasamine?
  Answers: Stalker, predator, creepy, weird
- Is Mary going to want to talk to Yasamine again?
  Answer: No, too creepy, too awkward

Use Good Body Boundaries

Video

- Don't stand too close or too far when talking to someone.
- Standing about an arm's length away is a good distance.

Social Vignette: Standing Too Close

The following social vignette is a transcript of the video demonstration from the accompanying DVD of standing too close.

Mary: (texting on mobile phone)
Yasamine: (walks up to Mary, stands too close) "Hey, Mary, how's it going?"
Mary: (startled, moves back) "Hey, Yasamine. How are you?"
Yasamine: (moves forward) "I'm good, what did you do this weekend?"
Mary: (moves back more) "Um, I went hiking."
Yasamine: (moves forward again) "That's cool; who'd you go hiking with?"
Mary: (looking annoyed, trying to escape) "Oh my gosh . . . um, I don't know . . . with my sister."
Yasamine: (standing too close) "What trail did you go to?"

Mary: (looking annoyed, trying to escape) "Um, I don't . . . I don't know. I don't remember."

Perspective-Taking Questions

- What was that interaction like for Mary?
  Answers: Uncomfortable, awkward, creepy, weird
- What do you think Mary thought of Yasamine?
  Answers: Stalker, creepy, weird
- Is Mary going to want to talk to Yasamine again?
  Answer: No, too creepy, too uncomfortable

Social Vignette: Standing Too Far Away

The following social vignette is a transcript of the video demonstration from the accompanying DVD of standing too far away.

Mary: (reading a book)

Alex and Lara: (looking at mobile phone)

Yasamine: (standing across the room) "Hey, Mary. How's it going?"

Mary: (startled, confused) "It's good."

Yasamine: (standing across the room) "What did you do this weekend?"

Alex and Lara: (looking annoyed)

Mary: (looking confused) "Um, nothing."

Yasamine: (still standing across the room) "I went to the aquarium. It was so much fun. They have this new shark exhibit. It's amazing."

Mary: (looking confused and embarrassed) "That's cool."

Yasamine: (still standing across the room) "Yeah, you totally have to check it out. There's all sorts of colorful fish. It's so cool."

Mary: (apologizes to Alex and Lara, looking around the room, trying to escape) "That sounds interesting."

(*continued*)

Yasamine: (standing across the room) "Yeah, they have one down the street; it's in walking distance. It's awesome."

Mary: (bored and annoyed) "Okay."

Perspective-Taking Questions

- What was that interaction like for Mary?
  Answers: Uncomfortable, awkward, embarrassing, strange, weird
- What do you think Mary thought of Yasamine?
  Answers: Weird, odd, embarrassing (other people could hear)
- Is Mary going to want to talk to Yasamine again?
  Answer: No, too embarrassing, too awkward

Use Good Volume Control

Video

- Don't speak too softly or too loudly; this may be annoying to the listener.

Social Vignette: Talking Too Loudly

The following social vignette is a transcript of the video demonstration from the accompanying DVD of talking too loudly.

Alex: (speaking very loudly) "Hey, Ben, how's it going?"

Ben: (startled, moves back) "Good."

Alex: (speaking very loudly) "What'd you do last night?"

Ben: (looking annoyed, moving farther away) "Uh, I went to the basketball game."

Alex: (speaking very loudly) "Oh yeah? I was there, too. Wasn't it crazy?"

Ben: (looking around, covering ear) "Uh, yeah."

Alex: (speaking very loudly) "Do you watch any other sports?"

Ben: (looking annoyed, covering ear) "I watch baseball."

Alex: (speaking very loudly) "Oh yeah? I used to play baseball. What else do you watch?"

Ben: (cringing, holding ear) "Geez, I watch football."
Alex: (speaking very loudly) "Oh, yeah, I love football."
Ben: (looking annoyed, trying to escape)

Perspective-Taking Questions

- What was that interaction like for Ben?
  Answers: Annoying, uncomfortable, awkward, embarrassing
- What do you think Ben thought of Alex?
  Answers: Weird, strange, odd, maybe angry
- Is Ben going to want to talk to Alex again?
  Answer: No, too obnoxious, too annoying

Social Vignette: Talking Too Quietly

The following social vignette is a transcript of the video demonstration from the accompanying DVD of talking too quietly.

Alex: (whispering) "Hey, Ben, how's it going?"
Ben: (straining to hear) "What?"
Alex: (whispering) "How's it going?"
Ben: (looking confused) "How's it going?"
Alex: (whispering) "Yeah. How are you?"
Ben: (looking bored) "I'm good. How are you?"
Alex: (whispering) "I'm good. What'd you do last night?"
Ben: (straining to hear) "What?"
Alex: (whispering) "What'd you do last night?"
Ben: (appears annoyed) "Well, I went to a basketball game."
Alex: (whispering) "Oh, yeah, I was there, too. It was unbeliev-able. Oh my gosh. That ending was crazy."
Ben: (looking around, appears annoyed) "What?"
Alex: (whispering) "You saw the ending. It was unbelievable."
Ben: (straining to hear, moving closer) "The ending?"
Alex: (whispering) "Yeah the ending, it was . . ."
Ben: (looking around, appears bored) "Oh, yeah. Uh, yeah, it was crazy."

(*continued*)

Alex: (whispering) "Oh, that's cool. Do you watch any other sports?"

Ben: (straining to hear, moving closer) "Um, what?"

Alex: (whispering) "Do you watch any other sports? Do you watch any other sports?"

Perspective-Taking Questions

- What was that interaction like for Ben?
  Answers: A struggle, too much work, annoying, frustrating
- What do you think Ben thought of Alex?
  Answers: Shy, timid, introverted, depressed, sad
- Is Ben going to want to talk to Alex again?
  Answer: No, too much work, too much trouble

Don't Be a Conversation Hog

Video

- Don't just talk about yourself and what you're interested in.
- Give the other person a chance to talk, too.

Social Vignette: Don't Be a Conversation Hog

The following social vignette is a transcript of the video demonstration from the accompanying DVD of being a conversation hog.

Alex: "Hey, Ben. How's it going?"

Ben: "Good. How are you?"

Alex: "I'm good. I just got back from the comic book convention."

Ben: "Ah, no way, you . . ."

Alex: (interrupts) "Yeah, it was unbelievable. It was downtown and everyone was there. We all dressed up."

Ben: "I really wish I could've . . ."

Alex: "Yeah, I wore the coolest outfit. I met all the famous authors. It was awesome."

Ben: (trying to get a word in) "Oh yeah?"

Alex: (interrupts) "It was really cool. Everyone was dressing up, and I think I'm going to go next week also. Uh, but I'm not sure what I'm going to wear because I don't want to wear the same thing, but maybe I'll get a new one. Maybe . . ."

Ben: (trying to get a word in) "Well, actually . . ."

Alex: (interrupts) "I should go on eBay to buy something. But everyone was wearing the coolest costumes. I got a ton of pictures, so maybe I'll get some ideas from there."

Ben: (appears bored, looks around) "Um, yeah."

Alex: "I think there's one also the weekend after. I'm going to try to go to that too. . . ."

Ben: (trying to get a word in) "Well . . ."

Alex: ". . . and get a bunch of autographs . . ."

Ben: (trying to get a word in) "Well, maybe . . ."

Alex: ". . . with a bunch of people. So, we'll see. Yeah, so a lot of my friends want to go, so I figure I'll just go with them."

Ben: (appears bored, looks around) "Yeah."

Alex: "It's a bit of a drive, but, you know, it's so worth it because it's a really big comic book convention. But, yeah . . . so it'll be fun. I really can't wait for it."

Ben: (appears annoyed, looks away)

Perspective-Taking Questions

- What was that interaction like for Ben?
  Answers: Annoying, frustrating, boring
- What do you think Ben thought of Alex?
  Answers: Selfish, boring, obnoxious, self-centered
- Is Ben going to want to talk to Alex again?
  Answer: No, too obnoxious, too self-centered

Video

Don't Be an Interviewer

- Don't ask question after question without sharing anything about yourself; it will feel like an interview or an interrogation.

(continued)

Social Vignette: Don't Be an Interviewer

The following social vignette is a transcript of the video demonstration from the accompanying DVD of being an interviewer.

Alex: "Hey, Ben. What did you do this weekend?"

Ben: "I went to the movies. What about you?"

Alex: "Oh, what did you see?"

Ben: "Um, I saw that new sci-fi movie."

Alex: "Ah, yeah? Do you like sci-fi movies?"

Ben: (nodding his head) "Um, yeah, I do."

Alex: "What else do you like?"

Ben: "I also like action movies."

Alex: (interrupts) "Oh, cool."

Ben: "Um . . ."

Alex: "Do you go to the movies a lot?"

Ben: (appears bored) "Uh, yeah. Yeah, I go a lot."

Alex: (interrupts) "Oh, yeah, when else do you go?"

Ben: (appears bored) "Um . . ." (pause) "I go on the weekends. . . ."

Alex: (interrupts) "Oh, on the weekends?"

Ben: ". . . a lot."

Alex: "Oh, cool, cool. Who do you go with?"

Ben: (appears bored, looking around) "Um, I usually go with friends. . . ."

Alex: (interrupts) "Which theater do you go to?"

Ben: "Um, man. I don't know."

Alex: "Do you go close by you or far away?"

Ben: (appears annoyed) "Whichever one they're playing . . ."

Alex: (interrupts) "What else did you do this weekend?"

Ben: (appears disinterested) "Um, I played some basketball."

Alex: "Oh, where'd you play?"

Ben: (bored) "Um, I played at the park."

Alex: "With who?"

Ben: (looking around, appears annoyed) "Ah, man." (under his breath) "Um, I played with some of my other friends. . . ."

Alex: "Oh, cool. Did you guys . . . was it competitive . . . or was it easy? Did you win?"

Perspective-Taking Questions

- What was that interaction like for Ben?
  Answers: Annoying, exhausting (a lot of work), frustrating, boring
- What do you think Ben thought of Alex?
  Answers: He was like a drill sergeant, interrogator, nosy, annoying, weird
- Is Ben going to want to talk to Alex again?
  Answer: No, too exhausting, too much work

Don't Be Repetitive

- Don't talk about the same topic all the time.
- Just because you have a common interest with someone doesn't mean that's all you can talk about.

Video

Don't Police

- Don't criticize or point out the other person's mistakes; this will be annoying to the person and you'll look like a know-it-all.

Social Vignette: Don't Police

The following social vignette is a transcript of the video demonstration from the accompanying DVD of policing.

Alex: "Hey, Ben. How's it going?"
Ben: "Oh, I'm doing good."
Alex: "It's actually, 'You're doing *well.*' *Well* is an adverb and *good* is an adjective and in this situation you actually want to use the adverb *well.*"
Ben: (appears annoyed) "Okay, well, sorry. I'm doing well."

(continued)

Alex: "Well, I mean, you know . . . it's for your benefit. It's for you, so . . ."
Ben (annoyed) "Yeah."
Alex: "So, what'd you do this weekend?"
Ben: "Um, I went and played basketball."
Alex: "Oh."
Ben: (appears bored, looking around)
(Long awkward pause)

Perspective-Taking Questions

- What was that interaction like for Ben?
  Answers: Annoying, obnoxious, embarrassing
- What do you think Ben thought of Alex?
  Answers: Rude, arrogant, know-it-all
- Is Ben going to want to talk to Alex again?
  Answer: No, too annoying, too rude

Don't Tease
Video

- Teasing or bantering is risky behavior if you're trying to make and keep friends.
- When you tease, you may offend, hurt, or upset the other person.

Social Vignette: Don't Tease

The following social vignette is a transcript of the video demonstration from the accompanying DVD of teasing.

Alex: "Hey, Ben. What did you do this weekend?"
Ben: "Oh, I actually went to dinner with my parents."
Alex: (in a teasing manner) "You went to dinner with your parents? What are you, kidding me? What are you, like, a momma's boy or something?"
Ben: (uncomfortable) "No."
Alex: (teases) "Who goes to dinner with their parents on a weekend?"

Ben: (quietly responds) "We just got . . . like a . . ."

Alex: (interrupts) "What, did your mom help you lay out these clothes on the bed?"

Ben: (appears uncomfortable) "Um, no . . . gosh, uh . . ."

Alex: (interrupts) "Does she know where you are right now?"

Ben: (trying to avoid Alex, pulls out phone) "No."

Alex: (teases) "Are you texting your mom? Is that your mom?"

Ben: (on phone) "Ah, no . . . no . . ."

Alex: (interrupts) "Make sure she knows where you are. You gotta tell your mom where you are. She's going to be worried." (in a sarcastic tone) "She's your mommy." (teases) "Do you still wear diapers? Are you a little baby?"

Ben: (looking around, on the phone, appears uncomfortable) "Uh, no . . ."

Alex: "What's wrong? How old are you . . . like four?"

Ben: (uncomfortably shifts sideways, looking around, pretends to be on the phone)

Alex: (teases) "What's wrong with you? Does she know where you are? Make sure . . ."

Ben: (uncomfortable) "What?"

Alex: (teases) ". . . she's probably really worried!"

Perspective-Taking Questions

- What was that interaction like for Ben?
  Answers: Irritating, annoying, hurtful, embarrassing
- What do you think Ben thought of Alex?
  Answers: Mean, unfriendly, unkind, rude, annoying
- Is Ben going to want to talk to Alex again?
  Answer: No, too mean

Video

Don't Get Too Personal at First

- If you share too much personal information about yourself or ask too many personal questions, you may make the other person feel uncomfortable.

(continued)

Social Vignette: Don't Get Too Personal at First

The following social vignette is a transcript of the video demonstration from the accompanying DVD of getting too personal at first.

Alex: "Hey, Ben. What are you doing this weekend?"

Ben: "I'm going to my mom's and step-dad's; they're having a party."

Alex: (questioning) "Your step-dad? Are your parents divorced?"

Ben: "Um, yeah."

Alex: "Oh, when did that happen?"

Ben: (hesitant) "Um, when I was twelve."

Alex: "Oh, why?"

Ben: (uncomfortable, crosses arms) "Um, I don't know, . . . can we talk about something else?"

Alex: (being persistent) "When you were twelve; was that hard on you?"

Ben: (hesitant) "Uh, yeah, yeah."

Alex: "Oh, did they tell you why or do you just don't know?"

Ben: "Um." (pause) "I . . . ah . . . can we talk about something else?"

Alex: "I'm just curious ya know? Is it weird going to your mom's and dad's? I'm just curious."

Ben: (uncomfortable, looks around) "Yeah, yep."

Alex: "What? Do you like see one of them more than the other? Or do they like get jealous? Is it weird?"

Ben: (appears uncomfortable, hands crossed) "Um, I don't know."

Alex: "Do they fight over you still? Is it awkward there?"

Ben: (pause, looks uncomfortable)

Perspective-Taking Questions

- What was that interaction like for Ben?
  Answers: Uncomfortable, awkward, embarrassing, creepy, weird

- What do you think Ben thought of Alex?
  Answers: Creepy, stalker, nosy, weird
- Is Ben going to want to talk to Alex again?
  Answer: No, too uncomfortable, too creepy

CHAPTER EXERCISES
for Teens, Young Adults, and Parents

Teens and young adults should complete the following exercises with parents:

- Practice trading information and having a two-way conversation with your parent using all of the rules of good conversations outlined in this chapter.
  - Review the rules of good conversations summarized in this chapter prior to practicing.
  - Your goal while trading information will be to find a common interest with your parent.
  - After you've traded information with your parent, identify what your common interests were and what you could do with that information if you were to hang out.
- Practice trading information and having a two-way conversation with someone around your age whom you feel comfortable with using all of the rules of good conversations outlined in this chapter.
  - Begin by reviewing the rules of good conversations. Using the FriendMaker mobile app to review the steps just beforehand might be helpful.
  - Your goal while trading information will be to find a common interest.
  - After you've traded information, share the details of the conversation with your parent and identify what your common interests were and what you could do with that information if you were to hang out with that person.

4

Starting and Entering Conversations

LEARNING HOW TO MAKE NEW FRIENDS CAN seem like a mysterious and enigmatic process for some, particularly those with social challenges who may experience the social world as puzzling and perplexing. Yet even among those who find it easy to make friends, few would actually be able to identify the steps they take in meeting new people. Aside from meeting people through introductions from mutual friends and acquaintances, there are in fact concrete steps people follow to meet new people. Yet, few people have actually consciously mapped out the route they take or the steps they follow.

Imagine a teen at a party where he doesn't know anyone. He'd like to talk with the other teens, but he's unsure how to approach them. Imagine this teen has a history of peer rejection, with a tendency to be impulsive and hyperactive. What do you think he'll do to meet the other teens? Based on our experience and what research suggests, this teen is likely to be intrusive when he enters the conversation. He'll most likely walk up to the other teens, barge into their conversation, and start talking about something completely off topic. What will he talk about? He'll probably talk about what he's interested in, even though that's not what the group is talking about. What will this interaction be like for the other teens whose conversation has been hijacked? They'll probably feel annoyed, irritated, and perhaps a little confused. What will they think of the teen who just interrupted their conversation? They'll probably think he's weird, annoying, obnoxious, and a little oblivious. Do you think they'll want to talk to him? The chance that such an awkward and intrusive start would result in a nice conversation is highly unlikely. It's more likely that the group will politely make one or two replies before going back to their original conversation, or they may ignore him entirely, or worse, laugh and make fun of him. If this intrusive and odd behavior becomes a pattern, the teen is likely to get a bad reputation, making it all the more difficult to develop friendships.

Now imagine a different teen at this same party. Like the other boy, he doesn't know anyone, hopes to talk with the other teens, but is also unsure how to engage them. This time, however, imagine this teen has a history of social neglect, with bouts of depression and anxiety. What do you think he'll do to meet the other teens? Based on what we know of similar teens and from what research suggests, this teen will probably stand alone along the perimeter of the room, not talk to the other teens, rarely make eye contact with the other party-goers, and make no or few attempts to engage others. Assuming he wants to meet the other teens, he'll probably wait for someone to come up and talk to him, which may or may not happen. His body language is not likely to be inviting: perhaps standing with his head held down, eyes looking away from the crowd, with no smile on his face, appearing as if he wants to be left alone.

In one final scenario, imagine another teen at this same party accompanied by an adult. Like the other teens, this boy doesn't know anyone at the party but wishes to meet the other teens. What do you think the adult will tell this teen to do to meet the other kids? We've asked this question to countless teens and young adults through the UCLA PEERS Clinic and routinely hear the same two answers. They're told to "go up and say hi" or to "go up and introduce yourself." Now imagine if this teen actually followed this advice. Picture him walking up to an unsuspecting group of teens and entering their conversation by saying, "Hi!" or "Hi, my name is Dan." What will happen to the conversation? This interruption will stop the conversation. All attention will now be focused on this strange boy who out of nowhere, with no apparent reason, walked up and interrupted a conversation to say hello and tell the group his name. What will this interaction be like for the other teens? They'll probably feel confused, annoyed, or even a little creeped out. What will they think of the teen that just interrupted them? They'll probably think he's weird, annoying, obnoxious, or creepy. Do you think they'll want to talk to him? The chance that this awkward and intrusive beginning will result in a new acquaintance is doubtful. It's more likely that the group will politely say hello and then go back to their conversation or just ignore the awkward teen altogether, maybe even laughing at his odd behavior. This example is a good illustration of how well-intentioned adults will often give teens the wrong advice when it comes to making and keeping friends. If you've given your child advice like this before, don't worry—it happens to the best of us. Don't beat yourself up about it. Instead, let's focus on the right advice to give your teen or young adult in the future, using ecologically valid social skills for starting and entering conversations.

The following steps are based on scientifically supported research evidence of how socially successful people initiate or join conversations. You'll quickly recognize that these steps are applicable not only to teens and young adults with social difficulties but also may be applied to anyone involved in the act of starting or entering a conversation, so feel free to use them yourself!

Steps for Starting Individual Conversations

Video

The following steps should be used when your teen or young adult is trying to start an individual conversation with someone he or she either doesn't know or knows only slightly. For people your child is well acquainted with, it's perfectly acceptable to go up and say hello and ask how they're doing, rather than follow these steps. These steps should be followed in the order presented without skipping any steps.

1. **Casually look over at the person.** When your teen or young adult is considering starting a conversation with someone, it's helpful to first show interest in this person while covertly gathering information about him or her. This can be done by casually making periodic eye contact with the person (if possible) or casually looking over at him or her from time to time. This shows that your teen or young adult is interested in the person. It's important not to stare at the person when looking at him or her. This would feel uncomfortable and creepy to the person being watched. Just a little brief look on a couple of occasions is plenty.

2. **Use a prop.** As your teen or young adult is casually attempting to make eye contact or show interest in the person, it's helpful to use a prop to make it seem like he or she is occupied with something other than noticing the person. For example, using a mobile phone, gaming device, laptop, book, or magazine will help give the appearance of being engaged in some activity.

3. **Look for a common interest.** While your teen or young adult is casually and covertly watching the person, it's critical to find some kind of common interest that they both appear to share. For example, if the other person is looking at a mobile phone and your child has the same phone or is considering getting one, this would be a common interest. If the other person is wearing a gaming T-shirt and your child happens to know and like that video game, this would be a common interest. If the person is reading a science textbook and your child likes science, this may be a common interest. Or if the person is carrying a comic book and your child likes comic books, this would be a common interest.

4. **Make a reference to the common interest.** Once your teen or young adult has identified an interest, he or she will want to make a reference to the common interest. This might involve making a comment, asking a question, or giving a compliment about the interest shared. For example, if the common interest is mobile phones, commenting on the phone and asking whether he or she likes the phone would be appropriate. If the common interest is a particular video game, pointing out the logo on the T-shirt and complimenting the choice of video game might be a good move. If the common interest is science, commenting on the science textbook and asking if he or she likes the subject would be a good idea. Or if the common interest is comic books, making a reference to the magazine and commenting about the characters or storyline would be smooth.

5. **Trade information about the common interest.** After making a comment about the apparent common interest, your teen or young adult should try to trade information about the topic. This will involve asking follow-up questions, answering his or her own questions, and sharing relevant information about the topic. Following the rules for conversational skills will be important, remembering

observing the execution of these three steps, they'll often appear to be occurring simultaneously. However, in order to simplify this sequence of behaviors into easy-to-digest steps for your teen or young adult, we'll consider these behaviors separately, although occurring within in the same general time period. So how close should your child move? Typically about an arm's length or two away is appropriate. Anything closer would feel intrusive. Anything further may seem too distant. Often when your child moves closer to the group, the group members will naturally look over, noticing that someone has entered their circle. This change in spatial dynamics will sometimes create a natural pause in the conversation, which leads to the next step for joining the conversation.

8. **Wait for a brief pause in the conversation.** The next important step for entering a group conversation will be to wait for a brief pause in the conversation just before joining. The reason your teen or young adult should wait for a brief pause is that he or she shouldn't be interrupting the conversation. As indicated in the previous step, although never a guarantee, this pause may occur as a natural response to moving closer. Ideally, though, the best time to join is when the conversation is shifting from one person to the next. Because there will never be a perfect pause in the conversation, your teen or young adult is simply looking for a good entry point. A transition from one conversational partner to the next is usually a good time to enter. The goal of waiting for a brief pause is not to find a moment of silence. Instead, the hope is just not to interrupt the conversation too much. In our experience at the UCLA PEERS Clinic, the most common problem teens and young adults with social challenges run into with this strategy is that they wait for the perfect pause. Again, there will never be a perfect pause, and if your child waits for one, he or she may wait forever. Instead, when coaching your child, just encourage him or her to try to join when the conversation is switching between partners and try not to interrupt too much.

> *The reason your teen or young adult should wait for a brief pause is that he or she shouldn't be interrupting the conversation.*

9. **Make a comment or ask a question about the topic.** The next step might be considered the most important in the process of entering a group conversation. It's in this step that your teen or young adult will engage the group by making a comment or asking a question that's on topic. In other words, your teen or young adult needs a reason for joining, and the reason is that he or she has something interesting to contribute to the conversation. The point about being on topic cannot be stressed enough because it may virtually make or break success in joining the conversation. The common social error committed by teens and young adults with social challenges is that they enter conversations armed with their own topic of interest (unrelated to the theme of the current conversation). In most cases, this error results in some kind of peer rejection because being off topic causes a disruption or disturbance in the conversation. Instead, the goal of entering a group conversation should be to join in a way that neither disrupts the flow of the conversation nor disturbs its participants.

> *Engage the group by making a comment or asking a question that's on topic.*

10. **Assess interest.** Once your teen or young adult has joined the conversation, it will be important to assess the interest of the group members to determine if he or she should remain in the conversation. Remember that the behavioral signs that tell you if someone is interested in talking to you include verbal cues, body language, and eye contact. Verbal cues relate to whether the group is actually talking to your child, speaking nicely, and giving extended responses to questions and comments. Body language relates to whether the group is facing your child after his or her attempt to join. When people talk in groups, they often talk in circles. When they're interested in talking to your child, they'll open the circle (turn their bodies toward

> *The behavioral signs that tell you if someone is interested in talking to you include verbal cues, body language, and eye contact.*

your child). When they're not interested, they'll close the circle (turn their bodies away) or give the cold shoulder. When they're interested, they will also look at your child and maybe even smile. To keep it simple, your teen or young adult should consider the following questions:

    a. Are they talking to me?

    b. Are they facing me (or did they close the circle)?

    c. Are they looking at me?

11. **Introduce yourself.** The final step in the process of entering a group conversation is for your teen or young adult to introduce him- or herself to anyone unfamiliar. This step happens only if your child has been accepted into the conversation and he or she has had a lengthy conversation (usually for several minutes). Notice again, introductions are the last step of the process, not the first step as many will wrongly suggest. Remember that introductions are often done by saying something like, "By the way, my name is Jennifer" or "I should probably introduce myself. I'm Jennifer." This may be followed by a handshake (more often with adults; more rarely with teens) but this will depend on the context and habits of the conversational partners.

    Social coaching tip: In order to learn these steps, you and your child should jointly read the social vignettes in the chapter summary for teens and young adults, view the DVD demonstrations for inappropriately and appropriately entering group conversations, and discuss these demonstrations using the perspective-taking questions.

    Social coaching tip: In order to help your child learn these skills, we recommend that you organize many opportunities to practice these steps with you and eventually with potential friends. The most common difficulty for peer-rejected teens and young adults when joining conversations is that they don't listen and watch the conversation, joining too quickly and off topic. For socially neglected teens and young adults, the most common problem involves waiting for the perfect pause. Although you may remind your child that there's never a perfect pause, they still may try to wait for one. As your child's social coach, it's important for you to know that your teen or young adult can follow these steps (even if only the abbreviated steps listed on the following page). They may not get it perfectly right away but you know what they say: practice makes perfect. So plan lots of opportunities to practice.

Social coaching tips: Some parents we've worked with through the UCLA PEERS Clinic have expressed skepticism that their child would be able to follow the steps described here. In our experience, the vast majority of teens and young adults are able to follow these steps with few problems, but if your child has trouble remembering all the steps, a simpler version is as follows:

1. Watch and listen for the topic.
2. Move closer.
3. Wait for a pause.
4. Make a comment or ask a question that is on topic.

Success Story: Morgan Makes Friends

Knowing how to start and enter conversations is a skill required of us all, though few not privy to these ecologically valid steps could describe how it's done. Although anxiety provoking for even the most socially savvy person, conversational entry is even more difficult for socially challenged teens and young adults who don't naturally know how to act in these situations. To make matters more confusing, well-meaning adults will sometimes give the wrong advice about what to do in these situations. Such was the case of Morgan, a fourteen-year-old girl with a history of social phobia and school refusal.

Morgan was an attractive young girl with an angelic face, who loved music and movies, and was obsessed with *Twilight*, like many girls her age. On the surface, Morgan seemed like a typical young girl. Yet, Morgan suffered from paralyzing social anxiety, finding it so frightening to be around others her age that her parents homeschooled her for two years before coming to PEERS. Despite her extreme social anxiety, Morgan did want to make friends. She owned to feeling lonely and isolated and secretly hoped that she'd be able to go back to school one day.

Although Morgan had many fears about socializing, the idea of talking to people she didn't know well was perhaps most frightening. She claimed that whenever she tried to meet new people "it never worked" and that no one wanted to talk to her. It probably wasn't that people didn't want to talk to Morgan but that she was approaching them the wrong way. For years Morgan had been told by well-meaning adults that if she wanted to meet new people she should go up and say "hi" and introduce herself. On the occasions when she was able to build up the nerve to use these improper strategies, she was often met with confusion and blank stares, not surprisingly. Morgan attributed these reactions to people not wanting to talk to her, only increasing her anxiety and social confusion.

As you can imagine, learning the ecologically valid steps for starting conversations and entering group conversations was pivotal in Morgan's transformation from a socially anxious to a socially successful teen. Although the process was lengthy—taking several weeks for Morgan to even summon the courage to practice these steps outside of our social skills group—eventually she was successful in entering a conversation. And how did she do it? She found a group of girls in her new community choir who loved to discuss the merits of Team Edward or Team Jacob as much as she did; her love of *Twilight* ultimately provided the key to unlocking the doors of social exclusion. Many months later when reminded of this first success, a more confident Morgan commented, "I used to think people didn't like me. Nobody wanted to talk to me at my old school. I tried to make friends at first, . . . but I didn't know I was doing it wrong. I didn't know what to say. I'd kinda stand there, and they wouldn't say anything, . . . and they'd look at me like I was weird. Then I just stopped trying. I used to cry about it, too. But now I know how to talk to people. I just find stuff that we like and talk about that. Like when they were talking about *Twilight* that day, I was like, 'I can talk about that.' So I did . . . and then they starting asking me questions. Now I know that's how it works, . . . that's how you make friends."

Morgan's story is not so different from other socially anxious teens and young adults who've gone through PEERS. If you're concerned that your child may be too fearful to overcome the obstacles of social angst, just remember Morgan—a vibrant young girl who now attends high school, joined the school choir, and has a close group of girlfriends, most of whom share her love of all things *Twilight*.

STARTING AND ENTERING CONVERSATIONS
Chapter Summary for Teens and Young Adults

The following information is intended to be read by teens and young adults and contains a brief summary of the chapter.

Video

Steps for Starting Individual Conversations

The best way to meet new people when we don't have mutual friends or acquaintances is to start a conversation. Adults will sometimes give the advice to go up and introduce yourself or go up and say "hi", but that's not really how it's done. The following steps outline how socially successful teens and young adults start individual conversations with people either unknown or only known slightly.

1. **Casually look over at the person.** When you're considering starting a conversation with someone, it's helpful to first show interest in the person by casually looking at him or her for a second or two—but not staring.
2. **Use a prop.** As you're casually looking over (attempting to make eye contact), it's helpful to use a prop such as a mobile phone, gaming device, or a book to give the appearance that you're focused on some other activity.
3. **Look for a common interest.** While you're casually and covertly watching the person, you need to find some kind of common interest that you both appear to share. Maybe you have the same mobile phone or you like the video game the person is playing.
4. **Make a reference to the common interest.** Once you've identified an interest that you both appear to share, you should make a comment, ask a question, or give a compliment about the common interest. This is your excuse for talking to the person.

5. **Trade information about the common interest.** Next you need to trade information about the common interest by asking follow-up questions, answering your own questions, and sharing relevant information about yourself.

6. **Assess interest.** Then you need to assess the interest of the person you're trying to talk to. If he or she doesn't seem interested in talking to you, move on. You can tell if people want to talk to you by asking yourself the following questions:

   a. Are they talking to me?
   b. Are they facing me (or giving me the cold shoulder)?
   c. Are they looking at me?

7. **Introduce yourself.** The final step for starting an individual conversation is to introduce yourself if you've never met before and if that person seems interested in talking to you.

Social Vignette of Starting Individual Conversations: Bad Example

The following social vignette is a transcript of the video demonstration from the accompanying DVD of inappropriately starting an individual conversation.

Ben: (watching a game on his phone, making a fist in the air) "Yes!"
Alex: (walks up, interrupts) "Hey, did you go to the comic book convention last night?"
Ben: (confused) "The what?"
Alex: "The comic book convention. Were you there?"
Ben: (pointing to phone) "I'm watching the game, uh . . ."
Alex: "But did you go there last night?"
Ben: "Ah, no . . . no."
Alex: "Oh, I was there. It was awesome. You should've been. Do you like comic books?"
Ben: (appears annoyed, looking at phone) "Um, yeah, I do. But, well, I'm watching . . ."

(continued)

Alex: (interrupts) "Why didn't you go then? You should've been. Everyone was there."

Ben: ". . . the game right now."

Alex: "Oh, yeah, so are you going next week?"

Ben: (annoyed) "Um, I don't know."

Alex: "It's gonna be really good. You should definitely check it out."

Ben: (looking at phone) "Okay, okay."

Perspective-Taking Questions

- What was that interaction like for Ben?
  Answers: Uncomfortable, annoying, awkward, confusing, weird
- What do you think Ben thought of Alex?
  Answers: Weird, odd, obnoxious
- Is Ben going to want to talk to Alex again?
  Answer: No, too weird and obnoxious

Social Vignette of Starting Individual Conversations: Good Example

The following social vignette is a transcript of the video demonstration from the accompanying DVD of appropriately starting an individual conversation.

Ben: (watching a game on his phone, making a fist in the air) "Oh, yes!"

Alex: (puts book on shelf, sees the game on Ben's phone) "Oh, is that the game?"

Ben: "Oh, yeah, yeah."

Alex: (leaning in toward Ben) "Oh, wow. What's the score?"

Ben: "Um, three–zero. There's a minute left."

Alex: "Oh, my gosh, that's crazy. Has it been an entertaining game?"

Ben: "Oh, yeah, it's been awesome. Did you see the one last night?"

Alex: "No, I was in the library and didn't get service. How do you get that on your phone?"

Ben: "Well, I have this app. It's free."

Alex: "Oh, my gosh, that is so cool. Does it take up a lot of battery?"

Ben: "Um, yeah, but you know it's worth it."

Alex: "Oh, that's awesome. Wow."

Ben: "Yeah."

Alex: "I gotta get one of these so I can watch the games in the library."

Ben: "Oh, you should. It's awesome!"

(After some time talking, Alex would introduce himself to Ben.)

Perspective-Taking Questions

- What was that interaction like for Ben?
  Answers: Nice, comfortable, pleasant
- What do you think Ben thought of Alex?
  Answers: Nice, friendly, cool, social
- Is Ben going to want to talk to Alex again?
  Answer: Probably yes, seems cool

Video

Steps for Entering Group Conversations

Another way to meet new people is to enter group conversations. This strategy is particularly helpful when you're at extracurricular activities or gatherings where you don't know people yet. Just like with starting an individual conversation, adults will sometimes give the advice to go up and introduce yourself or go up and say "hi" to the group, but that's not what socially successful teens and young adults do. Instead, you should use the following steps to enter a group conversation with two or more people you either don't know or only know slightly.

1. **Discreetly listen to the conversation.** Before you try to enter a group conversation between people you either don't know

(continued)

or only know slightly, you first need to discreetly listen to the conversation and try to figure out what they're talking about.

2. **Inconspicuously watch from a distance.** While you're listening, you should also be inconspicuously watching from a distance. This means you should occasionally look over toward the group for a second or two at a time without staring at them.

3. **Use a prop.** While you're listening and watching the conversation, it's helpful to use a prop such as a mobile phone to make it look like you're focused on something else.

4. **Identify the topic of conversation.** The most important goal of listening to the conversation will be to identify the topic being discussed. Topics shift a lot, so it's important to make sure you're following the topic the whole time.

5. **Make sure you share a common interest in the topic.** Before you attempt to join a conversation, you need to make sure you share a common interest in the topic. Your common interest will be your excuse for joining.

6. **Make a bit more eye contact.** Once you've decided that you share a common interest, you can start to make a bit more eye contact with the group. This shows your increased interest in them and what they're saying. Be sure not to stare though— no more than four to five seconds each time you look over.

7. **Move closer to the group.** Around the time you start to make a bit more eye contact and you've decided to join the conversation, you should move a bit closer to the group. Usually about an arm's length away or two is good.

8. **Wait for a brief pause in the conversation.** The next step is to wait for a brief pause in the conversation just before joining. There's never a perfect pause, so just try not to interrupt too much.

9. **Make a comment or ask a question about the topic.** You should join the conversation by making a comment or asking a question about the topic. This is your reason for joining the conversation.

10. **Assess interest.** Make sure the group wants to talk to you by asking yourself the following questions:
    a. Are they talking to me?
    b. Are they facing me (or did they close the circle)?
    c. Are they looking at me?
11. **Introduce yourself.** The final step for entering a group conversation is to introduce yourself to anyone you don't know. You only do this after you've been talking for a while (at least several minutes) and you're sure you've been accepted into the conversation.

Social Vignette of Entering Group Conversations: Bad Example

The following social vignette is a transcript of the video demonstration from the accompanying DVD of inappropriately entering a group conversation.

Mary, Alex, and Lara: (standing around and talking)

Lara: "So, Alex, you'll never believe it, . . . I ran into Mary at my piano lesson place."

Alex: (turns to Mary) "Oh, no way, I didn't know you played piano."

Mary: "Well, I didn't know that she played piano." (gesturing to Lara) "Then we ran into each other. It was the craziest thing."

Lara: "It really was."

Alex: "Wow."

Lara: (turns to Alex) "Do you play anything?"

Alex: "Yeah, I play . . ."

Yasamine: (walks up and interrupts) "Have you guys been to the water park?"

Mary, Alex, and Lara: (startled)

Mary: (confused) "Water park? No."

Alex: (turns to Mary) "Um, what did you say?"

(continued)

Yasamine: (interrupts) "The new water park that just opened up."

Lara: (turns to Alex, ignoring Yasamine) "Do you play anything, Alex?"

Yasamine: "It's so awesome!"

Alex: (talking over Yasamine) "Uh, yeah. I play guitar."

Yasamine: (interrupts) "There's this slide that starts at the very top, . . . and you just go round and round and round all the way down, . . . it's so much fun."

Mary, Alex, and Lara: (look annoyed)

Mary: (talking over Yasamine) "Um, so . . ."

Alex: (talking over Yasamine) "Um, I play electric."

Mary: (turns to Alex) "Cool."

Lara: (turns to Alex) "Very nice. Do you ever play out?"

Yasamine: (talking over others) "And you go really fast down the slide. It's so fun!"

Alex: (confused) "Um, in my garage."

Yasamine: (still talking over others) "There's also this place where you can kind of body surf. Have you guys been body surfing before?"

Lara: (turns to Alex, annoyed by Yasamine) "In your garage? I'm sorry, you play in your garage?"

Alex: (trying to talk over Yasamine) "Um, yeah . . . in my garage."

Yasamine: (still talking over others) "It's so much fun and it's so close, too."

Perspective-Taking Questions

- What was that interaction like for Mary, Alex, and Lara?
  Answers: Uncomfortable, awkward, confusing, weird
- What do you think they thought of Yasamine?
  Answers: Weird, odd, annoying, obnoxious
- Are they going to want to talk to Yasamine again?
  Answer: No, too weird and annoying

Social Vignette of Entering Group Conversations: Good Example

The following social vignette is a transcript of the video demonstration from the accompanying DVD of appropriately entering a group conversation.

Mary, Alex, and Lara: (standing around and talking)

Yasamine: (standing several feet away, looking at phone)

Lara: "So, Alex, you'll never believe it! Yesterday, I ran into Mary when I was leaving my piano lesson."

Alex: "No way?" (turns to Mary) "You play piano?"

Mary: "Yeah, I've been playing. It's the craziest thing, . . . I've never run into her before."

Lara: "I can't believe it."

Alex: "Oh, that's so funny."

Lara: (turns to Alex) "Do you play an instrument?"

Alex: "I play guitar."

Mary: "Cool."

Lara: "Oh, cool. I just started to play guitar."

Alex: "Ah, that's awesome. Electric or acoustic?"

Lara: "No, I play acoustic. How about you?"

Alex: "I play electric."

Yasamine: (looking over at Mary, Alex, and Lara periodically, starting to show interest)

Lara: "Oh, cool."

Alex: (turns to Mary) "Do you play?"

Mary: "No, I really want to learn though."

Lara: "It's really fun; you should definitely take lessons."

Mary: "I feel like it'd be good."

Yasamine: (moves closer, waits for a brief pause) "Do you play the guitar?"

Lara: (looking over at Yasamine): "Yeah, we were just talking about it. Alex and I play."

Alex: (looking over at Yasamine): "We both play."

(continued)

Yasamine: "Ah, that's so awesome! What do you play?"

Lara: "I play acoustic."

Alex: "And I play electric."

Yasamine: "Oh, nice. I play acoustic."

Lara: "Oh, cool."

Yasamine: "Yeah, I've been playing for like five years now."

Mary and Alex: "Wow."

Lara: "That's awesome. I just started, . . . so."

Alex: "Yeah, it's really fun."

Yasamine: "Yeah, I like it a lot." (looking toward Mary) "You should definitely learn."

Mary: "I know. I really want to."

Yasamine: "Yeah, it's so cool."

Lara: "We should all jam some time. That'd be fun."

Alex: "Definitely."

Yasamine: "Yeah, I'd really love that."

(After some time talking, Yasamine would introduce herself to the group.)

Perspective-Taking Questions

- What was that interaction like for Mary, Alex, and Lara?
  Answers: Nice, pleasant, interesting
- What do you think they thought of Yasamine?
  Answers: Nice, pleasant, cool, friendly, social
- Are they going to want to talk to Yasamine again?
  Answer: Probably yes, seems friendly

CHAPTER EXERCISES
for Teens, Young Adults, and Parents

Teens and young adults should complete the following exercises with parents:

- Practice starting an individual conversation with your parent following the steps outlined in this chapter.
  - With your parent, begin by reviewing the steps for starting an individual conversation.
  - Practice following the steps for starting an individual conversation with your parent.
- Practice entering a group conversation with your parent and at least one other person following the steps outlined in this chapter.
  - With your parent, begin by reviewing the steps for entering a group conversation.
  - Practice following the steps for entering a group conversation with your parent and at least one other person.
- Practice starting an individual conversation with a peer you don't know or know only slightly following the steps outlined in this chapter.
  - Begin by reviewing the steps for starting an individual conversation. Using the FriendMaker mobile app to review the steps just beforehand might be helpful.
  - You may want to choose someone from the social group you identified or someone enrolled in an extracurricular or social activity you belong to.
- Practice entering a group conversation with two or more peers you don't know well following the steps outlined in this chapter.
  - Begin by reviewing the steps for entering a group conversation. Using the FriendMaker mobile app to review the steps just beforehand might be helpful.
  - You may want to choose peers from the social group you identified or someone enrolled in an extracurricular or social activity you belong to.

5

Exiting Conversations

KNOWING HOW TO START AND ENTER CONVERSATIONS with unfamiliar people is one of the first steps in making new friends and acquaintances. The technical term for this kind of interaction is *peer entry*, which refers broadly to attempts to engage others through conversation, play, or other types of interactions. Research suggests that nearly 50 percent of peer entry attempts with unfamiliar people are turned down in some form. This means that if the average person were to try to join ten different conversations with people either unknown or only slightly known, nearly half of these attempts would end in some form of refusal. The type of refusal will vary. At best the person might be initially accepted into the conversation but somewhere along the way become excluded. At worst he or she might be completely ignored, utterly disregarded, or even laughed at or teased. The latter example is probably more likely to happen if the person trying to join makes a mistake when entering or has a bad reputation, as is sadly not uncommon for teens and young adults with social difficulties. In order for your child to enhance his or her chances at being accepted, it will be important to follow the steps that socially successful teens and young adults use for starting and entering conversations described in chapter 4.

Even still, being prepared for what to do when attempts are not accepted is part and parcel of the science of making friends.

> *Nearly 50 percent of peer entry attempts with unfamiliar people are turned down in some form.*

Although using the steps for starting and entering conversations will certainly improve the chances of being accepted, even when these steps are followed, from time to time your teen or young adult will be turned down during peer entry. Although it may be painful for you to imagine this kind of rejection, try to remember that not being accepted is actually a normal part of being social. Friendship is a choice. We don't get to be friends with everyone and everyone doesn't get to be friends with us. That means some attempts at being friendly will be accepted and some won't. It doesn't have to be a big deal and it's not the end of the world. Rather than feeling hurt and protective because someone may not want to talk, you might try to normalize this experience for your teen or young adult, explaining that it happens to everyone from time to time. In our experience through the UCLA PEERS Clinic, normalizing this experience is a big first step toward moving past it. When our teens and young adults are told that half of their attempts to join conversations will not be accepted, that it's not a big deal and happens to everyone, they learn not to take it so personally. As your teen or young adult's social coach, it will be important for you to convey this point, too.

In order to help normalize the experience of being turned down when trying to enter conversations, it might be helpful to consider some of the reasons why other teens or adults may not want to talk at any given time. If this is a hot button issue for your teen or young adult, remember that many times these reasons aren't even personal. So try not to get upset. Instead, take a deep breath, then think about why this might happen and what your child might do differently next time.

One reason for being turned down when joining a conversation is that the other people may want to talk privately, which means your teen or young adult might try again later when it's a better time. Another reason might be that the group is talking about things your child doesn't understand, which suggests he or she might want to listen more carefully next time before joining. Perhaps the other people are in a clique and aren't interested in talking to other people, which means your teen or young adult should probably choose a different group to join next time. Maybe the group didn't understand that your child was trying to join the conversation, which means he or she should try again later, following the steps for entering a conversation. Or perhaps your teen or young adult has a bad reputation with that particular group, which means joining a conversation with people that are unaware or unconcerned with your child's reputation would be a good strategy for next time.

Whatever the case and whatever the plan, we must all expect and be prepared not to be accepted into conversations from time to time. Yet, what if your child isn't even aware of not being accepted? Some teens and young adults who have difficulty reading social cues will fail to notice they're not being accepted into the conversation and may even persist. What would this look like? Imagine a young man walks up to a group of fellow classmates after a science lecture and tries to engage them by mentioning their most recent science experiment. The group is disinterested, talking instead about some party they went to over the weekend. Their backs are turned, the circle is closed, and they're not looking at the young man or talking to him. Rather than picking up on these behavioral signs, the young man persists. He speaks louder, moves closer, assuming they didn't realize he was there. How does the group react? They feel annoyed and irritated, begin to make faces at the young man, and roll their eyes to each other. The young man may eventually give up and walk away or perhaps he'll get upset and angry. In the latter case, he may question their rudeness and ask them why they won't talk to him, thereby causing a scene and drawing more negative attention. However this scenario plays out, the young man has committed a major social error in not successfully assessing the interest of the group and then appropriately exiting the conversation. Even worse, he may have done great damage to his reputation by persisting, and most certainly by exploding. Yet these are the social errors sometimes committed by teens and young adults with social challenges. You'll need to help your teen or young adult expect that he or she will not be accepted into every conversation, that this experience is perfectly natural, happens to everyone, and shouldn't be taken personally. Although not being accepted into conversations can feel embarrassing, using the steps outlined in the following for exiting these conversations can help your teen or young adult save face.

> We must all expect and be prepared not to be accepted into conversations from time to time.

In general, there are three types of scenarios for exiting conversations. The first involves conversations in which your teen or young adult doesn't feel accepted. The second involves conversations in which he or she initially feels accepted, maybe even sharing a few conversational exchanges, but then feels excluded. The third involves conversations in which your teen or young adult is fully accepted into the conversation but

> There are three types of scenarios for exiting conversations.

just needs to leave for other reasons. The concrete steps for how to handle each of these social scenarios are presented in the following pages with accompanying social vignettes, including transcripts of DVD video demonstrations and perspective-taking questions.

Assessing Interest: Should You Stay or Should You Go?

Before outlining the steps for exiting conversations, it's important to review the behavioral cues we've identified that tell us if your teen or young adult is accepted in a conversation. Recall that those behaviors include verbal cues, body language, and eye contact.

Verbal Cues

One of the simplest ways of assessing interest when joining conversations involves paying attention to verbal cues. Verbal cues include whether the group is talking, speaking nicely, and giving extended responses to your teen or young adult's questions and comments. If they're not talking, not speaking nicely (perhaps even teasing or making fun), or giving short replies to questions and comments, your teen or young adult will need to exit the conversation using the steps outlined in the following sections.

> Verbal cues include whether the group is talking, speaking nicely, and giving extended responses to your teen or young adult's questions and comments.

Body Language

Another important clue to determining whether a group is interested in talking involves body language. Body language is a form of nonverbal communication, consisting of body posture, gestures, and facial expressions. Reading body language can be a complicated process. To simplify things, we'll focus on the positioning of the bodies of the people your teen or young adult is trying to talk to. Remember that when people are interested, they turn their bodies toward the people they're including in the conversation. If their bodies are turned away, sometimes described as giving the cold shoulder, this is usually a sign of disinterest. You may also remember that when people talk in groups, they often talk in circles. When they're interested in talking, they open the circle (turn their bodies toward the other people). When they're not interested in talking, they close the circle (turn their bodies away). If they turn away, give the cold shoulder, or close the circle, your teen or young adult will need to exit the conversation using the following steps.

> Another important clue to determining whether a group is interested in talking involves body language.

Eye Contact

Another way of determining interest when joining conversations involves eye contact. Eye contact is an important clue when assessing interest because it gives hints about the attention of the people we are trying to talk to. When people are interested in talking, they look at their conversational partners, maybe nodding their heads up and down or smiling. Not making eye contact, making faces, or rolling their eyes are signs that they're not interested in talking, in which case your teen or young adult will need to exit the conversation using the following steps.

> Eye contact is an important clue when assessing interest because it gives hints about the attention of the people we are trying to talk to.

Remember, to help your teen or young adult simplify the cues for assessing interest, have him or her consider the following three questions:

- Are they talking to me?
- Are they facing me (did they open the circle or close the circle)?
- Are they looking at me?

Steps for Exiting Conversations When You Don't Feel Accepted

Video

The harsh reality about peer entry is that from time to time your teen or young adult will attempt to join conversations and he or she won't be accepted. Remembering that nearly 50 percent of entry attempts result in some form of refusal, you need to help your child be prepared to handle these situations in order to avoid injury to his or her reputation. The following strategy represents ecologically valid steps used by socially successful teens and adults who've attempted to enter a conversation but have not felt accepted. These steps should be followed in the sequence presented.

1. Keep Your Cool

The first step in handling any form of peer rejection is to keep your cool. This means your teen or young adult needs to avoid getting upset or angry in the moment and act as if the rejection didn't bother him or her. Getting upset would only draw negative attention, possibly hurting his or her reputation with any onlookers. Different people have different strategies for keeping cool. Some teens and young adults we've worked with have said they mentally count to ten to help cool down; others have said they take deep breaths. Whatever the strategy, the first step in exiting a conversation in which your teen or young adult has never felt accepted is to regulate emotions and keep cool. Although emotion regulation is very much intertwined with social acceptance, this book is not intended to provide tools to regulate emotions. Should your teen or young adult require further assistance in this area, there are many resources with useful information about emotion regulation.

> *Your teen or young adult needs to avoid getting upset or angry in the moment and act as if the rejection didn't bother him or her.*

2. Slowly Look Away

The next step in exiting conversations when you don't feel accepted is to look away. In this case, your teen or young adult should casually and slowly look away from the group, focusing his or her gaze in another direction—usually no more than a 90-degree angle from where he or she is standing. If your child is unsure where to look, using a prop such as a mobile phone or gaming device can also be a useful method for looking away. What impression does it give the group when your teen or young adult looks away? It shows that your child's attention is elsewhere and that he or she is no longer interested in the conversation.

> *Your teen or young adult should casually and slowly look away from the group, focusing his or her gaze in another direction—usually no more than a 90-degree angle from where he or she is standing.*

3. Slowly Turn Away

After your teen or young adult has begun to look away, the next step is to turn away. This involves casually and slowly turning his or her body in the same direction he or she is looking. When your child turns away, what impression does that convey? It shows that his or her attention and interest is now completely focused elsewhere and he or she is just about to leave.

> *Casually and slowly turn his or her body in the same direction he or she is looking.*

4. Slowly and Casually Walk Away

The final step in exiting conversations when you don't feel accepted is to walk away. This means your teen or young adult should casually and slowly walk in the direction he or she is looking and facing. What impression does it give the group when your child casually and slowly walks away? It shows he or she is no longer interested in the conversation and has something more interesting and important to do.

> *Your teen or young adult should casually and slowly walk in the direction he or she is looking and facing.*

Social coaching tip: Although it may seem obvious, from our experience working with teens and young adults with social challenges, it's important to clarify that the process of looking away, turning away, and walking away should occur with each of these behaviors following the same direction. Looking to the left, turning to the right, and then walking in an entirely different direction looks more like a complicated dance move than a subtle attempt at exiting a conversation! Although a humorous mental image, as the social coach, you actually may need to clarify with your teen or young adult that these behaviors should all be focused in one direction on one identified target.

Social coaching tip: Be sure to go over the steps for exiting conversations when you don't feel accepted with your teen or young adult and facilitate opportunities to practice these steps with you and another person. It will also be important to jointly read the social vignette in the chapter summary for teens and young adults, view the DVD video demonstration of exiting conversations when you don't feel accepted, and generate a discussion using the perspective-taking questions.

Steps for Exiting Conversations When You Initially Feel Accepted and Then Excluded

Video

Sometimes when entering conversations with people either unknown or known only slightly it will appear as though your teen or young adult is initially accepted. He or she might even share a few polite conversational exchanges with these people but then something may happen that gives the impression that the group is no longer interested in talking. The group members may begin to look away or turn their bodies away, no longer directing their conversation toward your child. Remember that these types of exchanges are relatively normal and occur frequently, so try not to feel too upset if this has happened to your child. Chances are it happens to all of us more than we even realize and may be the most common type of refusal in conversations. Consequently, your teen or young adult should try not to get upset or take these situations too personally. Instead, he or she should exit the conversation following the ecologically valid steps used by socially successful teens and young adults. These steps should be followed in the sequence provided.

1. Keep Your Cool

Just as before, the first step in exiting conversations when initially accepted and then excluded is to keep your cool. As a reminder, this

> *Your teen or young adult needs to avoid getting upset or angry and instead act as if he or she isn't bothered.*

means your teen or young adult needs to avoid getting upset or angry and instead act as if he or she isn't bothered.

2. Slowly Look Away

The next step is to casually and slowly look away. This may involve your teen or young adult looking in a direction to one side (no more than a 90-degree angle away) or using a prop such as a mobile phone or gaming device. Remember that looking away gives the impression that your child's attention is now elsewhere and that he or she is no longer interested in the conversation.

> Looking away gives the impression that your child's attention is now elsewhere.

3. Wait for a Brief Pause in the Conversation

The next step in exiting conversations when initially accepted and then excluded is to wait for a brief pause in the conversation. Because he or she was initially accepted into the conversation, to simply walk away without saying something would seem strange and rude. Instead, he or she should wait for a very brief pause before saying a few short words. If your child doesn't wait for this brief pause before speaking, he or she will be interrupting, which will seem rude and disruptive. Yet, just as with the steps for entering conversations, remember that there is never a perfect pause. During this step, your teen or young adult is just trying not to interrupt too much before leaving.

> To simply walk away without saying something would seem strange.

4. Give a Brief Cover Story for Leaving

Just as your child finds a brief pause in the conversation, he or she should give a brief cover story for leaving the conversation. Cover stories are reasons why we do certain things. To clarify, using the buzzword cover story doesn't signify any kind of deception, like a cover-up or lie. A cover story is simply the reason your teen or young adult has to leave the conversation. The reason for leaving could be real or just an excuse. Either way, it's important to provide some sort of acknowledgment for leaving because to simply walk away without saying anything would seem odd because your teen or young adult was initially accepted into the conversation. Cover stories need to be very short. Simply saying something like, "Well, gotta go" or "Gotta get to class" is enough. Even just a few words of acknowledgment that your child is leaving is fine. Saying something like, "Take care" or "See you later" is also acceptable. If your teen or young adult were to say much more than a few words it would be too much and would interrupt the conversation. The reality is that the group is no longer accepting your teen or young adult in the conversation, so they're unlikely to be concerned with where he or she is

> *If your child says nothing before leaving, that would seem odd or rude.*

going. Yet, if your child says nothing before leaving, that would also seem odd or rude.

5. Walk Away

The final step in exiting conversations when you initially feel accepted and then excluded is to walk away. If your teen or young adult followed the earlier step of looking away in a specific direction, he or she should start walking in that direction. If your child looked away to glance at his or her mobile phone or gaming device then it's less relevant where he or she walks but looking back at the item that captured his or her attention while walking away would be appropriate. Following these steps will give the impression that your teen or young adult is no longer interested or able to participate in the conversation and has something else to do. Often,

> *The final step in exiting conversations when you initially feel accepted and then excluded is to walk away.*

when handled appropriately, the group will acknowledge the departure in a friendly manner, keeping the door open for the possibility of future communication.

Social coaching tip: To help your teen or young adult understand this strategy and when to use it, you will want to share these steps with him or her and facilitate opportunities to practice these steps with you and another person. It will also be important to jointly read the social vignette in the chapter summary for teens and young adults, view the DVD video demonstration of exiting a conversation when initially accepted and then excluded, and generate a discussion using the perspective-taking questions.

Video

Steps for Exiting Conversations When You Feel Fully Accepted

A final type of peer exiting that your child will need to become familiar with involves leaving conversations in which he or she has been fully accepted. Generally speaking, this may be the most common type of peer exiting.

People have to exit conversations all the time. Perhaps they have to get to class or they have somewhere else they need to be. Yet, consider the common mistakes made by teens and young adults with social difficulties when they have to leave a conversation. What might they do? A common response reported by parents at the UCLA PEERS Clinic is that their teens or young adults walk away without even acknowledging that they're leaving or where they're going. Because simply walking away would appear odd and even rude to others, you'll need to help your teen or young adult use an alternative strategy. The following strategy represents ecologically valid steps used by socially successful teens and young adults who've been fully accepted into a conversation but just need to leave. The steps should be followed in the sequence described.

> A final type of peer exiting that your child will need to become familiar with involves leaving conversations in which he or she has been fully accepted.

1. Wait for a Brief Pause in the Conversation

The first step in exiting conversations when fully accepted is to wait for a brief pause in the conversation. The pause doesn't need to be long, just a brief moment during the transition between speakers is enough. Like before, there's never a perfect pause, so your teen or young adult shouldn't wait for the perfect opportunity to leave because that moment may never come. Instead, your child should simply try not to interrupt the conversation too much before saying good-bye.

> The first step in exiting conversations when fully accepted is to wait for a brief pause in the conversation.

2. Give a Specific Cover Story for Leaving

The next step is to give a specific cover story for leaving the conversation. Remember that cover stories are reasons for doing certain things. In this case, the reason is related to why your teen or young adult needs to leave the conversation. However, this cover story is different from the ones used when excluded from conversations. Rather than giving a brief cover story, your child's cover story will need to be specific. For example, if your teen or young adult were simply to say, "Well, gotta go" or "Gotta get to class" and walk away from an accepting group of peers, that would seem strange and possibly rude. Brief remarks like that are only acceptable when being excluded because the group probably isn't concerned with where your child is going. However, accepting peers do care where your child is going and if he or she simply says, "See you later," the group may reply with, "Where are you going?" Consequently, cover stories with accepting peers should be a bit longer and more specific. For example, if your teen or young adult needs to get to class he or she might say, "Well, the bell is about to ring. I better get to class" or "I've got a science midterm, so I better get going."

> Cover stories with accepting peers should be a bit longer and more specific.

In these cases, your child has given the accepting peers a specific reason for leaving, so they're less likely to think your child doesn't want to talk to them anymore.

3. Tell Them You'll See or Speak to Them Later

The next step is to say you'll see or speak to them later. This is a nice social gesture that lets others know that your teen or young adult would like to continue talking in the future. Your child might say something like, "Talk to you later" or "See you later" or "I'll text you later" (if they do in fact text one another). Again, this doesn't have to be a long good-bye in which the exact time and place of the next communication is planned out. Unless friends are making specific plans to meet up, that degree of information isn't usually necessary.

4. Say Good-bye

As your teen or young adult is saying, "See you later," he or she will then want to say good-bye. These two steps generally go hand-in-hand, but to avoid confusion and make the steps more concrete for your child, the two steps are kept separate in this sequence of behaviors. Good-byes are usually quite brief and may include a simple, "Bye," possibly followed by a brief

> He or she will then want to say good-bye.

wave, perhaps a hug or kiss on the cheek (more common among females) or perhaps a fist bump or a pound, which is a gesture similar to a handshake or a high-five in which two people lightly tap closed fists (more common among males).

5. Walk Away

The final step in exiting conversations when fully accepted is to walk away. In this case, your teen or young adult doesn't have to pay as much attention to which direction to go or how slowly or casually to walk; he or she can just simply leave.

> The final step in exiting conversations when fully accepted is to walk away.

Social coaching tip: When coaching your teen or young adult on giving specific cover stories, it's important to clarify that although these cover stories are specific and a bit longer, they shouldn't be too long. For example, your child doesn't want to say something like, "Well, the bell is about to ring and I have a science midterm. I don't want to be late because I've been late five times this semester and I don't want to get in trouble. My professor gets really uptight when people show up late and I don't want to make her mad right before an exam. So I better get going." What's the problem with giving such a long cover story for leaving? When people go on and on trying to explain why they have to do something it often sounds fake or made up. We don't want your teen or young adult to give the impression of being disingenuous or dishonest, so make sure he or she keeps these cover stories specific and a little longer (but not too long).

Social coaching tip: Share the steps for exiting conversations when fully accepted with your teen or young adult and as always facilitate opportunities to practice these steps together and with another person. It will also be important to jointly read the social vignette about exiting conversations when fully accepted and generate a discussion using the perspective-taking questions. View the DVD video demonstration of exiting a conversation when fully accepted.

Success Story: Ryan Reads the Conversational Cues

Knowing how to enter and exit conversations can be hard for anyone, but when you're a fifteen-year-old boy with a history of peer rejection and trouble reading social cues, it's a lot more difficult. Such was the case for Ryan. He explained, "I was in high school when one day my so-called friends decided to literally vote me out of their circle because someone hated me for no reason. I was by myself for the rest of the school year. That was the summer my parents signed me up for PEERS." For Ryan, entering and exiting conversations was something he struggled with in particular. It didn't help that he had a history of being rejected, which made him apprehensive about making new friends. He experienced tremendous anxiety when he had to talk to a new group of people, so he would often avoid interacting altogether. When reflecting on which skills helped him to get over this anxiety, Ryan said, "What stuck out to me the most was slipping into conversations and slipping out of conversations." Learning the concrete steps for entering group conversations and knowing how to read the cues for when he wasn't accepted into conversations made it easier. He stopped worrying about whether he would be accepted, expecting that half the time he wouldn't be and it wasn't a big deal. "It made it easier to talk to people," he said.

His mother explained, "PEERS was a challenge for Ryan because at first he really didn't see the value of it. I think now that he's matured a little he recognizes the necessity of these skills. He's still pretty shy and complains that he 'has to be the one to go up to people' but he's made good progress."

Since going through PEERS, Ryan graduated from high school, got his driver's license, and is in his second year of college. By using the skills he learned to enter and exit conversations while reading the cues, Ryan found a new group of friends whom he enjoys spending time with on the weekends and who appreciate all of his wonderful qualities.

EXITING CONVERSATIONS
Chapter Summary for Teens and Young Adults

The following information is intended to be read by teens and young adults and contains a brief summary of the chapter.

The focus of this chapter is on how to exit conversations appropriately. The first part of this strategy involves paying attention to whether or not you're accepted into a conversation you've tried to join. Remember, there are three types of clues you can look for that will help you decide if you're accepted:

- Verbal cues
  - Are they talking nicely to you?
- Body language
  - Are they facing you or giving you the cold shoulder?
  - Did they open the circle or close the circle?
- Eye contact
  - Are they looking at you nicely?

Steps for Exiting Conversations When You Don't Feel Accepted

The sad truth is that about half the conversations we try to join we're not going to be accepted. There are lots of reasons why this happens but the bottom line is it isn't a big deal and it happens to everyone. Because you obviously don't want to force yourself on people, you need to get out of these conversations as smoothly as possible. Here's what you should do and the order you should follow when you don't feel accepted into a conversation:

1. **Keep your cool.** Don't get mad or upset because that will only cast a negative spotlight on you and could give you a bad reputation.
2. **Slowly look away.** Slowly look away from the group at some other point of interest. When you look away it shows that your interest is somewhere else.
3. **Slowly turn away.** Slowly turn in the direction you're looking. This gives the impression that whatever you're looking at is more interesting than the conversation you just tried to join.
4. **Slowly and casually walk away.** Slowly and casually walk away in the direction you've been looking and facing. You can also

(*continued*)

use a mobile phone, gaming device, or some other item that can appear to catch your attention, taking you away from the group.

Social Vignette: Exiting When You Don't Feel Accepted

The following social vignette is a transcript of the video demonstration from the accompanying DVD of exiting conversations when you don't feel accepted.

Mary, Alex, and Lara: (standing around and talking)

Yasamine: (standing several feet away, looking at her phone)

Lara: "So, Alex, Mary, and I just ran into each other at our piano lesson place yesterday."

Alex: (turns to Mary) "You play piano?"

Mary: "Yeah, I have been, and I've never run into her before."

Alex: "Ah, that's so funny."

Lara: "Yeah, it was totally crazy. We didn't . . . I bet . . . how long have you been going there for?"

Mary: "For like six years now."

Lara: "Ah, I've been there for seven. I can't believe I've never seen you."

Mary: "Yeah, that's crazy."

Lara: (turns to Alex) "Do you play any instruments?"

Alex: "I play the guitar."

Mary and Lara: "Oh, cool."

Lara: "I just started to play the guitar."

Yasamine: (looking over at Mary, Alex, and Lara periodically, starting to show interest)

Alex: "Ah, what, acoustic or electric?"

Lara: "Acoustic. How about you?"

Alex: "Electric."

Lara: "Oh, cool, that's really cool."

Yasamine: (moves closer, waits for a brief pause) "Do you play the guitar?"

Alex: (turns to Mary, ignoring Yasamine) "Uh, do you play the guitar?"

Mary: (also ignoring Yasamine) "No, I really want to learn though."

Yasamine: (begins to look away)

Lara: (turns to Mary) "Oh, you should totally learn."

Yasamine: (slowly turns away)

Alex: (turns to Mary) "It's really rewarding."

Yasamine: (casually walks away)

Mary, Alex, and Lara: (don't appear to notice that Yasamine has left)

Mary: "I feel like it's just a really cool instrument to learn."

Lara: "It is. It's fun!"

Alex: "Yeah."

Lara: "Well, we should all jam sometime."

Mary: "Yeah, that'd be fun."

Alex: "Definitely."

Perspective-Taking Questions

- What was that interaction like for Mary, Alex, and Lara?
  Answers: Fine, unmemorable
- What do you think they thought of Yasamine?
  Answers: Indifferent, no particular impression
- Are they going to want to talk to Yasamine again?
  Answer: Unknown, may not be opposed to talking to her

Steps for Exiting Conversations When You Initially Feel Accepted and Then Excluded

Video

Sometimes when you join conversations with people it seems like they want to talk to you at first and then they push you out of the conversation. When that happens, there are different steps you need to follow to exit the conversation. These are the steps

(continued)

for leaving a conversation when you initially feel accepted and then excluded:

1. **Keep your cool.** Just like before, you need to stay calm and not get upset.
2. **Slowly look away.** Slowly look away as if you're distracted by something. When you look away, make sure that you don't look all the way behind you. Instead, look to one side or the other or look at a personal item such as a mobile phone.
3. **Wait for a brief pause in the conversation.** Wait for a pause in the conversation before you say anything. Just like with entering a conversation, there's never a perfect pause; just try not to interrupt too much.
4. **Give a brief cover story for leaving.** Remember, cover stories are reasons you have to do something. You need to give a brief cover story for leaving the conversation. For example, you could say, "Well, gotta go" or "Gotta get to class" or you could say a few words of good-bye such as, "Take care" or "See you later." If you don't give some acknowledgment that you're leaving, it will seem weird to the group.
5. **Walk away.** After you've given a brief cover story, don't wait for the group to respond, just casually and calmly walk away.

Social Vignette: Exiting When You're Initially Accepted and Then Excluded

The following social vignette is a transcript of the video demonstration from the accompanying DVD of exiting a conversation when you initially feel accepted and then excluded.

Mary, Alex, and Lara: (standing around and talking)
Yasamine: (standing several feet away, looking at her phone)
Lara: "So, Alex, you'll never believe it. I ran into Mary yesterday when I was leaving my piano lesson."
Alex: (turns to Mary) "No way. I didn't know you played piano."

Mary: "Yeah, I've been playing for a while now. It's the craziest thing." (turns to Lara) "I've never run into you before."

Lara: "I know. It was so crazy."

Alex: "Wow, that's funny."

Mary: "It was . . . it was so funny."

Lara: "I know." (turns to Alex) "Do you play anything?"

Alex: "Uh huh. I play the guitar."

Yasamine: (looking over at Mary, Alex, and Lara periodically, starting to show interest)

Lara: "Oh, cool. I just started playing."

Alex: "Oh, that's awesome. Acoustic or electric?"

Lara: "Acoustic, how about you?"

Alex: "Electric."

Lara: "Oh, cool."

Alex: "It's so much fun though."

Lara: "Yeah."

Yasamine: (moves closer, waits for a brief pause) "You play the guitar?"

Lara: "Yeah, Alex and I do."

Yasamine: "That's so awesome. I play acoustic."

Lara: "Oh, me too."

Yasamine: "Cool. How long have you been playing for?"

Lara: "Uh, I just started, so maybe a couple months . . ."

Yasamine: "Oh, nice. I've been playing for five years."

Lara: "Oh, that's really cool."

Mary: (turns to Alex) "But anyways, how long have you been playing for?"

Mary, Alex, and Lara (begin to turn away and look away from Yasamine)

Alex: "Uh, about eight years. A long time."

Yasamine: (begins to look away)

Mary: "What? That's a really long time."

Lara: (turns to Alex) "Eight years?" (turns to Mary) "Mary, have you ever played the guitar?"

(continued)

Mary: "No, but I really want to get into it though."

Alex: "Oh, you should, it's so fun."

Lara: "You totally should."

Yasamine: (slowly turns away, waits for a brief pause) "Gotta go guys. Bye."

Mary, Alex, and Lara: (turn to Yasamine) "Bye."

Yasamine: (casually walks away)

Lara: "Yeah, you totally should. We should jam sometime guys."

Alex: "Absolutely."

Mary: "That'd be really cool."

Perspective-Taking Questions

- What was that interaction like for Mary, Alex, and Lara?
  Answers: Nice, pleasant, fine
- What do you think they thought of Yasamine?
  Answers: Nice, friendly, pleasant
- Are they going to want to talk to Yasamine again?
  Answer: Probably, seems friendly

Steps for Exiting Conversations When You Feel Fully Accepted

Video

Another example of a time when you're going to need to exit a conversation is when you're fully accepted but you just have to go. In that case, you don't want to walk away without doing a few important things:

1. **Wait for a brief pause in the conversation.** You need to wait for a brief pause in the conversation because it would be rude to interrupt someone unless it was urgent.
2. **Give a specific cover story for leaving.** In this case you also need to give a cover story but this time your cover story will be specific and a little longer. This is because if you just say, "Gotta go," your friends are probably going to ask, "Where

are you going?" Instead, be more specific by saying something like, "Well, I better get to class."

3. **Tell them you'll see or speak to them later.** If you're planning on seeing these friends again, you might say something like, "Talk to you later" or "See you later."

4. **Say good-bye.** As you're leaving, it's nice to say, "Bye." Some people will also wave, give a hug or kiss, or give a fist bump or a pound.

5. **Walk away.** After you've followed all these steps, the last step is to walk away.

Social Vignette: Exiting When You're Fully Accepted

The following social vignette is a transcript of the video demonstration from the accompanying DVD of exiting a conversation when you feel fully accepted.

Mary, Lara, and Yasamine: (standing around and talking)

Yasamine: "So, what'd you guys do this weekend?"

Mary: "I actually went and saw that new sci-fi movie. Uh, I forget what it's called."

Lara: "That fantasy sci-fi one that's in the theaters right now and just came out on Friday?"

Mary: "Yeah."

Lara: "Oh, I want to see that."

Yasamine: "I know what you guys are talking about, yeah."

Lara: "Did you see that one?"

Yasamine: "Yeah, yeah I saw it last weekend."

Lara: "Oh, really, how was it?"

Mary: "It was good, I liked it." (turns to Yasamine) "Did you like it?"

Yasamine: "Yeah, I thought it was really good actually."

Lara: "I'm going to try to go this weekend I think."

Mary: "You really should. It's cool."

(continued)

Lara: "It's worth it?"

Mary: "Yeah, it's worth it."

Lara: "It's worth the ticket?" (said playfully)

Mary: "It's a good movie."

Lara: "Cool."

Yasamine: "It's totally fun; you should see it."

Lara: "Awesome, it sounds exciting. I will definitely see it."

Yasamine: (begins to look away) "Hey, guys, my ride's here, so I've got to get going."

Mary: "Okay."

Lara: "Alright."

Yasamine: (begins to turn away) "It was good talking to you guys."

Mary and Lara: "You, too."

Yasamine: "See you tomorrow." (waves, casually walks away)

Mary: "Bye, see you."

Lara: (turns to Yasamine) "Bye." (turns to Mary) "So maybe you want to see it again?"

Mary: "Yeah, that'd be cool."

Lara: "Well, alright; maybe we'll go this weekend?"

Mary: "Yeah, that'd be fun."

Perspective-Taking Questions

- What was that interaction like for Mary and Lara?
  Answers: Nice, fun, interesting, enjoyable
- What do you think they thought of Yasamine?
  Answers: Nice, friendly, interesting, pleasant
- Are they going to want to talk to Yasamine again?
  Answer: Yes

CHAPTER EXERCISES
for Teens, Young Adults, and Parents

Teens and young adults should complete the following exercises with parents:

- Practice entering a group conversation with your parent and some other person following the steps outlined in chapter 4, and then practice exiting a conversation using each of the possible scenarios outlined in the current chapter.
  - With your parent, begin by reviewing the steps for entering and exiting group conversations.
  - Practice each of the three scenarios with your parent and some other person:
    - Don't feel accepted into the conversation
    - Initially feel accepted but then excluded from the conversation
    - Fully accepted into the conversation
- Practice following the steps for entering a group conversation with two or more peers you don't know well and use the steps for exiting a conversation if needed.
  - Begin by reviewing the steps for entering and exiting conversations. Using the FriendMaker mobile app to review the steps just beforehand might be helpful.
  - You may want to choose peers from the social group you identified or from those enrolled in an extracurricular or social activity to which you belong.

6

Managing Electronic Communication

WITH EACH NEW GENERATION, modes of electronic communication become more sophisticated and more all-encompassing. With the vast majority of communication between teens and young adults now occurring electronically, it is important for you to be familiar with some of the common forms of electronic communication and the general rules associated with them.

Although some teens and young adults with social challenges may be technology savvy and even have an inclination toward technology, it's been our repeated observation that these young people rarely engage in the more social forms of electronic communication, such as text messaging, instant messaging, video chatting, and using social networking websites. Perhaps the same is true for your teen or young adult. Yet, as your child becomes more socially engaged, it may become necessary for him or her to be familiar with the different forms of social media and the general rules related to using them.

Countless forms of electronic communication exist, each rapidly evolving, with newer and more sophisticated forms constantly replacing older, soon-to-be-obsolete forms. It would be useless to spend much time providing a comprehensive overview of the different forms of social media because between the time of my writing these words and you actually reading them, the information will surely be outdated. Instead, we'll stick to a cursory overview of common forms of social media currently used by teens and young adults.

Common Forms of Social Media

The term *social media* refers to web-based and mobile-based technologies used to create interactive electronic communication among people. Social media technologies take on various forms, and according to research published in 2010, may be categorized into six major forms: collaborative projects, such as Wikipedia; blogs, such as Twitter; content communities, such as YouTube; social networking sites, such as Facebook; virtual game worlds, such as *World of Warcraft*; and virtual social worlds, such as *Second Life*. Don't worry if you don't know what these are; this chapter will help clarify what you need to know.

At the time of writing this book, the following five social media technologies are the most frequently used forms of electronic communication for making and keeping friends. Popular technologies such as text messaging, instant messaging, video chatting, social networking sites, and e-mail will be briefly summarized to make sure you understand the general concepts. Although virtual game worlds and virtual social worlds such as *World of Warcraft* and *Second Life* are also known to be frequented by young people, they're not generally considered to be a good source of real-life friends, unless used to interact with preexisting friends, so they will not be covered extensively in this chapter.

Text Messaging

Also referred to as short message service (SMS), text messaging is by far the most common form of electronic communication used by teens and young adults. Even if you're a fan of old-fashioned letter writing, chances are you've heard of text messaging. It's just the sending of short written messages (usually no more than a few sentences) back and forth on a cell phone or smartphone. Recent research suggests that more than 75 percent of electronic communication between teens and young adults and their peers is conducted via text messaging.

> *More than 75 percent of electronic communication between teens and young adults and their peers is conducted via text messaging.*

Instant Messaging

Another common form of electronic communication used by teens and young adults includes instant messaging (IM). Usually conducted over the Internet, instant messaging involves instantaneous transmission of text messages (usually no more than a few sentences) between two or more people using personal computers or other devices when they're online at the same time. Instant messaging is most often used through computers and sometimes through social networking sites such as Facebook—unlike text messaging, which is more often used through mobile phones. Both instant messaging and text messaging offer real-time, text-based communication. Some IM systems also allow enhanced modes of electronic communication, such as live voice or video chatting. Google Chat and AIM (America Online Instant Messaging) are examples of IM platforms.

Video Chatting

Another common form of electronic communication used by teens and young adults to facilitate social interaction includes video chatting. Video chatting, also known as *video calling* (telephone-based video chatting), uses technology to receive and transmit audio-video signals between users in real time. Whether using computers or mobile phones, callers can see and hear each other instantaneously using this mode of electronic communication. Although video chatting (or video conferencing) is also common in commercial and corporate settings to facilitate conferences and meetings, this visually dynamic form of electronic communication is gaining great popularity among teens and young adults. FaceTime and Skype are examples of video chatting platforms.

Social Networking Sites

Currently, one of the most popular forms of electronic communication used by teens and young adults is social networking sites. Social networking sites are Internet websites that facilitate the building of social networks and social relationships among people who may be acquainted or who share similar interests and backgrounds. Users post profiles and pictures on personal pages, which others can view and comment on. Most social networking sites are web-based and therefore often provide other forms of electronic communication as part of their platform, including IM and e-mail. Popular websites such as Facebook and Myspace are examples of social networking sites. Dating websites such as Match and eHarmony are also examples of this form of social media.

> *Currently, one of the most popular forms of electronic communication used by teens and young adults is social networking sites.*

E-mail

Chances are, you're very familiar with e-mail and may even use it more than your teen or young adult. But for those of you who don't use the Internet, electronic mail, more commonly known as e-mail, is a method of exchanging digital text-based messages between a sender and one or more recipients. E-mail operates across the Internet and allows users to send, forward, accept, and save messages. Unlike IM, users need not be online simultaneously, and message length is relatively unlimited with the capacity to send large files and attachments. Gmail (also known as Google Mail) and Yahoo Mail are examples of e-mail service providers.

General Rules for Using Electronic Communication

Given the universal and pervasive nature of electronic communication as a form of social interaction, particularly among teens and young adults, it will be important for you to establish some basic rules about using electronic forms of communication when helping your teen or young adult make and keep friends. The following general rules relate directly to the use of the five forms of social media described previously. Phone calling is also included in these general rules, although used less frequently by teens and young adults at present.

Don't Get Too Personal

An important rule for electronic communication involves the tendency to get too personal. A common social error made by many people of all walks of life who use social media is the tendency to get too personal in their electronic communications, either through sharing too much or asking too much. The difficulty with electronic communication is that there is very little control over who sees, hears, or reads what is shared. Your teen or young adult might imagine that the information he or she is sharing is private, when in fact that information could easily be shared with others, either intentionally or unintentionally. A good rule of thumb for using electronic communication is to have your teen or young adult avoid sharing information he or she wouldn't be willing to share with anyone, almost assuming that others will be viewing, hearing, or reading the images and words. Rather than getting too personal over electronic communication, private or per-sonal conversations should be saved for in-person interactions. If your teen or young adult fol-lows this important rule, he or she is more likely to avoid poten-tially embarrassing and hurtful situations.

> *A common social error made by many people of all walks of life who use social media is the tendency to get too personal in their electronic communications.*

Use Cover Stories When Contacting People You Don't Know Well

As a reminder, cover stories are reasons or excuses for engaging in cer-tain social behaviors. Although an excuse, cover stories aren't necessarily made up or fake—they're just a reason for doing something. When your teen or young adult contacts people he or she does not know well, it's important to give a reason for being in contact. Cover stories legitimize your teen or young adult's need to be in touch by providing an excuse for contact. Cover stories decrease or eliminate any awkwardness that might arise around new communication during the early stages of acquaint-ance. Socially successful teens and young adults often use cover sto-ries when contacting people they don't know well either by text message, instant message, video chat, e-mail, or phone.

> *Cover stories decrease or eliminate any awkwardness that might arise around new communication during the early stages of acquaintance.*

The first time your teen or young adult gets in touch with people who have given him or her their contact information, the cover story will probably relate to whatever the reason was for exchanging contact information. For example, if your child exchanged phone numbers with someone in order to make plans to get together for the weekend, your teen or young adult might call the person using the cover story, "I'm just following up to see if you still want to get together" or "I'm calling to see if you're still free this weekend." If your teen or young adult forgets to give a cover story, there's a chance the other person might ask, "What do you want?" or "What are you calling for?" Obviously, we never want to start any form of communication with questions like those. Instead, your teen or young adult can avoid these awkward questions by providing cover stories or reasons for getting in touch with people not known well. With good friends, it's less necessary to use cover stories when texting or instant messaging, although cover stories are still very common with phone calls and during contact with people less close in acquaintance.

Use the Two-Message Rule

Another common social error committed by teens and young adults with social challenges relates to the number of messages left in a row with no response. In sharing this rule with your teen or young adult, you might begin by asking the simple question, "About how many messages in a row can we leave someone without getting a response?" When we ask that question in our PEERS social groups, we get answers ranging from one to twenty! So what could be the problem with leaving twenty messages in a row without hearing back? What's that going to be like for the person picking up those twenty messages? They're probably going to be creeped out. What are they going to think of the sender? They're probably going to think he or she is weird, creepy, or a total stalker! Are they going to want to talk to the sender again? It's highly unlikely they'll talk again. The receiver may even block the number and will probably tell his or her friends about the creepy stalker who left twenty messages in a row, undoubtedly damaging the reputation of the sender.

In order to avoid your teen or young adult making this social error, you should share and help to enforce the two-message rule. This rule asserts that your teen or young adult shouldn't leave more than two messages in a row without hearing back from the receiver. That's not to say that your teen or young adult must leave two messages; one message is perfectly fine but leaving more than two messages in a row is a big no-no. The two-message rule crosses all forms of electronic communication, including text messaging, instant messaging, video chatting, e-mail, and phone calls. That means your teen or young adult can't leave two text messages, two instant messages, two e-mails, two voicemails, and so on without receiving a response! A humorous example but it's happened more than once in our clinic. One text message and one voicemail message would be the maximum allowed by the two-message rule, for instance.

> *Your teen or young adult can't leave more than two messages in a row without hearing back from the receiver.*

One exception to the two-message rule relates to social networking sites such as Facebook and Myspace. In this case, your teen or young adult should only send one friend request (not two). That's because when someone tries to "friend" another person on a social networking site, the receiver has the option of either accepting the request or ignoring the request. Although many people frequently make this mistake, a second attempt to connect through this social medium is too much. If the person ignores your teen or young adult's first request, he or she needs to let it go and move on. This would be a good time to remind your teen or young adult that friendship is a choice. We don't get to be friends with everyone, and everyone doesn't get to be friends with us.

Another important point to make about the two-message rule is that it also applies to calling someone's phone and not leaving a message. More than two missed calls on a caller ID is a violation of the two-message rule, and anything more than two missed calls will be too much. What's more, failing to leave a voicemail during a missed call and expecting the person to call you back is a mistake and may not result in a returned phone call. Consequently, it's best to leave a voicemail on the first call if your teen or young adult wants a call back.

Avoid Cold Calling

Cold calling is a marketing term used to describe the act of contacting prospective customers for the purposes of advertising or sales. The term *cold*

> One of the rules for appropriate use of electronic communication is to avoid cold calling.

is used because the recipients of these calls didn't give prior consent to be contacted. We can all relate to how annoying these calls can be, so consequently, one of the rules for appropriate use of electronic communication is to avoid cold calling.

Some teens and young adults with social difficulties mistakenly believe that access to a school, work, or online directory gives them permission to contact anyone listed. They may call, text, IM, video chat, e-mail, or send friend requests through social networking sites to people who've never given them their contact information, not realizing the tremendous social error they are making. Imagine the following scenario. A teenage boy with social difficulties contacts a female classmate whose phone number he got from a social networking site. He believes that because her cell phone is listed on her Facebook page, and her Facebook page has no privacy settings, that it's okay to call her. In reality, the boy just cold called the unsuspecting girl. Keeping this example in mind, think back to your perspective-taking questions and imagine what this interaction will be like for the girl. She's probably going to be confused and startled by a random call from a stranger. She may even be a little scared and creeped out. What will the girl think of the boy who just cold called her? She'll probably think he's creepy and maybe even a stalker. At best she might think he's weird. Will the girl want to talk to the boy again? Probably not. In fact, she'll probably tell all of her friends the story of the creepy guy who got her number off Facebook and randomly called her, possibly doing great damage to this boy's reputation.

This social error is not uncommon. In our clinic at UCLA, we encounter endless stories of teens and young adults with social challenges who cold call their peers, particularly those they're attracted to, not realizing the social faux pas they make. In some cases the error has been so egregious that it even resulted in criminal charges, such as the case of a young man who went to the home of a girl he liked whose address he got off the Internet. The girl was naturally frightened by the sight of the strange man standing on her doorstep, professing his love for her. She quickly notified the police, landing the young man in trouble with the law and charged with stalking, even though he intended no harm and simply wanted to meet the girl. This extreme example demonstrates the importance of the no cold calling rule.

Social coaching tip: As your teen or young adult's social coach it's important for you to stress this rule, possibly even sharing stories like the ones just described, and asking your teen or young adult what could be the problem with doing such things.

Exchange Contact Information

Obviously, because cold calling is out of the question, you need a strategy for helping your teen or young adult make contact with people he or she would like to get to know better. This can be done by exchanging contact information. Contact information includes phone numbers, screen names, e-mail addresses, and user names. Many teens and young adults with social challenges know they need to exchange contact information; the problem is they often don't do it appropriately. So what are the common social errors committed? For those experiencing peer rejection, walking up to an unsuspecting peer and randomly asking for his or her phone number is fairly common. How would the unsuspecting peer react? He would probably be startled, confused, perhaps even a little weirded out. What would the peer think of the socially awkward teen or young adult? He would probably think him or her strange, odd, and a bit creepy. Would the peer want to give out the requested contact information? It's highly unlikely that contact information would be exchanged, and more likely that the peer would avoid the awkward teen or young adult in the future. What about those experiencing social neglect? How would they go about seeking contact information from their peers? The reality is that it's unlikely these teens or young adults will even attempt to exchange contact information with others because of anxiety and discomfort. Instead, socially neglected teens and young adults will often wait for someone to offer his or her contact information, which sadly may not happen, leading to further isolation.

Assuming your child is inclined to exchange contact information with someone, the following six steps used by socially successful teens and young adults should be followed:

1. **Trade information.** The first step in exchanging contact information is to trade information. In other words, your teen or young adult should have talked with this person before asking for his or

her contact information. Simply walking up to a random person and asking for his or her phone number would be highly inappropriate. In fact, your teen or young adult should probably have traded information with this person on multiple occasions before asking for his or her contact information.

> *The first step in exchanging contact information is to trade information.*

tion. It's rare that people exchange contact information before a strong acquaintance has been formed.

2. **Find common interests.** Just like anytime your teen or young adult trades information, the goal is to find common interests. Remember that common interests are important because they give your teen or young adult things to talk about and things to do with others, forming the foundation of a friendship. If your teen or young adult has trouble finding common interests with the person he or she is talking to, it's probably useless to exchange contact information because they'll have little to talk about and little to do together.

> *Find common interests.*

3. **Use a cover story to suggest further contact.** The next step for exchanging contact information is to use the identified common interest as a cover story for suggesting further contact. For example, imagine through the course of trading information with an acquaintance, your teen or young adult discovers a mutual love for *Warhammer* (a table-top science fantasy miniature war game). This common interest could be used as a reason for interacting in the future and exchanging contact information. He or she might say, "That's cool you like *Warhammer*, too. We should play sometime." If it feels too soon for a get-together, another cover story might be to say, "That's cool you like *Warhammer*, too. I know a games workshop nearby. I could send you the info." Proposing further contact before actually suggesting the exchange of contact information is a nice way to avoid possible rejection because the process gives your teen or young adult an opportunity to see if the other person seems interested.

> *Use the identified common interest as a cover story for suggesting further contact.*

4. **Assess interest.** After using a cover story to suggest some type of further contact, the next step is to assess the person's interest about further communication. If the person seems interested (for example, agrees to future contact, smiles, shakes his or her head to indicate yes), then your teen or young adult should proceed to the next step and actually suggest exchanging contact information. If the person doesn't seem interested in the suggestion (for example, doesn't agree to future contact, makes a face, looks nervous or flustered, stalls, changes the subject), then your teen or young adult shouldn't proceed any further. Although this kind of rejection can feel bad, it's important to remember that friendship is a choice. We don't get to be friends with everyone, and everyone doesn't get to be friends with us. The nice thing is that by using a cover story and assessing interest, your teen or young adult managed to avoid rejection because he or she never actually asked for the person's contact information.

> *Assess the person's interest about further communication.*

5. **Suggest exchanging contact information.** Assuming the person seems interested in future contact, the next step is to suggest exchanging contact information. For example, your teen or young adult might say, "Why don't I get your number" or "Let me give you my e-mail." Some young people prefer to communicate electronically over social networking sites such as Facebook. In this case, your teen or young adult might say, "Are you on Facebook?" and if the person is, he or she might say, "I'll look you up." Your teen or young adult would then need to follow up with a Facebook friend request shortly after.

> *Suggest exchanging contact information.*

6. **Exchange contact information.** The final step in the process is to actually obtain the other person's contact information and offer contact information in return. If the other person is hesitant to give your teen or young adult his or her contact information, but is willing to accept your child's, this is not a good sign of interest. In this case, your teen or young adult should go with the flow, not make a big deal out of it, and give his or her contact information

> *Obtain the other person's contact information and offer contact information in return.*

without pressuring the other person to do the same.

When exchanging phone numbers, it's common for teens and young adults to enter the new number into their mobile phone and let it ring to the other person's phone so that both numbers are saved in the phone memory, to be labeled in the phone contacts at some point. Another common way of exchanging contact information is to have the other person enter his or her information directly into your phone. That means if someone suddenly hands your teen or young adult his or her phone during the process of exchanging contact information, that person is expecting your teen or young adult to input the information him- or herself.

Finally, when your teen or young adult actually does contact this person, whatever cover story was used for exchanging contact information should be the reason he or she is calling. That means, if your teen or young adult's cover story was to offer to send information about a nearby games workshop for *Warhammer*, then this needs to be the reason given when your teen or young adult eventually contacts that person (see the section "Steps for Beginning Phone Calls" for more information).

Rules for Using the Telephone

Over the last several years, electronic forms of communication such as text messaging, instant messaging, and e-mail have replaced our reliance on phone calls. In fact, some teens and young adults will even think it's weird to call up a friend on the phone just to chat. Yet even with the rise in text messaging, at this point in time it's still difficult to get through

> *The common issues related to using the phone involve beginning and ending calls and leaving voicemail messages.*

life without knowing how to use the phone. Many parents of teens and young adults with social challenges report that their kids don't know how to talk on the phone properly. Some even experience tremendous anxiety when using the phone. In our experience working with families through the UCLA PEERS Clinic, the common issues related to using the phone involve beginning and ending calls and leaving voice-mail messages.

To illustrate this point, imagine a socially challenged young woman attempting to make a phone call to a new friend. She dials the number, the friend picks up the phone and says "hello," and then the young woman begins speaking as if in mid-conversation. Does this sound familiar? Perhaps your teen or young adult has done the same thing. So what could be the problem with starting a phone call in mid-conversation? What will this experience be like for the new friend? She's likely to feel confused, maybe wondering who's on the line and whether the person has the right number. What's the friend likely to say? After a few moments of confusion, she might ask, "Who is this?" possibly followed by, "What do you want?" What's the friend going to think of the young woman? She'll probably think the young woman is strange or odd. Will the friend want to talk to the young woman on the phone again? It's difficult to know for sure, but the chances are lessened with this awkward start.

Steps for Beginning Phone Calls

In order to help your teen or young adult avoid social awkwardness, share the following steps for beginning phone calls. A social vignette highlighting these steps is provided in the chapter summary for teens and young adults.

1. **Ask for the person you're calling.** Unless calling a personal cell phone and your teen or young adult is certain the person he or she is calling will answer, the beginning of a phone call generally begins by asking for the person you're calling. This might include saying something like, "Hi. May I please speak to Jennifer?" or "Hi. I'm calling for Jennifer."

2. **Say who you are.** Unless the receiver of the call greets your teen or young adult by name when answering the phone (perhaps because of caller ID), the next step in beginning a phone call is to have your teen or young adult identify him- or herself by name. Simply saying, "It's

me" is not enough identifying information. Instead, saying something like, "This is Carrie" or "It's Carrie" would be good.

3. **Ask how he or she is doing.** The next step typically involves having your teen or young adult briefly ask how the other person is doing. For example, saying, "How's it going?" or "How are you?" is sufficient. This will usually be met with a brief, "I'm fine. How are you?" or something to that effect.

4. **Ask if the person can talk.** After these brief greetings, the next step will be to ask if the other person can talk right now. Although it seems like the person should be free because he or she picked up the phone, many people still answer the phone even when they're unavailable. To avoid the slight embarrassment of being told the other person is too busy to talk, have your teen or young adult ask, "Can you talk right now?" or "Is this a good time?" If it's not a good time, your teen or young adult can make arrangements to speak later and avoid a little awkwardness.

5. **Give a brief cover story for calling.** The final step for beginning a phone call is to give a brief cover story for calling. Remember, cover stories are reasons for engaging in certain behaviors and they're almost always brief. In this case, the cover story will be the reason for calling. Examples of cover stories include, "I was just calling to see how you've been doing" or "I was calling to get the homework assignment" or "I was calling to see what you're doing this weekend." Whatever cover story your teen or young adult chooses, make sure that it's not too personal. For example, when practicing making a phone call as part of the chapter exercises, your teen or young adult shouldn't use the cover story, "I'm calling you for a practice assignment." Even though it's true, that would be an example of too much information. When in doubt, simply saying, "I was just calling to see what you've been up to" or something to that effect is nice.

Social coaching tip: A social vignette highlighting the steps for beginning phone calls is provided in the chapter summary for teens and young adults. Feel free to go over this vignette with your child and have him or her practice following these steps as described in the chapter exercises.

Steps for Ending Phone Calls

How a phone call ends is equally as important as how it begins. Once again, teens and young adults with social challenges often struggle with these kinds of transitions. The result is that endings of phone calls can be rather awkward. In our clinic at UCLA, many parents will report that when their kids get stuck in phone conversations and don't know what to say, they hang up, usually without even saying good-bye. Imagine our socially challenged young woman from before, coming to the end of her phone call. Imagine that when lost for words, she hangs up, without a word of good-bye. What is her friend going to think? Although it's possible she might think there was a bad connection and the phone dropped out, if this were to happen often, it's likely she'd become suspicious. What would the friend think of the young woman? She might think the young woman was strange or weird. Would the friend want to talk to the young woman on the phone again? It's possible that in time she'd grow tired of the awkwardness of the calls and the frequent hang-ups.

To avoid awkward good-byes, share the following steps for ending a phone call with your child. A social vignette highlighting these steps is provided in the chapter summary for teens and young adults.

1. **Wait for a brief pause in the conversation.** Before ending a phone call, your teen or young adult should wait for a brief pause in the conversation, some type of transitional moment when the topic of conversation is winding down. It's important to wait for a brief pause because interrupting the other person would be rude.

2. **Give a brief cover story for ending the call.** After a brief pause in the conversation, the next step is to give a brief cover story or a reason for hanging up. If your teen or young adult doesn't give a reason, the other person may ask, "Why do you have to go?" or "What do you have to do?" The other person also might think your teen or young adult just doesn't want to talk to him or her anymore. Remember that cover stories are almost always brief because if they're too long they'll seem untrue. For example, imagine your teen or young adult were to say, "I think my mom wants to use the

phone, and actually I have a big midterm tomorrow and I've hardly studied, so if I don't get off the phone now I'm going to be up all night, and I don't do well on exams when I'm tired. So I better get going." What do you think the person on the receiving end of that cover story would think? They'd probably think it was made up, and your teen or young adult didn't want to talk to them anymore. Instead, giving a brief cover story such as, "I have to finish my homework" or "I need to study" or "My mom needs to use the phone" would be more appropriate. Finally, cover stories should not be too personal. For example, saying, "I have to go to the bathroom" is way too much information, even if true. If your teen or young adult doesn't want to lie, saying, "I've gotta go" is enough to get the point across.

3. **Tell the person it was nice talking.** The next step in ending a phone call is to tell the other person that it was nice talking to him or her. Assuming your teen or young adult enjoyed the conversation, saying something nice such as, "It was good talking to you" or "Nice catching up" may make the other person feel good.

4. **Tell the person you'll see or speak later.** If your teen or young adult expects to see or speak to the other person again, this would be a good point in the call to say so. For example, saying, "I'll talk to you soon" or "I'll speak to you later" or "See you in class" are nice things to say to let the friend know that your teen or young adult is interested in talking again.

5. **Say good-bye.** The final step for ending a phone call is to say good-bye. Different people have different ways of signing off on phone calls but customarily saying, "Good-bye" or "Bye" is appropriate. It's important to say good-bye with some type of verbal acknowledgment before hanging up; otherwise, the friend may not realize your teen or young adult has gone.

Social coaching tip: A social vignette highlighting the steps for ending phone calls is provided in the chapter summary for teens and young adults. Feel free to go over this vignette with your child and have him or her practice following these steps as described in the chapter exercises.

Steps for Leaving Voicemail

Voicemail in some form or other has been around since the 1980s, yet people continue to struggle with the act of leaving voicemail messages. Uncertain what to say, concerned that they'll stumble on their words or sound awkward, many people will avoid leaving voicemail altogether, preferring to text or e-mail. Not surprisingly, many teens and young adults with social difficulties also struggle with this particular skill, either completely refusing to leave voicemail or leaving rather awkward and somewhat confusing messages. Perhaps your teen or young adult is the same. The reality is that leaving voicemail messages doesn't need to be awkward or anxiety provoking if we know the steps to follow.

To help your child avoid awkward or confusing messages, share the following steps for leaving a voicemail:

1. **Say whom you're calling.** Unless calling someone's personal cell phone or private phone line, the first step in leaving a voicemail is for your teen or young adult to say whom he or she is calling. Many land lines, for example, are still shared lines. Consequently, saying whom you're calling is an important step in making sure the correct person receives your teen or young adult's message.

2. **Say who you are.** The next step is to identify yourself. Simply saying, "It's me" is insufficient and saying, "My name is Carrie," for instance, would sound strange. Instead, your teen or young adult should identify him- or herself during phone calls and over voicemail by simply saying, "It's Carrie" or "This is Carrie," for example.

3. **Give a brief cover story for calling.** The next step in leaving a voicemail is to give a brief cover story for calling. As always, cover stories should be short. This is particularly true for voicemail because people don't usually like receiving long messages, and if your teen or young adult goes on for too long, he or she might even get cut off. One brief sentence describing the reason for the call is enough.

4. **Leave the day and time.** With the advent of time stamps on messaging services, many people have fallen out of the habit of leaving the day and time when they're calling. However, your teen or young adult shouldn't assume that every person has a time

stamp feature on his or her phone, that the time stamp is accurate, or that the person will even bother to check the time stamp if it's not available by audio. To be safe, it's best to briefly leave the day and time of the call on the message. This way if your teen or young adult has spoken to his or her friend since leaving the message, confusion and miscommunication will be minimized.

5. **Leave your phone number.** Unless leaving a message for someone spoken to regularly, it's also important to leave your phone number on the voicemail message. Similar to the issue of time stamps, with the introduction of caller ID features and contact lists on phones, the practice of leaving phone numbers has fallen by the wayside to a certain extent. Still, it's never certain that every person has a working caller ID or has your teen or young adult's phone number programmed in their contact list. To avoid communication snafus, it's safer for your teen or young adult to leave his or her phone number when recording a voicemail message with someone not spoken to regularly.

6. **Say good-bye.** The final step for leaving a voicemail is to say good-bye. Just as with ending phone calls, a simple "Good-bye" or "Bye" is sufficient.

Social coaching tip: A social vignette highlighting the steps for leaving voicemail is provided in the chapter summary for teens and young adults. You should go over this vignette with your child and have him or her practice following these steps as described in the chapter exercises.

Rules for Using the Internet Safely

Since the mid-1990s, the Internet has had a tremendous impact on our culture and our way of interacting with one another. Many teens and young adults won't even remember a time when the Internet didn't exist. Yet even with all this online familiarity, some teens and young adults with social challenges may still fall prey to the anonymous and sometimes dangerous cyber world.

We've all heard tales of the exploitative and predatory practices occurring in various dark corners of the Internet. Sometimes less obviously, predators and those who wish to do harm often choose to skulk in

Internet locations frequented by young people. In order to protect your teen or young adult from potential danger, it's important for you to establish very specific rules about using the Internet. A few key rules are presented in this section to help provide a guideline. Additional rules specific to your teen or young adult may also be needed.

The Internet Shouldn't Be Used for Making New Friends for Teens

Perhaps the most important overarching rule for teens using the Internet is that this virtual homestead and conveyor of social media should not be used for making new friends. Instead, for teenagers, the Internet is best used for developing stronger friendships, making plans, and communicating with preexisting real-life acquaintances. This is because attempting to make new friends online can be a dangerous business for teens. None of us can ever be certain whom we're talking to online, which can make teens in particular easier targets for predators and people wishing to do them harm. If the thought of these predators is something that keeps you up at night, you're not alone. Many parents we've worked with through the UCLA PEERS Clinic express similar concerns about their socially naive teens and young adults. The good news is that if you establish clear, concrete rules about how your teen should use the Internet (such as the ones described in this chapter), you'll significantly improve the odds that your teen won't fall victim to your fears. You may have noticed that this rule has only been extended to teens and not adults. This is because of the common occurrence of online dating that has become quite usual among young adults. Given your experience and concerns about your child's safety online, you may need to decide whether this rule should be extended to include your young adult.

> *Attempting to make new friends online can be a dangerous business for teens.*

In our experience, when communicating the rule that the Internet shouldn't be used for making new friends, most adolescents will quickly agree with the idea. Yet, some teens may be resistant to the rule, particularly as it relates to online friends. Some teens and young adults struggling to make friends will have an extensive social network of online friends, those whom they're only connected to through the Internet. Many online friends are developed through gaming sites in which guilds or clans are formed. If these terms are unfamiliar, a guild or clan is an organized group of players, ranging from a few friends to thousands of players who regularly play together around a particular online multi-player game. Although your child's association with guilds and clans in and of itself may not be a problem, it will be important for you to stress that these online friends are not the same as real-life friends. More important, teens should never meet in person with online friends because these friends may not be who they say there are, potentially placing your child in danger.

The notion that online friends should not develop into real-life friends may be confusing for some teenagers, particularly if they've seen friends or relatives engaging in activities such as online dating. Yet, online dating occurs between consenting adults for the purposes of developing romantic relationships. In other words, the rules are different for adults, like so many things in life. The complicated safety aspects of online dating for adults will be discussed later in this section.

Avoid Giving Contact Information to Strangers Online

As a general rule, teens and young adults should avoid giving contact information to strangers online. This is always true for teenagers, and generally true for adults, even in the early stages of online dating. Contact information includes your teen or young adult's full name, home address, birth date, and social security number but may also include identifying e-mail addresses that include your teen's full name, place of school or business, and phone numbers, which can sometimes be easily traced to an address through reverse directories. Social networking sites and online directories should also be free from your teen's identifying contact information (including Facebook and Myspace pages). Your teen or young adult's screen names (pseudonyms used for Internet communications) should also be gender neutral when possible to avoid identification and minimize targeted harassment or attempts at exploitation. Discussing these important points with your teen or young adult will be an important aspect of keeping him or her safe online.

Use Privacy Settings on Social Networking Sites

Given the personal nature of content often posted on social networking sites (including pictures and personal accounts of whereabouts) it's very important that you ensure that your teen or young adult is using privacy settings on these sites. That means people from outside your teen or young adult's network of friends shouldn't be able to view his or her personal profile or obtain identifying information or contact information. In our experience, many teens and young adults need some assistance from parents in setting up these privacy settings, so be prepared to become familiar with these social networking sites if you're not already, or consider enlisting help from another supportive family member familiar with social networking sites.

Don't Accept Friend Requests from Strangers

If your teen or young adult is using social networking sites such as Facebook or Myspace, it will be important for you to stress the rule that he or she shouldn't accept friend requests from strangers online. Friend requests are requests or invitations from others to connect via a social network. Although it may be tempting to be linked to hundreds of friends through these websites (people often compete over who has the most friends), your teen or young adult opens him- or herself up to possible victimization or exploitation by potential predators when accepting friend requests from strangers. This is because when people friend your teen or young adult, they have access to personal information about his or her interests, whereabouts, and appearance. It's important for you to have a candid discussion about these potential threats and even periodically go through your teen or young adult's friend list to identify who is there and what his or her connection to your child is.

Safety Suggestions for Online Dating for Adults

Although the rule for teens is that the Internet shouldn't be used for making new friends, the rule for adults is less black and white given the fact that many young adults are involved with social networking sites such as Match or eHarmony that focus on the development of romantic relationships through online dating.

Because of the popularization of online dating and the likelihood that many young adults (even with social difficulties) will be involved with online dating, the following safety suggestions are provided as a guideline for *adults*:

- Avoid giving your date your personal contact information at first.
- Meet your date in a public place where there are lots of people around.
- Don't go anywhere alone with your date at first.
- Drive yourself to and from the date, or find your own alternative form of transportation.
- Don't get in the car with your date or have him or her take you home at first.
- Let your friends and family know where you are and whom you are with.
- Check in with your friends and family before and after the date.

These are just a few simple but important suggestions you might offer your adult son or daughter if he or she is interested in online dating. Because the process of online dating (as well as other forms of dating) is complex and complicated, you may need to provide additional assistance and coaching in this area. Although dating skills are of course very important, the purpose of this book is to help socially challenged teens and young adults learn to make and keep friends. So any additional assistance in the rules and steps of dating etiquette will require outside resources, of which there are many.

Parent Social Coaching Tips for Online Safety

The following tips are suggestions for parents whose teens or young adults are engaged in the use of social media.

Monitor Social Networking Sites and Online Activity

It's highly recommended that you monitor the social networking sites and online activity of your child, particularly when teens are concerned. You need to be educated about these sites and monitor the goings on, not only to protect your child from being victimized or exploited but also to ensure that your teen or young adult is behaving appropriately and not engaging in behaviors that could get him or her in trouble or create a bad reputation. This means you might friend your teen or young adult on social networking sites (making that a condition of their enrollment if they're a minor) and regularly monitor their activity there. Some families also limit Internet use to shared family computers in common areas where behavior can be monitored. Other parents may have open access to their child's personal computers, allowing them to monitor the comings and goings of their teen or young adult's online activity. Whatever your level of involvement, it's probably best to have an honest discussion about your expectations and how you plan to monitor your child's behavior. If you have a particularly hard time navigating the online world, having these online activities monitored by an older sibling, cousin, or some trusted family member or friend who is more familiar with these social forums might be a good alternative idea.

Be Familiar with Textese

If your teen or young adult is using text-based messaging, you should familiarize yourself with textese, also known as *SMS language*. Remember that *SMS* is another term for text messaging. With the huge popularity of text messaging and IM flooding our culture and community, an entirely new language known as *textese* has developed. This language is also known as *text talk* or *chatspeak*. *Textese* is a term for the common abbreviations and slang used when sending SMS or IM. Due to the brevity of this text-based communication (usually including only a couple of sentences per message), abbreviations have developed into an entirely new dialect. As your teen or young adult's social coach and guardian, it will be important for you to be familiar with this language if he or she texts or IMs. You may already be familiar with some of the vernacular and may not even know it. For example, OMG is now widely recognized as translating to "oh my God," just as LOL is widely known to stand for "laugh out loud" (although it might also mean "lots of love"). Some of these textese abbreviations may be less innocent, like those used for sexting, which is the act of sending sexually explicit messages or photographs. Other less innocent abbreviations may be used to stave off impending trouble such as the popular POS ("parent over shoulder") or PAW ("parents are watching"). Consequently, if your teen or young adult is involved with this type of electronic communication, you should familiarize yourself with this terminology. For assistance, long glossary lists of textese translations can easily be found on the Internet.

> *If your teen or young adult is using text-based messaging, you should familiarize yourself with textese, also known as SMS language.*

Success Story: Steven Stays Safe Online

Staying safe online is an important goal for anyone actively using the Internet. Yet those with social challenges may be easier prey for online predators. Such was the case for Steven, a twenty-four-year-old man diagnosed with ASD. When Steven and his mother came to PEERS, he was a recent college graduate, was unemployed, and spent the majority of his time talking to his "girlfriend" online. His "girlfriend," we later discovered, was a woman he had never met whom he paid to talk to—a relationship carrying a hefty bill of over $10,000 in unpaid credit card debt.

Unbeknownst to his family, while away at college, Steven had fallen victim to an online scam in which he was coaxed into believing that he was in a relationship with a woman whom he paid several hundred dollars per month to talk to. Although he had never met the woman in person, he spent several hours each day "talking" to her over group video chat with dozens of other men he believed to be her "friends." This chatting consisted of the men typing in questions as the woman sat in front of a web camera, answering their questions one-by-one, as if speaking to each individually. By the time Steven came to PEERS, he had become quite obsessed with this pastime.

Although a disturbing tale highlighting the dangers of the Internet, Steven's story actually has a happy resolution. After several discussions about the difference between online friends and real-life friends, and multiple conversations about the characteristics of good friendships (which do not require financial payment), Steven began to understand that his online girlfriend was no friend at all. Once free from the chains of his cyber obsession, Steven began to channel his energy into making real-life friends. He joined a gaming club and a musical ensemble group, quickly making friends with a few of its members, whom he began having regular get-togethers with. He joined Facebook and Instagram—relishing in posting comments and sharing online pictures with his real-life friends. He eventually got a part-time job, which enabled him to pay off his credit card debt, and even began online dating. When looking back on how far he'd come, Steven commented, "I used to go through every day wondering when my life was going to start. I always wanted to have friends and a girlfriend, and I thought I did back then. But I didn't understand what friendship was. Now I do, and it doesn't feel lonely anymore. I like to go online and talk to my friends, but it's not the same. These are real friends. We hang out and do things, and I know I can trust them. It's safe now."

Although a rather dramatic tale, Steven's story is not that uncommon for teens and young adults with social differences. We've met many young people with similar stories through our clinic; the vast majority of whom were able to develop meaningful relationships with real-life friends. So if your child has also fallen victim to dangers of the Internet or simply struggles to use electronic communication appropriately, remember Steven's story and his inspirational journey of learning to be safe.

GENERAL RULES FOR USING ELECTRONIC COMMUNICATION
Chapter Summary for Teens and Young Adults

> The following information is intended to be read by teens and young adults and contains a brief summary of the chapter.

This chapter is focused on the rules for electronic communication. Social media such as text messaging, instant messaging, video chatting, e-mail, social networking sites, and even the phone are common ways you might keep in touch with friends. Like most things, there are rules for how to act when using this technology. Some of the rules used by socially successful teens and young adults are listed in the following.

(continued)

Don't Get Too Personal

A common mistake people make when using electronic communication is they forget that anyone could read or hear what they have to say. Don't make that mistake. Be smart and avoid sharing or asking anything too personal. Just imagine that anyone could be reading or listening to you, and only share what you're comfortable having everyone know.

Use Cover Stories When Contacting People You Don't Know Well

When you're contacting someone you don't know well using electronic means, you need to give them a reason why you're in touch. That's called a *cover story*. Cover stories are usually short, not too personal, and they're not necessarily made up. Some examples are, "Texting to see what you're doing this weekend" or "Calling to see what you've been up to" or "Thought I'd drop you a note to see if you're going to the game."

Use the Two-Message Rule

Have you ever thought about how many messages in a row you can leave without hearing back from someone? Well, the answer is two. It's called the *two-message rule*, and it means you shouldn't leave more than two messages in a row with no response or you might creep out the other person. This includes text messages, instant messages, e-mail, voicemail, and even missed phone calls. One message is fine, but never leave more than two in a row or they might call you a stalker!

Avoid Cold Calling

Cold calling is a term used to describe a person who contacts someone without ever asking for his or her contact information. When you ask for someone's contact information, you're basically asking for permission to get in touch. If you never get permission and instead call him or her out of the blue, you're likely to creep that person out, which is not a good start. Instead of doing that, you should exchange contact information before getting in touch. The steps for how to do that follow.

Exchange Contact Information

1. Trade information with the person (usually on several different occasions).
2. Find common interests with the person.
3. Use a cover story based on your common interest to suggest getting together or talking again.
4. Notice whether he or she seems interested in your suggestion to get together or talk again.
5. If he or she seems interested, suggest exchanging contact information. If that person doesn't seem interested, don't ask for his or her contact information.
6. Exchange contact information with the person by sharing phone numbers or screen names.

RULES FOR USING THE TELEPHONE

The following rules are specific to when you're using the telephone. You may not use the phone much, but when you do, here are some steps for avoiding awkwardness.

Steps for Beginning Phone Calls

1. Ask for the person you're calling.
2. Say who you are.
3. Ask how he or she is doing.
4. Ask if the person can talk.
5. Give a brief cover story for calling.

(*continued*)

Social Vignette: Beginning Phone Calls

The following social vignette is an example of how to appropriately begin a phone call.

(phone ringing)
Jennifer: (picks up the phone) "Hello?"
Carrie: "Hi. Can I speak to Jennifer please?"
Jennifer: "This is Jennifer."
Carrie: "Hi, Jennifer. This is Carrie."
Jennifer: "Oh, hi Carrie."
Carrie: "How's it going?"
Jennifer: "Pretty well. How are you?"
Carrie: "I'm fine, thanks. So can you talk right now?"
Jennifer: "Sure."
Carrie: "I was just calling to see what you've been up to."
Jennifer: "Oh, not much. Just going to school."
Carrie: "Oh, yeah. How's school going? I haven't seen you around lately."
Jennifer: "It's okay. I've been kind of busy, and we have the homecoming game this weekend."
Carrie: "I know. I can't wait! Are you going?"
Jennifer: "I was thinking about it."

Steps for Ending Phone Calls

1. Wait for a brief pause in the conversation.
2. Give a brief cover story for ending the call.
3. Tell the person it was nice talking.
4. Tell the person you'll see or speak later.
5. Say good-bye.

Social Vignette: Ending Phone Calls

The following social vignette is an example of how to appropriately end a phone call.

(conversation picks up where it left off)

Carrie: "So, who's going to the game?"

Jennifer: "I'm not sure. I haven't decided if I'm going to go."

Carrie: "Oh, you should. Do you like football?"

Jennifer: "Yeah, I do. What about you?"

Carrie: "Yeah, me too. Maybe we should go together."

Jennifer: "That would be fun! Let's do it."

Carrie: "Great. I'm excited!"

Jennifer: "Me too!"

Carrie: (brief pause) "Well, my mom needs to use the phone, so I should probably get going."

Jennifer: "Okay."

Carrie: "But it was good talking to you."

Jennifer: "You too. Thanks for calling."

Carrie: "I'll talk to you tomorrow, and we can make plans for the game."

Jennifer: "Sounds good."

Carrie: "Take care."

Jennifer: "You too."

Carrie: "Bye!"

Jennifer: "Bye!"

Steps for Leaving a Voicemail

1. Say whom you're calling.
2. Say who you are.
3. Give a brief cover story for calling.
4. Leave the day and time.
5. Leave your phone number if you don't talk regularly.
6. Say good-bye.

Social Vignette: Leaving a Voicemail

The following social vignette is an example of how to appropriately leave a voicemail.

(continued)

(phone ringing)

Voicemail message: "Hi, we can't get to the phone right now. Please leave a message." (beep)

Carrie: "Hi, this message is for Jennifer. It's Carrie. It's about 7 o'clock on Thursday night. I was just calling to see what you've been up to. Give me a call at 555–1212. Talk to you soon. Bye." (hangs up phone)

RULES FOR USING THE INTERNET SAFELY

The following rules are specific to when you're using the Internet.

The Internet Shouldn't Be Used for Making New Friends for Teens

Many teens and young adults talk about having online friends. Although these friends are fine in guilds and clans for online gaming, it's dangerous to turn online friends into real-life friends, especially when you're a teenager. You've probably heard stories about predators on the Internet, preying on teens and unsuspecting young people. Well, it's true that they're out there, and because you can never be sure whom you're talking to online, it's better to be safe and only use the Internet for talking with current friends. If you're an adult and you're online dating, we have some tips for how to stay safe in this section.

Avoid Giving Contact Information to Strangers Online

Because there's no way of knowing for sure that someone you meet online is who they say they are, it's really important that you never give your contact information to strangers online, including online friends. That means you don't share addresses, phone numbers, or even names because there are ways people can find you by just knowing your name. If you're on social networking sites such as Facebook, you should also keep your contact information off your profile page because lots of people have access to that information.

Use Privacy Settings on Social Networking Sites

If you're on social networking sites such as Facebook or Myspace then you probably know about privacy settings. They limit the people who can look at your profile page and keep you safe from predators and all kinds of creepy people. It's really important for you to use privacy settings on these sites or else anyone can have access to your personal information such as what you look like, things you like to do, and places you go. If you need help adjusting your privacy settings, talk to your parents and they should be able to help you out.

Don't Accept Friend Requests from Strangers

Another important rule about social networking sites is that you should never accept friend requests from strangers. That means if someone you don't know wants to be part of your social network, you need to ignore that person's request. The scary truth is you don't really know who that person is because he or she could be pretending to be someone else. So be safe and only friend people you actually know in real life.

Safety Suggestions for Online Dating for Adults

Although the safety rule for teens is that the Internet should never be used for making new friends, the reality is that a lot of adults use the Internet for activities such as online dating. Because online dating is so popular, we've provided the following safety suggestions as a guideline for *adults:*

- Avoid giving your date your personal contact information at first.
- Meet your date in a public place where there are lots of people around.
- Don't go anywhere alone with your date at first.

(continued)

- Drive yourself to and from the date or find your own alternative form of transportation.
- Don't get in the car with your date or have him or her take you home at first.
- Let your friends and family know where you are and whom you are with.
- Check in with your friends and family before and after the date.

CHAPTER EXERCISES
for Teens, Young Adults, and Parents

Teens and young adults should complete the following exercises with parents:

- Practice exchanging contact information using the steps outlined in this chapter.
  - With your parent, begin by reviewing the steps for exchanging contact information.
  - Practice following the steps for exchanging contact information with your parent.
  - Practice following the steps for exchanging contact information with a peer you feel comfortable with.
    - Using the FriendMaker mobile app to review the steps just beforehand might be helpful.
    - You may want to choose peers from among the social group you identified or from those enrolled in an extracurricular or social activity to which you belong.
- Practice beginning and ending phone calls and leaving voicemail using the steps outlined in this chapter.

- With your parent, begin by reviewing the steps for beginning and ending phone calls and leaving voicemail.
- Practice following the steps for beginning and ending phone calls and leaving voicemail with your parent.
- Practice following the steps for beginning and ending phone calls and leaving voicemail with a peer you feel comfortable talking to on the phone.
  - Using the FriendMaker mobile app to review the steps just beforehand might be helpful.

> *Good sportsmanship primarily centers on three important behaviors: fellowship, fair play, and self-control.*

or negative way will cast a negative reflection on your teen or young adult's character, making it less likely that people will want to be friends. No one wants to play with a sore loser or a bad winner.

Rules for Good Sportsmanship

The following rules include concrete behaviors your teen or young adult can use to be a good sport when playing with people he or she wishes to be friends with. These rules aren't always followed in competitive team sports but are used by socially successful teens and young adults when playing games and sports for fun.

Praise the Other Players

One of the most basic ways to demonstrate good sportsmanship is to praise the other players. This is an example of the principle of fellowship. Praising others is simply the act of giving a compliment. A good sport not only praises members of his or her own team but also players from opposing teams. Although less common in competitive team sports, when playing games and sports with friends, it's perfectly appropriate for your child to praise players from opposing teams for good playing. A common social shortcoming we sometimes see in teens and young adults with social challenges is failure to praise or compliment others during game playing. This oversight may be due to poor perspective-taking abilities, in which the social benefit of praising others may not be so obvious. So what is the social benefit of praising others? It usually makes them feel appreciated, proud, special, even worthy to some extent, making them want to seek you out again.

> *One of the most basic ways to demonstrate good sportsmanship is to praise the other players.*

Although giving praise or compliments may not be something that comes naturally to teens and young adults with social difficulties, in our experience at the UCLA PEERS Clinic it can be easily learned. So if

7

Showing Good Sportsmanship

ACCORDING TO RESEARCH, THE AMOUNT OF TIME spent playing video games and computer games for teens far outweighs time spent on other recreational activities. Given the significant amount of time spent playing these games, sometimes several hours a day, it's important for your teen or young adult to be familiar with the rules for good sportsmanship. Good sportsmanship, although encompassing many values, primarily centers on three important behaviors: fellowship, fair play, and self-control.

- *Fellowship* involves supportive play between players, often involving the sense of unity, camaraderie, and connectedness. All players are playing toward an end goal. In the case of friendships, the goal shouldn't be to win at any cost but instead to make sure that everyone has a nice time. Competitive sports or professional sports don't necessarily follow the same guidelines. Instead, the goal there is usually to win. However, if your teen or young adult's goal is ultimately to make and keep friends, then when playing games and sports, the goal should always be to make sure everyone is having fun.
- *Fair play* involves the practice of playing ethically and justly. It includes playing by the rules and not bending or twisting the rules to your own advantage. No one wants to be friends with someone who cheats or doesn't play fairly.
- *Self-control* involves the ability to regulate your feelings and behaviors. In games and sports this involves avoiding getting upset or angry when you lose or gloating if you win. When playing games and sports, demonstrating poor self-control by behaving in an immature

you're concerned that it's not in your teen or young adult's nature to give praise to others, remember that if the goal is to make and keep friends, then once familiar with this rule, he or she may be more willing to try, as we've seen repeatedly with the teens and young adults in our clinic.

Social coaching tip: Be sure to read the chapter summary for teens and young adults, which provides examples of common forms of verbal and nonverbal praise often used by socially successful teens and young adults. Once familiar to your child, be sure to positively point out instances when your teen or young adult uses these types of praise, and prompt when he or she may forget by saying things such as, "Your sister just made a great shot. What could you say?" This reinforcement and prompting should only be done in the company of supportive family members and those your teen or young adult would not be embarrassed in front of.

Social coaching tip: You'll want to encourage your child to think about how it makes people feel to be praised when playing games or sports. Your teen or young adult may need to be reminded over and over of this skill. You may want to ask questions such as, "How do we feel about the person praising us?" and "Are we more likely to want to play with that person again?" Of course the answers to these questions are that when someone praises us, we might think the person is kind, thoughtful, fun, and generally a good sport, and we're more likely to seek that person out again because they make everyone feel good.

Play by the Rules

Another aspect of good sportsmanship is the principle that your teen or young adult must play by the rules. More simply put, this rule means don't cheat. In our experience working with teens and young adults with rigid thinking, this rule is often followed naturally, given their strong preference for following rules. Yet for some, playing by the rules will be more of a challenge, particularly for those with impulse control problems. The problem with this social mistake is that one intentional act of not playing by

> One intentional act of not playing by the rules has the capacity to end a friendship, and a pattern of cheating has the strong probability of leading to a bad reputation.

the rules has the capacity to end a friendship, and a pattern of cheating has the strong probability of leading to a bad reputation.

To illustrate the importance of this rule, imagine a teenage boy playing a friendly pick-up game of basketball with his friends. Not known for his gross motor skills and coordination, the boy frequently double dribbles, running with the ball rather than dribbling, yet refuses to admit his mistake when called on the play. He often runs out of bounds to flee his opponents but refuses to admit his wrongdoing, knowing full well he was out. Using your perspective-taking questions, consider this scenario from the point of view of the other players. What is this experience going to be like for the other players? They're likely to be annoyed, frustrated, and maybe even angry. What are they going to think of this boy? They're probably going to think he's a liar and a cheat. Are they going to want to play with him again? It's highly unlikely that this boy will be first choice for a pick-up game anytime in the near future, and if he continues to behave in this unsportsman-like way, he may get a reputation as a cheat.

Social coaching tip: You may need to coach your teen or young adult about the consequences of cheating. Parents in our program have found it very helpful to highlight the importance of this rule by going over the perspective-taking questions with their kids during teachable moments in their home when this rule is violated.

Share and Take Turns

Another essential rule of good sportsmanship is to share and take turns. This means that when playing games and sports with friends, it's important that everyone has a chance to play. Consider the previous example of the teenage boy playing basketball with his friends. How would his friends react if he were hogging the ball, not passing to other players? They'd likely feel annoyed, frustrated, and maybe even bored. What would they think of the boy who was being a ball hog? They'd probably think he was selfish, rude, and irritating. Would they want to play with him again? It's difficult to say if they'd want to play with him again but failing to share and take turns during games and sports isn't likely to lead to many future invitations to play.

> *When playing games and sports with friends, it's important that everyone has a chance to play.*

Social coaching tip: If your teen or young adult has a tendency to ball hog, or maybe he or she doesn't like to share the controller during video games, it will be important for you to coach this important rule of good sportsmanship during teachable moments. You may even want to set up opportunities for coaching this rule. For example, if the problem is sharing and taking turns, you might have your child play some preferred game with another member of the family, such as a sibling or a cousin around the same age. If there are no family members around the same age, you might want to practice with your teen or young adult yourself. When you notice he or she isn't sharing or taking turns, you might take the opportunity to remind him or her of this rule in a way that won't be embarrassing. Too often parents give in and let their children have their way. However, it's a good idea to play the role of a friend who won't be so forgiving.

Don't Referee

Some teens with social challenges have a tendency to think in concrete and literal terms. Consequently, they may examine the world through complicated sets of rules. They notice rules, often cite rules, and rarely break rules; and when they see someone break a rule, they might feel compelled to point out the rule violation, regardless of how embarrassing or rude their comments may seem. In conversations, we call this social error *policing.* In games and sports, we call this social error *refereeing.* We use the term *refereeing* because the act of pointing out rule violations in games and sports has the appearance of someone designated to preside over a game and enforce the rules of the game.

To illustrate the importance of this rule, imagine a young teen playing *Dungeons and Dragons* (a fantasy role-playing game) with his friends. At some point, another player makes a move that seems inconsistent with this player's character. The young teen feels compelled to point out this apparent rule violation, yet he's not the dungeon master (the referee and storyteller of the game). Using your perspective-taking questions, imagine how this young teen's comments and accusations might make his partner feel. It's likely that the partner will feel embarrassed, upset, and possibly even angry by the comments. What will he think of his accuser? He'll probably think he's arrogant, bossy, and a know-it-all.

Do you think he'll want to play with him again? If this pattern of ref-ereeing persists, it's unlikely that he'll want to play with him again, and the other players witnessing the refereeing may also choose not to play with him in the future. In fact, the young teen may get a reputation for being bossy, which will make it difficult for him to make and keep friends with anyone.

The tendency to referee others, although a strong urge for many teens and young adults with social difficulties, has the potential to create a huge barrier to developing and maintaining friendships. Perhaps your teen makes this mistake, like so many others. Although he or she may do this because it seems correct and factual to note rule violations, the problem with refereeing is that the receiver often experiences the scrutiny as an accusation or cen-sure, making the referee an unde-sirable companion.

> *The tendency to referee others, although a strong urge for many teens and young adults with social difficul-ties, has the potential to create a huge barrier to developing and main-taining friendships.*

Social coaching tip: If your teen or young adult has a tendency to referee, it's imperative for you to provide social coaching during teachable moments when these mistakes occur. Just as with the rule for no policing, once your teen or young adult is familiar with the social rule not to be a referee, it will be important for you to gently point out violations in the moment away from peers.

Don't Coach

Similar but different to the rule of no refereeing, another important social rule in games and sports is not to coach. Coaching is similar to refereeing in many ways, with one major exception: intent. The intent of a referee is to enforce the rules of the game and make sure the play-ers are playing fairly. The intent of a coach is to guide the players and help them to play better. Although both roles involve the identification and acknowledgment of rule violations, the actions of a coach are to help, whereas the actions of a referee are to enforce rules. To highlight this point, imagine two teenage boys playing video games. One is fairly proficient at the game being played and the other is more of a novice. As the novice struggles a bit with the game, having trouble reaching the next level, the more experienced player is attempting to guide him. He's providing verbal commentary, telling the other kid what to do and where to move, eventually grabbing the controller and saying, "Here let me show you how to get to the next level." Although the actions of the more skilled player may have been kindly meant, what do you think this experience was like for the player being coached? He probably felt annoyed, pressured, and perhaps even a bit embarrassed. What would he think of the teen doing the coaching? He's likely to think the coaching teen is bossy, rude, and a complete know-it-all. Is he going to want to play with the coach again? If this pattern persists, it's unlikely he'll want to play with the coach again. Even worse, if this coaching is pervasive and begins to be noticed by others, the teen may even get a bad reputation with his peers.

> The actions of a coach are to help, whereas the actions of a referee are to enforce rules.

Social coaching tip: If your teen has a tendency to coach others, you'll need to provide feedback during teachable moments including gentle reminders of how his or her friend might feel. Ironically, your social coaching during these moments will feel a bit like the behavior your teen or young adult is trying to avoid. Your teen may even call you out on the paradox. Just remember that in agreeing to learn the rules and steps of making and keeping friends, your child also agreed to be coached by you. It's unlikely his or her friends have a similar agreement.

Don't Be Competitive

A common social mistake committed by some with social difficulties is to be overly competitive during games and sports. Being overly competitive gives the appearance of being aggressively in pursuit of winning and is an example of a breach of the principle of self-control in sportsmanship. During organized games and sports (such as chess teams, science competitions,

> When playing recreational games and sports for the purpose of socializing and having fun with friends, being competitive is abnormal and socially frowned on.

or team sports), being competitive wouldn't be unnatural or even inappropriate. However, when playing recreational games and sports for the purpose of socializing and having fun with friends, being competitive is abnormal and socially frowned on.

If your teen or young adult has a tendency to be competitive, then the object of the game is probably to win, and he or she may get frustrated and upset if that doesn't happen. Yet, if the goal is to make and keep friends, what could be the problem with being overly competitive? To demonstrate, imagine a young man engrossed in a game of chess with his friend. Both are experienced players, skilled in the game, providing challenging competition for one another. Imagine that this young man is feeling frustrated by the game and the possibility that his opponent might win. He slams his fist on the table in frustration, grunts and groans, and his blood pressure rises and his face turns red. What is this experience going to be like for his partner? The friend might feel surprised, annoyed, or perhaps even scared by this strong overreaction. What is he going to think of the young man as he grunts and groans? He's likely to think he's weird, obnoxious, and maybe even a little crazy. Is he going to want to play with the young man again? If this behavior becomes a pattern, it's probable that he won't want to play with him anymore, no matter how great a challenger he is. What's more, if this young man continues to act in this way, he'll probably get a reputation for being a hot head and other people won't want to play with him either.

Social coaching tip: If this sounds like your teen, you will need to help him or her understand that an important rule for good sportsmanship is to avoid being competitive. If your teen or young adult needs support beyond this in managing his or her emotions, you may want to find additional resources for emotion regulation and avoid competitive social situations in the interim. Although the ability to regulate emotions and not lose your cool is very much intertwined with making and keeping friends, emotion regulation is a complicated process involving many different strategies. If your teen has trouble staying calm in difficult social situations and regularly loses his or her cool with peers beyond competitive sports, you may want to help him or her work on regulating emotions and decreasing behavioral outbursts before attempting some of the skills outlined in this book.

Show Concern and Offer Help When Someone's Hurt

When playing physical sports, the likelihood that someone will get slightly injured or fall down at some point is relatively high. When this happens, it's important to show concern and offer help if necessary. In some cases, it may even be necessary to stop the game. Although this may seem obvious, one of the common social errors exhibited by teens and young adults with social difficulties is that they sometimes don't show concern or offer help when someone's hurt.

> One of the common social errors exhibited by teens and young adults with social difficulties is that they sometimes don't show concern or offer help when someone's hurt.

To help underscore the importance of this rule, think of our previous group of teenage boys playing their game of pick-up basketball. Imagine while taking a shot, one of the players stumbles and falls to the ground, not immediately getting up. Picture our socially challenged teen walking by the player without acknowledging his fall, not asking if he's okay, and not offering to give him a hand to stand up. Even if the player's injury was minor, what would the others think of this behavior? They might think the behavior was odd, inconsiderate, and highly unusual. What would they think of the boy who walked by his injured friend without a moment's notice? They'd probably think he was thoughtless, rude, and unfeeling. Are they going to want to play with him again? The player who was injured might be less interested in playing with the boy again, and the other players may also be less inclined.

Perhaps this example sounds familiar to you. In our experience working with kids with social differences, it's probably not a lack of caring that causes these oversights but more likely a lack of awareness. Although showing concern and offering help may not be intuitive for your teen, our experience tells us that it can be easily learned in specific contexts, such as physical sports.

Social coaching tip: If your teen or young adult has a tendency not to notice or show concern, begin by explaining that he or she should expect that people may get injured from time to time during physical sports. Follow this up by telling your teen or young adult that if he or she wishes to be seen as a good friend, then he or she must show concern and offer help in these situations. By prompting your child to be on the look-out for these instances, it's far more likely that he or she will be able to respond appropriately.

Suggest a Change When Bored

It's not uncommon for people to become bored or tired during games and sports. In these instances, the ecologically valid skill used by socially savvy teens and young adults is to suggest a change in the activity. This might be done by saying something like, "How about when we're done with this game, we go get something to eat?" or "Anyone feel like play-ing something else?" These types of suggestions are infinitely preferable to saying, "I'm bored," which is a classic insult. When your teen or young adult suggests a change, it's not a guarantee that the others will want to do what's suggested, but by providing another option, the likelihood of moving onto another activity improves.

One of the more common social errors committed by teens and young adults with social challenges is to walk away from games and sports when they're bored or become disinterested. Think of our chess-playing young man for a moment. Imagine he's playing a game of chess with a slightly inferior partner. He feels unchallenged by his rival and so walks away from the game without saying anything. He doesn't intend to cause offense to the other man. He's just bored and wants to do some-thing else. Use your perspective-taking questions and consider what this experience will be like for his partner. He'll probably feel confused, not sure what's just happened, and may feel irritated by having been left alone in the middle of a game. What will he think of the young man? He'll prob-ably think he's weird, strange, and very rude. Will he want to play with the young man again? After being slighted in such a way, the chance that he'll want to play chess with this young man again is slim. Unfortunately, this type of behavior is quite common among teens and young adults with social challenges, who when they get bored, might make the mistake of walking away from activities, not realizing the offense they cause.

Social coaching tip: If your teen or young adult has a tendency to do this, the alternative to walking away is to suggest a change in activi-ty. To help change this habit, you may need to intervene during teachable moments and provide social coaching around this important social rule. Parents going through the UCLA PEERS Clinic have also described knowing when their child is reaching the point of boredom and have intervened during these critical times to help identify other options in the moment until their teen or young adult is able to manage these situations alone.

Don't Be a Sore Loser

A common social mistake committed by competitive teens and young adults involves being a sore loser. In games and sports, sore loser behavior includes getting upset, angry, or sad as a result of a defeat. This might include blaming others for the loss, making excuses for the defeat, or not taking responsibility for any part in the loss. Research tells us that young adults with social challenges are more likely to engage in this unsportsmanlike conduct. Take our chess-playing young man for example. Imagine he was back at the chessboard with his highly skilled rival. They manage to get through the game, despite the grunting and groaning and fist slamming on the table. Much to the young man's chagrin, his skillful challenger wins the game. The young man is visibly upset, launching into a tirade of excuses for the loss, including distractions during the game being the cause of his defeat. The young man goes on and on at length about how it wasn't a fair game and that he would have played better if it weren't for the distractions. He's being a sore loser. What's this experience going to be like for the young man's partner? He's probably going to feel irritated and annoyed that his triumph is being sullied by this unsportsmanlike behavior. What's he going to think of the young man who's acting like a sore loser? He's likely to think the young man is self-centered, arrogant, and rude. Is he going to want to play with the young man again? Assuming he has other opponents up to the challenge, it's highly unlikely that he'll want to play with the young man again. Moreover, the partner may share the details of this unsportsmanlike behavior with other chess-playing friends, possibly resulting in a bad reputation for the young man.

> Sore loser behavior includes getting upset, angry, or sad as a result of a defeat.

Social coaching tip: If your teen or young adult has a tendency to be a sore loser in games and sports, you're not alone. We've talked with scores of parents in the same boat. Fortunately, if your child (like theirs) has agreed to learn the rules for making and keeping friends described in this book, then he or she is socially motivated enough to benefit from the following advice. Explain that no one wants to be friends with a sore loser, so if the goal is to make and keep friends, then he or she needs to act like losing wasn't a big deal.

Don't Be a Bad Winner

Similar to the rule, *don't be a sore loser*, it's also important that when playing games and sports, your teen isn't a bad winner. Bad winner behavior involves gloating about victory either through excessive boasting, over-the-top displays of celebration, or rubbing the defeat in the opponent's face. The concept conjures up images of NFL football players doing the end zone dance after scoring a touchdown, spiking the ball to the ground, dancing around the field, and cheering themselves on. In many sports leagues, this kind of performance is now banned as unsportsmanlike behavior. Although not uncommon in professional sports, being a bad winner is also relatively common among teens and young adults playing recreational games and sports. For example, think of our competitive chess-playing young man under different circumstances. Imagine his game of chess with his arch rival took a different turn. In this case, despite any supposed distractions, he manages to win the game. His competitive spirit makes it difficult for him to contain his exuberance. On checkmate, he jumps up from the table, throws his fist in the air as if hitting some invisible target, and yells, "Yes!" He then proceeds to dissect every nuance of the game, describing in great detail the brilliance of his strategy and the genius of his every move. What will this display be like for the gloating man's opponent? He'll likely feel embarrassed, humiliated, and extremely annoyed by this obnoxious display of grandiosity. What will he think of the gloating young man? He'll probably think he's arrogant, rude, and obnoxious.

> *Bad winner behavior involves gloating about victory either through excessive boasting, over-the-top displays of celebration, or rubbing the defeat in the opponent's face.*

Will he want to play with him again? The opponent will probably be less likely than ever before to want to play with the young man because his behavior has caused him embarrassment and discomfort.

Social coaching tip: Perhaps your teen has a tendency to be a bad winner, too. It's not uncommon behavior, even among socially adept teens and adults, so don't feel bad. Yet even though this behavior isn't uncommon, it's rather risky for teens and young adults who have difficulty making and keeping friends. So in your case, help your teen or young adult understand the consequence of this behavior and adopt a less risky behavior, such as acting like winning wasn't a big deal and avoiding being a bad winner.

Say, "Good Game" at the End of the Game

Instead of behaving like a sore loser or a bad winner when playing games and sports with friends, a good rule of sportsmanship is to say, "Good game" at the end of the game and avoid acting like winning or losing is a big deal. Remember, when your teen's goal is to make and keep friends, then his or her goal during non-competitive games and sports is to make sure everyone is having a good time. The best way to achieve this goal is by being a good sport and following the rules established in this chapter.

> *A good rule of sportsmanship is to say, "Good game" at the end of the game and avoid acting like winning or losing is a big deal.*

Success Story: Carter Can Be a Good Sport

Being a good sport is a critical skill for any teen or young adult actively involved in sports or game playing. Although particularly important during games and sports with friends, good sportsmanship is also important when playing organized team sports. In fact, being a poor sport during team sports (even when competitive) can result in a bad reputation, making it difficult to make and keep friends. This was the case for Carter, a sixteen-year-old boy with a history of peer rejection and a bad reputation.

Carter was a very talented volleyball player—the best on his school team. Unfortunately, the school Carter was attending prior to coming to PEERS did not have a winning track record, despite Carter's athletic gifts. Because he was naturally competitive and took his sport very seriously, this frustrated Carter to no end. His mother explained, "Carter would have a meltdown at the end of the game if they didn't win—which was often. He would yell and throw things and even tell off his coach and the other players. His teammates couldn't stand him. They knew he was the best player on the team, but it didn't matter. They never invited him to parties, and even though he said he didn't care, I know he did. His reputation was awful."

Eventually Carter's parents decided to switch schools, enrolling him in another local high school with a better volleyball team—hoping that a fresh start would give him the chance he needed to succeed socially. This was about the time they brought him to PEERS. From the moment he walked in the door, Carter was exceptionally motivated to learn the skills we had to offer. He explained, "I wanted things to be different. I knew that was my chance to make things work for me, and I didn't want to blow it." Carter was the first to admit that his poor sportsmanship was the cause of his bad reputation and the reason he didn't have friends. "People thought I was a hot head. I guess I was," he admitted, "but I knew I could be different."

Although Carter was the new kid at a new school, this did not guarantee a fresh start. The community he lived in was small and his reputation preceded him. His new teammates were well aware of his unsportsmanlike conduct, having witnessed it firsthand in previous matches with his old school. His classmates were also aware of his tendency to "go ballistic" in games, and Carter suspected that everyone was waiting for him to do the same at his new school. Fortunately, Carter had a different game plan. Shortly after joining PEERS, he approached our team with his problem, asking for help. He said he wanted to make a new start but didn't know what to do. Quickly we devised a plan.

Even though our group had only just begun, Carter was given a crash course in the rules of good sportsmanship and the steps for changing a bad reputation (described in chapter 14). He quickly learned to praise his teammates (something that had never occurred to him to do before), not to referee or coach the other players, and not to act like a sore loser when his team lost a match. He said, "Good game" to his teammates and the opposing team after every match, and above all he kept his cool. He also laid low for the first couple of months at his new school while his reputation (which had followed him) died down. In the span of a semester (the length of our program), Carter not only overcame his bad reputation but he also actually became popular! By the time he left PEERS, he was having four to five get-togethers a week, being invited to parties and gatherings every weekend, and was even dating. His father commented, "It's like he's a different kid. We used to worry about whether he'd ever be able to have friends. Now we worry about him making curfew and whether he's driving safely—the usual stuff. The other day he got grounded for staying out too late. I had to do it, but secretly I was proud."

Although Carter's story isn't the typical one—most teens and young adults going through our program don't end up becoming popular—his story is a good example of what can come from good social motivation and a set of core skills. Carter was eager to change his social circumstances, and he did! Although the goal of this book isn't to make your teen or young adult the most popular person at school or work, it is the goal to help him or her make and keep friends. An important part of that process involves being a good sport, like Carter.

RULES FOR GOOD SPORTSMANSHIP
Chapter Summary for Teens and Young Adults

> *The following information is intended to be read by teens and young adults and contains a brief summary of the chapter.*

Playing games and sports is a common way teens and young adults socialize with friends. The problem is that if you act like a poor sport during these activities, you could push people away. The following rules of good sportsmanship are used by socially successful teens and adults.

(continued)

Praise the Other Players

One of the easiest ways to show people that you're a good
sport is to praise them. *Praise* is just another word for giving
compliments and can be given either through words or actions.
Here are some common types of verbal and nonverbal praise
used by teens and young adults.

Example of Verbal Praise
- Good job!
- Nice try.
- Great shot!
- Nice move.
- Nice kill.
- Awesome!

Examples of Nonverbal Praise
- High-five
- Pound or fist bump (lightly tapping closed fists)
- Thumbs up
- Clapping
- Handshake
- Pat on the back

Play by the Rules

Another important rule of good sportsmanship is to play by the
rules. This means you shouldn't cheat or try to make up different
rules in the middle of a game, which could be seen as cheating.
One of the biggest pet peeves people have in games and sports
is cheating. If you do this enough times, you could get a bad
reputation and fewer people will want to play games and sports
with you. So instead, play it safe and play by the rules.

Share and Take Turns

Another way to show good sportsmanship is to make sure
everyone has a chance to play. That means you shouldn't hog

the controller or be a ball hog. Instead, share and take turns with everyone. When all the players get a chance to play, it's more fun for everybody.

Don't Referee

A common mistake some people make during games and sports is that they referee others and tell them what they're doing wrong. So why is it bad to referee? Think about it. What do referees do? They call the plays, point out rule violations, and generally enforce the rules of a game. Now imagine someone doing that during a friendly game. How obnoxious would that be? Even though you may notice that your friends break rules from time to time, it's not your job to point that out. No one wants to play with a referee. Instead, you need to go with the flow and realize that rule enforcement isn't your business. If your goal is to make and keep friends, then your business is to have fun with your friends and don't referee them. But if you notice that your friend doesn't follow the rules and you don't like that— then remember that friendship is a choice. You don't have to hang out with that friend. Meanwhile, don't referee him or her if you want others to like you.

Don't Coach

It's also important that you don't coach others during games and sports. Coaching is similar to refereeing because both involve telling other people their business when they're not asking. But coaching is different from refereeing because the motive of a coach is to be helpful, whereas the motive of a referee is to enforce the rules. So what's the problem with coaching then? Think about it. What do coaches do? They help players play better. But if your goal is to make and keep friends, coaching your friends, even if it's to help them get to the next level in a favorite video game, can still seem bossy

(continued)

and controlling. Instead, you can offer to help your friend in those situations, but if your friend doesn't want your help, let it go.

Don't Be Competitive

Have you ever played a game with someone who's super competitive? What's that like for the other players? It's usually not that fun. Playing on teams and organized sports leagues is one thing but playing games and sports with friends is supposed to be about having fun. Focusing on winning at all costs is not a good way to make and keep friends, so if friendship is your goal, don't be competitive.

Show Concern and Offer Help When Someone's Hurt

Sometimes when you play physical sports, people can get hurt or injured in some way. When that happens, it's important for you to show concern and offer help when it's needed. That means if your friends fall down during a game, ask if they're okay and offer to help them up. If you just walk by and don't say anything, you'll look like you don't care and your friends may get upset with you. You could also get a bad reputation for being cold and uncaring, even if you're really not that way.

Suggest a Change When Bored

It's pretty common for people to get bored or tired during games and sports. It's probably happened to you many times. In those cases, you want to avoid saying things like, "I'm bored" or walking away. Even if true, that would seem rude and is insulting to your friends. Instead, you could suggest a change in the activity by saying something like, "How about

when we're done with this game, we go get something to eat?"
or "Anyone feel like playing something else?" Just because you
suggest a change doesn't mean your friends will want to do it.
But if your friends rarely want to do what you suggest, go with
the flow in the moment, and then remember that friendship
is a choice. You don't need to hang out with those friends
anymore, but you also don't need to be a poor sport in the
meantime.

Don't Be a Sore Loser

Some people get upset, angry, or sad when they lose a game.
We call that being a sore loser. The problem with being that
way is that no one wants to play with a sore loser. So even if
you're upset about losing a game, act like losing wasn't a big
deal.

Don't Be a Bad Winner

Another rule of good sportsmanship is to avoid being a bad
winner. Being a bad winner involves gloating about your victory
either through excessive bragging, over-the-top displays of
celebration, or rubbing the defeat in your opponent's face. It's
like the NFL football players who do the end zone dance after
scoring a touchdown. People don't like playing with bad winners
because it's obnoxious and embarrassing. So instead, act like
winning wasn't a big deal.

Say, "Good Game" at the End of the Game

One of the simplest ways to be a good sport is to say, "Good
game" at the end of the game. This is an alternative to acting like
winning or losing was a big deal and a nice way to make your
friends feel good.

CHAPTER EXERCISES
for Teens, Young Adults, and Parents

Teens and young adults should complete the following exercises with parents:

- Practice being a good sport using the rules outlined in this chapter.
  - Begin by reviewing the rules for good sportsmanship with your parent.
  - Practice following the rules for good sportsmanship with your parent or a family member around the same age as you, playing a game familiar to both of you.
    - Be sure to play by the rules, share and take turns, give lots of praise, and say, "Good game" at the end of the game.
- Practice following the rules for good sportsmanship with one or more peers with whom you play games (video games, computer games, card or board games, sports).
  - Using the FriendMaker mobile app to review the rules just beforehand might be helpful.
  - This practice may occur within the context of the following:
    - An extracurricular activity, sports team, or other social activity to which you belong
    - Game playing during get-togethers with friends
    - Gym class (if relevant)

8

Enjoying Successful Get-Togethers

The goal of this book is to help you provide the tools necessary for helping your teen or young adult develop and maintain meaningful friendships based on scientific evidence about what truly works. Organizing and having successful get-togethers with friends is one of the most important skills your teen or young adult will gain toward achieving ongoing meaningful relationships.

Get-togethers might be described as casual social gatherings organized among friends for the purpose of social interaction. Socially active teens and young adults have regular and frequent get-togethers with friends. They occur in a variety of locations including homes and places in the community, all outside of school or the workplace. Research suggests that teens and young adults with social challenges have significantly fewer get-togethers with their peers, often remaining socially isolated outside of the academic or vocational setting. In our experience through our clinic at UCLA, younger teens with social difficulties who do manage to have regular get-togethers with friends may still refer to them as *play dates*. Their parents may even call them *play dates*, too. Yet the term *play date* describes parent-organized playtime between younger children. To speak bluntly, teens and young adults aren't supposed to have play dates. Instead, they have what they describe as get-togethers or hangouts. Parents may be thinking, "Who cares what you call it?" The reason we highlight this for parents is because the major difference between a play date and a get-together or hangout is who is doing the organizing. For play dates, as we know, the interaction is parent organized. For get-togethers, the contact is organized by teens or young adults. Anything apart from this for teens and young adults without intellectual disabilities is probably not developmentally appropriate, and although well intentioned by parents may seem or feel socially immature.

> Teens and young adults with social challenges have significantly fewer get-togethers with their peers.

If you've been actively involved in helping your teen or young adult plan and organize get-togethers with friends, you've probably done this because he or she was having trouble doing this alone and the alternative was social isolation and loneliness. Your reasons are good and your instincts are fantastic—because being with peers is very important. Many teens and young adults with social difficulties do struggle with knowing how to organize social interactions with friends. But instead of taking on this responsibility for him or her, let's try a different approach and teach your teen or young adult how to organize and have successful get-togethers with friends in a more independent way that won't appear immature to his or her friends. Your role in helping to organize these activities will be just as important but will be slightly different.

Long after organizing play dates has ceased to be developmentally appropriate, parent assistance in facilitating social interactions for any teen is probably either not happening or happening behind the scenes at times. Yet for teens and even some young adults with social challenges, the role of organizer continues to be a component of the parent-planning process, often for years. One of the reasons for continued parent involvement may be that many teens and young adults with social differences don't know how to organize social gatherings on their own and often don't even think to plan them. We suggest that you can help your teen or young adult with this transition by offering social coaching on the steps needed to plan and organize get-togethers. Doing so, we've found, will probably be a better way to help him or her develop closer friendships and become more socially engaged in the future.

Moving forward, organizing and having successful get-togethers will be a critical step in your teen or young adult's pursuit of friendships. Because close friendships are developed by having get-togethers outside of the school and work setting, if your teen or young adult doesn't engage in these interactions, it will be very difficult (if not impossible) to develop close friendships with acquaintances. Recall from chapter 2 that friendships have varying degrees of closeness. For example, acquaintances are those only known slightly. Casual friendships are those that may involve some socializing but aren't particularly close. Regular friendships are those that include regular socializing and a slight degree of closeness. Close friendships or best friendships involve frequent socializing and a high degree of closeness. If your teen or young adult wishes to enhance current friendships and develop new friendships beyond those that are casual or simply acquaintance based, then organizing and having successful get-togethers is the way to do that.

> *Close friendships are developed by having get-togethers outside of the school and work setting.*

In the following, we'll outline the steps for planning, preparing, and having successful get-togethers for teens and young adults based on what science tells us works. Helping your teen or young adult learn and apply these skills will be an important key to unlocking the gateway to developing close friendships.

Steps for Planning a Get-Together

The following steps for planning a get-together should be put into action by your teen or young adult. You may want to provide assistance by helping identify the who, what, where, when (the *four Ws*), and how aspects of planning the get-together described in the following, but it will be important for your teen or young adult to follow through independently with the steps. This is when parents can be invaluable coaches. We have found that often socially isolated individuals are not by nature hermits and they don't want to be; rather, they're just not natural planners.

Who

The first step in planning a get-together is deciding whom to invite. Remember that friendship is a choice; there are good choices and bad choices. A good choice is someone your teen or young adult has common interests with. These common interests will give them something to talk about and something to do together during the get-together. So before even suggesting a get-together, it's important that your teen or young adult has traded information with the other person on a number of occasions, found common interests, and decided that this person seems interested in getting to know him or her (for a review of assessing interest see chapters 4 and 5). Some get-togethers involve just two people, and others include three or more people, sometimes referred to as *group get-togethers.* An important aspect of having a get-together (particularly group get-togethers) is to let everyone invited know who's going to be there. By making sure everyone knows who's invited, your teen or young adult ensures there are no surprises. For young adults in particular, when having friends over to their home, letting everyone know who will be there, including family members and roommates, is a very important part of the planning.

> *An important aspect of having a get-together is to let everyone invited know who's going to be there.*

What

The next step in planning a get-together is to figure out what to do. Get-togethers for teens and young adults with social challenges should be activity based. That's because planning a get-together around an activity takes the pressure off finding things to talk about, which may naturally be more difficult for those with social differences. When your teen or young adult organizes an activity-based get-together, much of the conversation will center on the activity, making it easier to talk and trade information. The choice of activity should always be based on the common interests of everyone attending the get-together. For example, if a shared common interest is video games, playing video games at someone's house might be a good activity. Friends sharing a common interest in computers might play on the computer together or go to a computer expo. Interest in science fiction might lead to going to a sci-fi movie, whereas interest in comic books might mean that going to a comic book convention or a comic book store would be good options. You get the idea. If your teen or young adult has

> *Get-togethers for teens and young adults with social challenges should be activity-based.*

traded information extensively with his or her friends, multiple common interests should have been identified that could lead to ideas for activity-based get-togethers.

Having a fun idea is the first step in organizing what to do during a get-together, but it's also important that your teen or young adult asks his or her friend if the activity is something he or she is interested in doing. If not, but the friend still wants to hang out, your teen or young adult should be ready to suggest other options of things to do based on common interests. Asking friends what they want to do is another option. Table 8.1 in the chapter summary for teens and young adults highlights some common activity-based get-togethers used by teens and young adults attending the UCLA PEERS Clinic. Remember that friendships are based on common interests, so if your teen or young adult has chosen his or her guest well, then finding an activity that is of interest to both should be no problem.

Where

The next step in planning a get-together is to consider where the get-together is going to take place. If appropriate and comfortable, your teen or young adult might have the first few get-togethers in a place where it's natural for you to be there, such as your home. This is helpful in the early stages because you can inconspicuously monitor the activities and step in if social coaching is needed (without the awareness of the guest, of course). If it's not appropriate to have the get-together in your home or someplace where you can unobtrusively observe, get-togethers in the community for teens and young adults are perfectly natural. Get-togethers may also take place in someone else's home, although in this case, your teen or young adult won't be the one planning the get-together. Whatever is decided, figuring out where the gathering will take place is a key ingredient to making sure the get-together happens. If your teen or young adult doesn't figure this out, there will probably be confusion and the get-together may never come together.

When

The next step in planning a get-together is to figure out when it will take place. Your teen or young adult might begin by thinking about what times work best with his or her schedule and the timing of the activity, then check with the friend to make sure that time works. If the friend is unavailable at the time suggested but still wants to get together, suggesting an alternative day and time or asking what works best is a good idea. Although this probably seems obvious to you, we've heard countless stories from our families whose teens and young adults have been heartbroken after get-togethers fell through because they never figured out when (or where) they were going to happen. To avoid the same fate, help your teen or young adult solidify these details by asking questions about the *four Ws*.

> *Help your teen or young adult solidify these details by asking questions about the* four Ws.

For the first few get-togethers with new friends, it's recommended that gatherings be more time limited, usually no more than two to three hours unless going to a movie, concert, sporting event, or some other lengthier activity. Sticking to shorter initial get-togethers is a good idea because it may be difficult for your teen or young adult to keep the conversation going for extended periods of time with people he or she doesn't know well. Keeping these initial gatherings shorter at first is a safer bet because hopefully guests will leave wanting more.

How

The final step for planning a get-together is to figure out how this is going to happen. That might include how everyone is going to get to where they need to be. If the get-together is not within walking distance and if no one has a driver's license or access to a car or public transportation, you might offer to drop off and pick up everyone if appropriate. The nice thing about offering to be the driver is that you get to be like a fly on the wall; you'll be privy to how the get-together is going. For young adults, though, having a parent driver may not be developmentally appropriate (depending on the level of functioning of the young adult) and public transportation may be a better option. Whatever is decided, identifying how to make the get-together happen will be a critical step in making sure your teen or young adult has a successful get-together.

Social coaching tip: Be prepared to help your teen or young adult work out the details of the *four Ws* as well as the *how* aspects of planning the get-together. For many parents, this is the most active role you will provide in social coaching for get-togethers. Don't expect your teen or young adult to know what to do or even think to organize these kinds of interactions on his or her own. More than likely, you will need to be an active participant in this process at first, helping to pull the strings behind the scenes.

Strategies for Preparing for a Get-Together

The following strategies highlight the things your teen or young adult needs to do when preparing for a get-together. Many of these strategies described involve organizing get-togethers at home because these gatherings usually require the most preparation. You may need to provide a little extra help or support to make sure these things get done but your teen or young adult should follow through independently with the preparations as much as possible.

Follow Up to Finalize Plans

When preparing for a get-together that's been planned at least a few days in advance, your teen or young adult needs to follow up to finalize the plans. In one way, a follow-up call (or text, IM, or e-mail) is a courtesy reminder about the get-together to make sure no one's forgotten and that your plans are still on. In other cases, this step may actually involve solidifying plans that were either tentative or never fully finalized. For example, your teen or young adult may have casually decided to get together with friends over the weekend but never settled on a day or time. In this case, a follow-up call with these friends to finalize plans is a must. Casual plans aren't final until they're confirmed. That means that if friends are suddenly unavailable to "hang out this weekend" as discussed, although unpleasant and disappointing, your teen or young adult will have to accept that because a particular day and time wasn't set, the chance that the plans would fall through was left wide open. Even finalized plans may be canceled for a variety of reasons, so your teen or young adult should be prepared for these eventualities and be willing to go with the flow and be flexible. Although it's not uncommon for plans to change or fall through, if you notice that your teen or young

When preparing for a get-together that's been planned at least a few days in advance, your teen or young adult needs to follow up to finalize the plans.

adult's friend is consistently canceling plans or rarely following through, you may need to have a conversation about whether this is a good choice for a friend.

Make Sure Personal Space Is Presentable

If your teen or young adult is planning a get-together at home or is driving a car, making sure that personal space is presentable is part of preparing for the get-together. Cleaning up personal space by removing trash and organizing clutter is an important part of making sure the space is comfortable for the friend. This doesn't mean that the space has to be immaculate, just not messy and gross. So what happens if this space isn't presentable? Imagine a young man who's having a friend over for a get-together and his home is a mess. He's had a busy week and has run out of time to clean up before his friend comes over. His friend arrives at the expected time, knocks on the door, and when greeted, enters his place only to find dirty dishes on tables, empty food cartons and wrappers scattered across the room, and dirty clothes strewn about furniture. Using your perspective-taking questions, consider what this experience will be like for the friend. The friend will probably feel immediately awkward and uncomfortable, not knowing where to sit or stand amidst the clutter. What will he think of the young man? He'll probably think the young man is a slob, possibly even inconsiderate and rude. Is the friend going to want to hang out with the young man again? Chances are he's probably not going to want to hang out in the young man's home again. In order to avoid this embarrassment and insult, it's important that when preparing for a get-together, your teen or young adult clean up and make any relevant personal space presentable. If for whatever reason it's not possible to clean up, you may want to suggest that the get-together happen outside of your home in the community.

Put Away Personal Items

Another important step for preparing for a get-together in your home is to put away any personal items your teen or young adult is either unwilling to share or doesn't want others to see or touch. Dirty clothes strewn about furniture would be a good example of something that needs to get put away. The same is true for precious or highly valued items. For instance, imagine the young man from the previous example owns a valuable collection of original *Star Wars* action figures, never removed from their original boxes and in pristine condition. Although very proud of his collection, he experiences tremendous anxiety when others attempt to hold or even touch his collectibles. Imagine his friend, arriving at his home and upon entering, quickly narrows in on the collection. An avid *Star Wars* fan, his friend is excited to see such an impressive collection. He quickly grabs one of the boxes as the young man anxiously yells, "No, don't touch that!" Use your perspective-taking questions to think about what this experience is going to be like for the friend. The friend is likely to feel confused and embarrassed, unsure why he's being yelled at. What is he going to think of the young man? He's going to think the young man is strange and rude, perhaps a little crazy. Is the friend going to want to hang out with the young man again? Because yelling at your friend is not a good way to begin a get-together, the young man will have to do some serious damage control if his friend is going to want to hang out with him again.

> Put away any personal items your teen or young adult is either unwilling to share or doesn't want others to see or touch.

Although this was a difficult situation, anticipating that his friend may naturally be curious about his collectibles, perhaps even wanting to touch or hold one of the action figures, what should the young man have done to prepare? If there are any concerns about a friend touching, handling, or seeing any personal effects, these items need to be put away before the friend ever arrives. The same thing is true for food and beverages. Although it's always polite to have food and beverages available for visiting friends, if your teen or young adult is concerned that there won't be enough leftovers, then only put out what he or she is willing to share. Putting away any personal items or things that he is unwilling to share will help to avoid any potential conflict that might damage the friendship.

Have Alternative Activities Available

If your teen or young adult has used the *four Ws*, he or she will have planned an activity-based get-together, providing a good idea of how the time will be spent. However, plans sometimes change during get-togethers. Friends may begin with one activity, get bored, and move onto another activity. The ebb and flow of activities is normal and should be expected. Reminding your teen or young adult of this likelihood and encouraging him or her to go with the flow and not get too tied down to one activity or one plan is a good way to avoid potential conflict. When anticipating changes in activities, it's helpful for your teen or young adult to have alternative activities available when the friend arrives. These alternative activities should be based on the common interests shared with the friends. For example, if the plan is to play video games with friends in your home, but your teen or young adult knows that everyone also likes science fiction movies, leaving out a selection of sci-fi movies would be a good alternative plan in case people get bored. Leaving these items out where friends can see them and more easily suggest a change in activities is helpful. Having alternative activities available is a useful strategy to prepare for the natural changes and adjustments that happen during get-togethers and will help your teen or young adult be prepared to go with the flow to keep activities interesting and fresh.

> *When anticipating changes in activities, it's helpful for your teen or young adult to have alternative activities available when the friend arrives.*

Social coaching tip: It will be helpful for you to go over the strategies for preparing for a get-together with your teen or young adult a few days prior to the hangout. This is because many of the strategies involved require advance time and can't be left to the last minute. Feel free to use the strategies listed here as a checklist to ensure that your teen or young adult is prepared for the get-together. Don't expect that he or she will be ready to fully take charge just yet.

Steps for Beginning a Get-Together

The following steps provide an outline for how socially savvy teens and young adults sometimes begin get-togethers in their homes. These steps are generally followed in the order presented but may be modified a bit according to context and preference. Although these steps may seem obvious to you, they may not be so obvious to your teen or young adult, which is why we've broken them down into very concrete and specific parts.

1. Greet Your Guest

Whether occurring in your home, a friend's home, or the community, get-togethers always begin with some type of greeting. This usually involves saying hello and asking the other person (or persons) how they're doing. In general, females sometimes give a hug or kiss on the cheek, whereas males might give a head nod, handshake, or a fist bump, but the manner in which friends greet each other will vary according to individual preferences.

2. Invite Them In

For get-togethers hosted by your teen or young adult at home, once he or she has greeted friends at the door, the next step is to invite them in. This is usually done by saying, "Come in," followed by moving away from the door to make space for them to enter. In our experience working with teens and young adults with social differences, after learning this step, some make the mistake of saying, "Come in" but not moving out of the doorway. This creates an awkward start with the friend self-consciously and uncomfortably maneuvering around the fixed body of our teen or young adult positioned directly in the middle of the doorway. To help your child avoid this awkward beginning, you might remind him or her to move away from the doorway when inviting guests into your home.

3. Provide Introductions

The next step for beginning get-togethers is to provide introductions to anyone who hasn't met. This includes not only friends attending a group get-together but also family members or roommates whom the friend hasn't met. Introductions typically involve saying something like, "Andy, this is my friend Dan. Dan, this is Andy." If your teen or young adult isn't sure if people have met, saying something like, "Andy, have you met Dan?" or "Andy, I'm not sure if you've met Dan." When providing introductions, it's also nice to provide a little background about the people being intro-duced, even something as simple as how you know them. For example, saying something like, "Andy and I work together, and Dan and I went to school together" would be enough. This will help guests break the ice and have something to trade information about.

4. Offer Refreshments

It's important for your teen or young adult to provide and offer refreshments when having friends over. What's served will depend on the type of get-together, time of day, and number of people. At the very least, light beverages and snacks should be offered when entertaining at home. Choosing food and beverages that the friends like is nice, and having options when unsure about preferences is safe. You'll probably have to help your teen or young adult identify appropriate food and beverages when preparing for the get-together because this may be new territory for him or her.

5. Give a Tour

For guests who are new to your teen or young adult's home, it's appropriate and polite to offer to give them a tour. This step will depend on the size of the home and the comfort level of those living there. For smaller homes, aside from the area where people will be socializing, it may only be necessary to point to the general location of the kitchen and bathroom. Most friends (particularly teens) will also want to see your teen or young adult's bedroom, especially if the home is shared with family members or roommates, making the bedroom his or her only personal space. When sharing a home with others, your teen or young adult may need to clarify beforehand where guests are free to go in order to avoid any awkwardness during the get-together.

6. Ask Your Guests What They Want to Do

Once guests have arrived and everyone has been properly greeted following the previous steps, it's always nice to either ask the guests what they want to do or check in to make sure they still want to do what was planned. For example, saying something like, "What do you want to do?" or "What do you feel like doing?" or "Do you still want to play video games?" would be a nice transition into an activity. Even though it should have been decided during the planning phase, as we'll soon discuss, when hosting a get-together at home, guests get to pick the activities. That means that even if the plan was to play video games, if the guests want to do something else, your teen or young adult needs to go with the flow and follow their lead.

General Rules During a Get-Together

The following rules provide some general guidelines for how to behave during get-togethers. Although teens and young adults should be able to follow these rules independently, if you observe significant violations of these rules during get-togethers, you may want to briefly and privately speak to your teen or young adult to provide some quick in-the-moment social coaching, using the buzz words and phrases described here, being particularly sensitive not to provide this feedback in front of peers.

Guests Pick the Activities

If your teen or young adult has correctly followed the steps for planning a get-together, there will be a good plan for how time will be spent. Yet no matter what's been decided, your teen or young adult needs to be willing to go with the flow and change plans if friends prefer to do something else. The rule of thumb is that during get-togethers in someone's home, the guests pick the activities. Very often the host will have made a suggestion for an activity when planning the gathering, but if guests find themselves bored, or even simply change their minds, it is the host's obligation to go with the flow and let the guest pick the activities. As long as these new suggestions aren't dangerous or inappropriate, and wouldn't result in someone getting injured or in trouble, your teen or young adult should allow his or her guests to choose how the time is spent. This is because it's the host's job to make sure everyone's having a good time. However, not everyone is familiar with this rule. That means when your teen or young adult is a guest in someone else's home, he or she may need to go with the flow if his or her host wants to choose all of the activities. For rigid thinkers, violations of this rule by friends may be difficult to understand and accept at first, and going with the flow may be more challenging in the beginning.

During get-togethers in someone's home, the guests pick the activities.

Social coaching tip: If through the course of several get-togethers, your teen or young adult finds that his or her friend rarely wants to do what others suggest and only seems interested in doing what he or she wants, it's still important to go with the flow in the moment but remember that friendship is a choice. Your teen or young adult doesn't need to be friends with everyone, and everyone doesn't need to be friends with him or her. That means if his or her friend never wants to do what others suggests, it might be time to reconsider whether this person is a good choice for a friend (for a review of choosing good friends see chapter 2).

Trade Information at Least 50 Percent of the Time

One of the most important lessons we've discussed throughout this book is the importance of trading information and finding common interests. *Trading information* is a term we use to describe the process of having a good conversation. It involves the exchange of information back and forth between two or more people with the goal of finding common interests; these are the things people talk about and do with friends. Trading information is also the process by which closer friendships develop with peers during get-togethers. Remember that the purpose of get-togethers is to develop and maintain close friendships. That means if your teen or young adult's friends were simply to come over to play video games, but never talked, they will have missed the purpose of the interaction. This doesn't mean we have to plan special time during the get-together to trade information. Instead, this should happen naturally during activities.

Because trading formation is so fundamental to developing closer friendships, one of the rules for having a successful get-together is to trade information at least 50 percent of the time. This rule was established for a very specific reason. Through our work with families through the UCLA PEERS Clinic, we've found that many teens and young adults with social challenges engage in a form of parallel play during get-togethers, where time is spent engaging in the same activity (such as playing video games) but rarely spent talking and getting to know one another. In a sense, the play was happening simultaneously, in parallel, but not interactively. Because this kind of interaction (or lack thereof) defeats the purpose of having get-togethers and developing closer friendships, we established the rule of trading information at least 50 percent of the time. The 50 percent portion of the rule is particularly important for our rule followers. In our experience, if we only present the rule to trade information and find common interests during get-togethers (without a percentage goal), many rule-driven teens and young adults would follow the rule but only to a small degree (perhaps a small fraction of the time). However, when we present the rule that we must trade information at least 50 percent of the time, we've noticed that our teens and young adults take this rule very seriously and make concerted efforts to converse more during get-togethers.

> One of the rules for having a successful get-together is to trade information at least 50 percent of the time.

Social coaching tip: If you notice that your teen or young adult tends to be on the quieter side during get-togethers, you may want to emphasize this rule even further and ask for ballpark estimates of the amount of time spent trading information after the get-together is over. You can do this by asking the questions, "Did you trade information during your get-together?" and "What percentage of the time did you trade information?" If your teen or young adult is a rigid thinker, you may be amused to find (like we have) that estimates can be surprisingly exact, with approximations even down to half percentage points (like 37.5 percent of the time spent trading information)! Funny as these calculations may be, use them as an opportunity to encourage more trading information during future get-togethers by trying to at least reach the benchmark of 50 percent.

Don't Ignore Your Friends

It's not uncommon for people to become bored or tired with whatever activity they're engaged in during get-togethers. One of the more common social errors committed by teens and young adults with social difficulties is to walk away from activities when they become bored or disinterested. For example, imagine a group of young men make plans to watch a football game together. The game is boring and dull with very little action, and the men grow tired of watching. Using the perspective-taking questions, imagine what would happen if the host of the get-together got up and walked away from the game without saying anything. Even though he doesn't intend to cause offense, he's simply bored and wishes to do something else;

what do you think this experience will be like for the other men? They'll probably feel confused, not sure what's just happened, and they may feel irritated by being left in the middle of a game. What will they think of their host? They'll probably think their host is strange and pretty rude. Will they want to hang out with their host again? After being slighted in such a way, the chance that they'll want to hang out at this man's house again is less

One of the more common social errors committed by teens and young adults with social difficulties is to walk away from activities when they become bored or disinterested.

likely. Unfortunately, this type of behavior is quite common among young people with social differences. Yet, there are alternatives to this behavior, such as suggesting a change in activity when bored or disinterested.

Another common mistake teens and young adults make during get-togethers is that they ignore friends to talk or text with other people. This mistake isn't just made by teens and young adults with social challenges, but is even committed by some socially savvy people. The problem is that talking or texting with other people (unless a group activity) can be boring for those not involved. It makes the other people feel ignored. So a good rule of thumb is to avoid texting and chatting with other people during get-togethers unless it's your friend's idea and everyone is involved.

Social coaching tip: If you notice that your teen or young adult has these tendencies, you'll want to intervene during teachable moments and provide social coaching around this important social rule, obviously out of earshot of the guests. Also, because not everyone knows or follows this rule, if your teen or young adult has friends who take calls, send texts, or ignore others during get-togethers, it's important for your teen or young adult to go with the flow in the moment and remember that friendship is a choice. It's not your teen or young adult's job to police the friend and point out the rudeness of this behavior; instead, he or she can choose whether or not to hang out with this person in the future.

Suggest a Change When Bored

It's important to expect that when having get-togethers with friends, activities will probably get boring after a while. It's not a big deal and doesn't mean the other people are boring. Rather than walking away or saying, "I'm bored," a better response would be to suggest a change in the activity. That might be done by saying something such as, "How about when we're done with this game, we go get something to eat?" or "How about when we're done with this, we do something else?" or "Anyone feel like playing something else?" When your teen or young adult suggests a change, it's not guaranteed that the friends will want to do whatever activity is suggested, but by providing an alternative suggestion, the likelihood of moving on to another more enjoyable activity is increased.

> *Rather than walking away or saying, "I'm bored," a better response would be to suggest a change in the activity.*

Social coaching tip: Chances are you know the signs for when your teen or young adult is getting bored. If you notice these signs during a get-together, you may want to inconspicuously pull your child aside, ask how things are going (out of earshot of friends), and remind him or her about alternative activities that might be suggested if they happen to get bored.

Defend Your Friends

Another important rule to follow during get-togethers is to defend your friends if someone is giving them a hard time. It's not uncommon during group get-togethers for friends to tease one another or give each other a hard time. Although an awkward situation, if your teen or young adult is hosting the get-together, it's his or her responsibility to defend friends in these instances. Remember that when having a get-together, it's the host's job to make sure everyone is having a nice time. That means your teen or young adult should stick up for friends who feel threatened, harassed, or teased. As the host, your teen or young adult has a bit more influence over the behaviors of guests, so simply saying something like, "Ease up," "Leave him alone," or "Don't give him a hard time" can be effective strategies for defending friends if they're feeling hassled. You don't have to be the host of a get-together to stick up for your friends either. Defending your friend is always a nice way to show loyalty, which is one of the characteristics of a good friend, but when you're the host of a get-together it's not only nice, it's expected. However, not defending friends as the host will make it less likely that others will want to go to your teen or young adult's gatherings in the future.

> *Stick up for friends who feel threatened, harassed, or teased.*

Social coaching tip: One of the more difficult social skills for teens and young adults to navigate is conflict resolution. The next several chapters provide concrete strategies for handling peer conflict and peer rejection, so if you're concerned about how to help coach your teen or young adult in these touchy situations, hang on—we're just about to get there. The tools provided in chapter 9 may be of particular use in helping coach your teen or young adult in how to handle disagreements during get-togethers.

Steps for Ending a Get-Together

The following steps provide an outline of how socially savvy teens and young adults end get-togethers in their home. These steps are generally followed in the order presented but may be adapted according to context and preference. Just like with beginning get-togethers, these steps may seem obvious to you, but many teens and young adults with social challenges struggle with these transitional moments. Breaking down these good-byes into concrete steps will make this potentially uncomfortable interaction far more manageable and less awkward for your teen or young adult.

1. Wait for a Pause in the Activity

The first step in ending a get-together where your teen or young adult is the host is to wait for a pause in the conversation or activity. It's best if this pause comes in the form of a transitional moment when one activity (or conversation) is coming to an end. Waiting for a pause in the activity is key to making sure no one feels insulted that he or she has to leave in the middle of something.

2. Give a Cover Story

Once an appropriate transitional moment or pause occurs in the activity, it's important to give a cover story for ending the get-together. Remember that cover stories are the reasons we give for engaging in certain behaviors. In this case, your teen or young adult's cover story is the reason why his or her friends have to leave and why the get-together must end. To illustrate the importance of cover stories here, imagine the young man watching football with his friends in his home. Picture at the end of the game, instead of giving a cover story, he says, "It's time for you to go." Using your perspective-taking questions, think about what that would be like for the young man's guests. They might feel confused or possibly insulted. What would they think of the young man? They'd probably think he was rude and kind of weird for having such little tact. Would they want to hang out with him again? Although it's hard to know if this rude behavior will be a deal breaker in the future, they'll probably feel less comfortable or welcome if they go to his home again. So instead of abruptly telling friends they have to leave, the young man might have said something like, "Well, it's getting kind of late" or "Well I guess we all have work tomorrow" or "I've got an early start in the morning." For adolescents, common cover stories for ending get-togethers include, "My mom said it's time for dinner" or "My parents said I need to start my homework" or "I've got to study for a test tomorrow." Whatever the cover story is, it shouldn't be a lie. Just a simple (not too personal) explanation for why the get-together has to come to an end is enough.

3. Begin to Walk Your Friends to the Door

The next step for ending a get-together is to begin walking your friends to the door. Walking friends to the door is an important step because if you don't, they may never leave! Guests are usually waiting to take cues from the host about how to act during get-togethers. Consequently, it's the job of the host to provide the social cue that things are ending by heading toward the door. Even if your teen or young adult gives a cover story for ending the get-together, his or her friend may not take the initiative to stand up and start walking to the door. It would also be impolite to expect friends to find their own way out. Instead, your teen or young adult should slowly stand up after giving a cover story for wrapping things up (friends will usually stand up on cue at this point) and then slowly begin to walk the friends toward the door.

4. Thank Them

There is usually a fair amount of conversation happening as your teen or young adult slowly walks the friends to the door. These slow good-byes can often take several minutes and include a number of formalities, such

232 THE SCIENCE OF MAKING FRIENDS

as thanking each other. Thanking your friends for coming to your home might include saying things like, "Thanks for coming over" or "Thanks for a fun night" or "Thanks for watching the game." If your teen or young adult is the guest, he or she might say something like, "Thanks for having me over" or "Thanks for the invitation."

5. Tell Them You Had a Good Time

If your teen or young adult had a good time hanging out with friends, it's nice to say so at the end of the get-together. These kinds of compliments usually happen on that slow walk to the door and include comments such as, "I had fun" or "That was fun" or "I had a good time." Whether your teen or young adult is the host or the guest, the same kind of comments can be offered.

6. Tell Them You'll See or Speak to Them Later

While slowly walking to the door, other small talk might include telling the friends that you'll see or speak to them later (if that's the plan). Depending on the context and degree of acquaintance, hosts and guests often say things like, "I'll see you at school tomorrow" or "I'll talk to you at work" or "I'll call you later this week."

7. Say Good-bye

The last step for ending a get-together is to say good-bye. People say good-bye differently based on personal preferences and degree of closeness. Some people will hug or give a kiss on the cheek (particularly girls). Others will give a slight wave, a casual head nod, a handshake, or even a pound or fist bump (more common among boys). Whatever the mode of saying good-bye, most people end by saying, "Good-bye" or "Bye" as they're walking away.

Social coaching tip: Like all of the chapters, the information in the parent section of this chapter is more detailed than the chapter summary for teens and young adults. This is because not all teens and young adults will be interested in reading at the level of detail that we're providing parents (although they're welcome to read all sections). So this means that you'll be filling in a lot of the details as you discuss the content of this chapter and provide social coaching during teachable moments.

Success Story: Harry Hangs Out with Friends

The purpose of this book is to help socially challenged teens and young adults learn to make and keep friends. The way in which close friendships are developed is through organizing and having successful get-togethers. Yet, many of the teens and young adults attending PEERS rarely have get-togethers with friends prior to our program. This was also true for Harry, a seventeen-year-old socially isolated boy who was described by his mother as a "computer shut-in."

Like many teens and young adults attending our groups, Harry had no source of potential friends when he came to our clinic. Through the help of his parents, he initially found a club he could attend once a week, but it was far away and no lasting connections were made. Harry wasn't interested in any of the clubs at his school, so instead of giving up, he started his own club! His mother admitted, "He was fearful that no one would come. I was secretly terrified that no one would come. But in the end he had a huge turnout. The principal of the school was amazed as well and came by and congratulated him. This success totally inspired him to join other clubs and actual friendships were made." Soon after, Harry began to have get-togethers and started to form close friendships with the people from these clubs. In his final year of high school, Harry continued along this path by joining the track team, winning second place in the school talent show with a friend, and trying out and securing a role in the school play. More friendships were made, and by the middle of his senior year, Harry even had his first girlfriend. They went to the spring dance that year, and a year later they're still together.

In a recent update Harry's mother shared, "Being in PEERS triggered emotions in him that changed his attitude, his self-esteem, and his life. Actually, it changed all of our lives. Harry is now in college. He is happy, learning how to live on his own, making friends, and joining clubs. He still has some challenges socially, but he has the great tools he learned in PEERS to help him navigate through. We miss him a lot, but we know he is happily becoming the man we always knew he could be."

ENJOYING SUCCESSFUL GET-TOGETHERS
Chapter Summary for Teens and Young Adults

The following information should be read by teens and young adults and contains a brief summary of the chapter.

If your goal is to make and keep friends, then one of the best ways to do that is by having get-togethers with friends or potential friends. Sometimes called *hangouts,* get-togethers are the way teens and young adults form close friendships. To put it bluntly, if you're not having get-togethers with your friends from school or work, you're probably not that close. But that doesn't mean you can't be. The way people get close is by hanging out outside of school, work, or extracurricular activities. When you were younger, your parent may have organized these get-togethers for you. Back then, we would've called them *play dates.* But teens and young adults don't have play dates, which means it's your job to organize these hangouts now. So how do you do that? The following rules and steps used by socially savvy teens and young adults will walk you through how to plan and have good get-togethers.

Steps for Planning a Get-Together

Think about the *four Ws* and the *how* for planning your get-together.

Who

Decide who is going to be there. You should invite people who seem interested in you and whom you have common interests with. If it's a group get-together, make sure everyone knows who's coming so there are no surprises.

What

Figure out what you're going to do. This should be based on everyone's common interests. You can make suggestions but let your friends come up with ideas, too. Table 8.1 highlights some common activities teens and young adults do during get-togethers.

Table 8.1. *Common Activity-Based Get-Togethers Identified by Teens and Young Adults*

Public Activities	Indoor Activities	Attractions
Movie theaters	Computer and video games	Gaming centers
Malls	Surf the Internet	Video arcades
Comic book conventions	Social networking sites	Laser tag
Comic book stores	Listen to music	Amusement parks
Gaming stores	Rent movies	Miniature golf parks
Science expos	Watch TV	Water parks
Science museums	Card games	Go-carting
Warhammer	Board games	Batting cages
Concerts	Ping-pong	Golf ranges
Bowling	Pool	Zoos
Dog parks	Air hockey	Aquariums
Beach, lake, river	Darts	State and county fairs
Mealtime Activities	**Pair Sports**	**Group Sports**
Restaurants	Swimming	Basketball
Ice cream shops	Skateboarding	Baseball
Frozen yogurt shops	Shooting baskets	Soccer
Order pizza	Bike riding	Touch football
Barbeque	Roller skating	Airsoft
Sushi	Tennis	Volleyball
Cook a meal	Skiing	Badminton
Picnic	Surfing	Water polo
Bake	Hiking	Bocce ball

(continued)

Where

Decide where the get-together is going to take place. If you don't figure out where you're getting together, it probably won't happen.

When

You also need to figure out when you're getting together. If you keep it causal and don't make plans about when you're getting together, your plans might fall through.

How

In addition to the *four Ws*, you need to figure out *how* this is going to happen. That usually includes how people are getting there and other details such as how to get tickets, for example.

STRATEGIES FOR PREPARING FOR A GET-TOGETHER

Before your get-together, here are a few things you should do to prepare.

Follow Up to Finalize Plans

If your plans are made a few days or more in advance, you need to follow up in person or with a call, text message, IM, or e-mail to finalize your plans. This will help avoid people forgetting.

Make Sure Personal Space Is Presentable

If your friends are going to be in your home or car, you need to clean up and make sure your space is presentable. That includes your bedroom, even if you don't think your friends are going to see it. Your friend's might think you're a slob if you don't clean up, and it's kind of rude, too.

Put Away Personal Items

If there's anything you don't want your friends to touch, see, or share, you need to put those things away before they get there. It's rude not to share your stuff or to tell people they can't touch your things, so put away personal items where they can't be seen to avoid any problems.

Have Alternative Activities Available

If you did your job planning the get-together, you should know what you're doing beforehand, but plans change all the time and people get bored, so have some alternative activities ready to go for you and your friends. These other options should be based on your common interests. Be prepared to be flexible and go with the flow. Try not to get too attached to one idea about what you'll do. As host, it will be your job to keep others happy.

Steps for Beginning a Get-Together

Sometimes it can be awkward to know how to get things going when you host get-togethers in your home. Don't feel bad; it happens to adults all the time. Instead of feeling uncomfortable, just follow these simple steps for beginning a get-together.

1. **Greet Your Guest.** This is usually done by saying, "Hi" and asking, "How are you doing?" Girls sometimes give a hug or kiss on the cheek, boys sometimes give a head nod, hand-shake, or a fist bump. You should do what feels comfortable.
2. **Invite Them In.** This is usually done by saying, "Come in," but don't forget to move out of the way. Standing in the middle of the doorway and not making room for the person to get around you can happen to the best of us—but it's awkward!
3. **Provide Introductions.** If your friends don't know everyone there, or if you're not sure they remember each other's names, make sure to introduce people.

(continued)

4. **Offer Refreshments.** If you're hosting the get-together, you probably need to offer refreshments such as food and drinks. Try to choose things you think your friends will like. Your parent can help you with this part.

5. **Give a Tour.** When your friend has never been to your house, offer to give a tour if it feels comfortable. Make sure your family or roommates are okay with this beforehand.

6. **Ask Your Guest What They Want to Do.** If you've planned well, you should already have an idea of what you're going to do with your friends but it's still nice to ask. You might say something like, "What do you want to do?" or "What do you feel like doing?" or "Do you still want to . . ."

Social Vignette: Beginning a Get-Together

The following social vignette provides an example of how to begin a get-together in your home.

(knock on the door)
Lance: (opens door) "Hey, Dan! How are you?"
Dan: "Hi, Lance! I'm fine. How's it going?"
Lance: "Pretty well, thanks. Come on in." (moves away from the door)
Dan: (enters through the doorway) "Thanks."
Lance: "So, Dan, I don't think you've met my friend Andy." (points to friend) "Andy and I work together. Dan and I went to school together."
Dan: "Oh, that's great. Nice to meet you."
Andy: "Yeah, nice to meet you, too."
Lance: "So, Dan, I know you've never been here before, so I should show you around real quick." (gives a quick tour while Andy is occupied)
Dan: "Thanks for showing me around."
Lance: "Sure. Make yourself comfortable. There are snacks on the table. Can I get you something to drink?"

Dan: "Thanks anyway. I'm okay."

Lance: (looking at Dan and Andy) "So should I put the game on? I think the preshow is about to start."

GENERAL RULES DURING A GET-TOGETHER

Here are a few general rules you'll want to follow during the get-together.

Guests Pick the Activities

If you're hosting a get-together in your home, your guests get to pick the activities. You can offer suggestions but let your friends decide. Your job is to make sure they have fun. Not everyone knows this rule, so if you're a guest at someone else's home, and they don't let you pick the activities, just go with the flow.

Trade Information at Least 50 Percent of the Time

Having get-togethers is how you form closer friendships. In order to do that you need to talk and trade information. You should be trading information at least 50 percent of the time. If you spend at least half your time talking and finding common interests, it will be easier to get to know one another.

Don't Ignore Your Friends

Sometimes when people get bored they walk away from what they're doing. If you walk away from your friends or ignore them during a get-together you're going to seem pretty rude, and they may not want to hang out with you again. The same is true for texting or talking to other people during your get-together. Make sure you focus on the people you're with instead.

(continued)

Suggest a Change When Bored

You should expect that you and your friends are going to get bored at some point during your get-together. Instead of walking away or saying, "I'm bored," try suggesting a change by saying something like, "How about when we're done with this game, we go get something to eat?" or "How about when we're done with this, we do something else?" or "Anyone feel like playing something else?"

Defend Your Friends

If you're hosting a get-together with two or more people and one of your friends is giving another friend a hard time, it's your job to defend your friend. Remember when you're the host it's your job to make sure everyone is having a nice time. That means sticking up for friends who feel threatened, harassed, or teased. Saying something like, "Ease up" or "Leave him alone" or "Don't give him a hard time" is usually enough.

Steps for Ending a Get-Together

It can feel awkward wrapping up get-togethers in your home. You might feel uncomfortable telling people that it's time to leave. If you've felt that way before, you're not alone. Lots of people feel that way. Instead of feeling uncomfortable, just follow these simple steps for ending a get-together.

1. **Wait for a Pause in the Activity.** When you're wrapping things up, wait for a little pause in the activity or conversation so it doesn't seem like you're interrupting in the middle of something.
2. **Give a Cover Story.** Give a cover story for ending the get-together. This is your reason for why your friends have to leave and why the get-together must end. For example, you could say something like, "My mom said it's time for dinner" or "My parents said I need to start my homework" or "I've got to study for a test tomorrow."

3. **Begin to Walk Your Friends to the Door.** The next step is to walk your friends to the door. If you don't do this, they may never leave! The truth is your friends are taking your lead, so if you don't get up and start slowly and casually walking them to the door, they're probably not going to get up and find their way out on their own.

4. **Thank Them.** As you're slowly and casually walking your friend to the door, it's nice to thank them for coming over. You might say something like, "Thanks for coming over" or "Thanks for a fun night" or "Thanks for watching the game." If you're the guest it's also nice to thank your host for having you over.

5. **Tell Them You Had a Good Time.** It's also nice to tell your friends you had a good time as you're walking them out. You might say, "I had fun" or "That was fun" or "I had a good time." You can say the same kinds of things if you're the guest.

6. **Tell Them You'll See or Speak to Them Later.** If you think you're going to see or talk to your friends later, you could say, "I'll see you at school tomorrow" or "I'll talk to you at work" or "I'll call you later this week" as you're walking them out.

7. **Say Good-bye.** As your friend is leaving, you should say your final good-byes. People say good-bye in different ways. Girls will sometimes hug or give a kiss on the cheek. Some people will give a slight wave, a casual head nod, a handshake, or even a pound or fist bump. Usually at the least, most people will say, "Good-bye" or "Bye" as they're walking away.

Social Vignette: Ending a Get-Together

The following social vignette provides an example of how to end a get-together in your home.

(football game on TV ends)
Lance: "That was a great game!"
Andy: "Yeah, it was!"
Dan: "Definitely."
(pause in the conversation)   (*continued*)

Lance: "Well, listen guys, I know we all have work early tomorrow."
   (stands up)
Andy: "Yeah, it's getting late." (stands up)
Dan: "Yeah, I probably should get going." (stands up)
Lance: (starts walking to the door) "So thanks for coming over!"
Andy: (follows to the door) "Thanks for having us over!"
Dan: (follows to the door) "Yeah, thanks for the invite."
Lance: "It was really fun!"
Andy: "Yeah, I had a good time, too."
Dan: "Me, too."
Lance: "We should hang out again soon."
Andy: "That would be cool."
Dan: "Sounds great."
Lance: (opens the door) "So I guess I'll talk to you guys later."
Andy: "Okay. Sounds good." (walks through the door)
Dan: "Okay, great." (walks through the door)
Lance: "Take care. Bye!" (nods head)
Andy and Dan: "Bye!" (nod heads, wave bye)

CHAPTER EXERCISES
for Teens, Young Adults, and Parents

Teens and young adults should complete the following exercises
with parents:

- With your parent, discuss the rules and steps for organizing
  and having get-togethers outlined in this chapter.
- Begin to plan how you might organize a get-together with the
  help of your parent.
  - Think of whom you would like to have a get-together with.
    - You may want to choose people from the social group
      you identified or people who are enrolled in an extra-
      curricular or social activity you belong to.

- Think about what activity you could suggest to do based on your common interests.
- Think about when and where this get-together might take place.
- Come up with some ideas of how everyone will get there.
- Plan a get-together with one or more friends or acquaintances. Choose people who seem interested in you and whom you share common interests with.
- When planning the get-together, follow the steps for preparing for the get-together outlined in this chapter.
  - Before the get-together, do the following with your parent:
    - Review and practice the steps for beginning a get-together.
    - Review and practice the steps for ending a get-together.
  - During the get-together, follow the rules and steps outlined in this chapter.
    - Using the FriendMaker mobile app to review the rules and steps just beforehand might be helpful.
  - After the get-together, do the following with your parent:
    - Discuss how the get-together went, whether you had a good time, if you think your friend had a good time, and whether you might want to hang out with this person or group again.
    - Consider whether you traded information at least 50 percent of the time and whether you found common interests. If you did, think about what you could do with those common interests if you were going to hang out again.
- Moving forward, make an effort to have at least one get-together per week. Most teens and young adults have approximately three to four casual get-togethers every week, so one per week shouldn't be too much.
- It's always good to try to get together with different people from time to time, but don't neglect closer friendships just to try new people. Quality (not quantity) is what's important here.

3

The Science of Handling Peer Conflict and Rejection: Helpful Strategies

9

Dealing with Arguments

Arguments and disagreements are relatively common among teenagers and young adults, and when infrequent and not too explosive, they don't need to result in the loss of a friendship. Some teens and young adults lacking conflict resolution skills may have difficulty finding their way out of arguments and disagreements, instead choosing to end the friendship. The tendency to end friendships over minor conflicts is not uncommon among those who think in concrete terms. This is because a concrete manner of thinking may lead to inflexibility, or black-and-white thinking, in which the teen or young adult may view the friendship as either working because of the absence of conflict or not working because a conflict suddenly arises. As your child's social coach, it will be important for you to normalize the experience of arguments and disagreements as being a natural component of relationships, and help your teen or young adult understand that occasional arguments with friends, when not too explosive, don't need to end friendships. By learning to resolve conflict, following the steps outlined in this chapter, teens and young adults should be able to maintain friendships despite periodic disagreements. In fact, in some cases, the successful resolution of arguments and disagreements may even strengthen these friendships.

> The tendency to end friendships over minor conflicts is not uncommon among those who think in concrete terms.

You may recall from chapter 2 that one of the characteristics of a good friendship is the ability to resolve conflict without hurting the friendship. The ability to resolve conflict is often determined by qualities such as caring, commitment, and trust. That is, your teen or young adult must care for the person whose friendship he or she is trying to save, must be committed to the friendship in order to want to save it, and must trust the friend enough to be willing to try to resolve the problem. In fact, arguments and disagreements, when handled appropriately, may actually strengthen a friendship by highlighting these special qualities. However, not all arguments and disagreements end with a stronger, healthier friendship. If your child appears to be entangled in frequent and explosive arguments or disagreements with friends, it might be time to reconsider the appropriateness of these choices of friends. It might also be important to consider whether your teen or young adult needs more focused help with emotional regulation and anger management. Although self-control issues are tightly bound with making and keeping friends, learning how to control emotions and behaviors is a lengthy process sometimes requiring professional help. If after reading this chapter you feel that your teen or young adult may not be able to adequately keep cool in stressful social circumstances, you may want to consider finding additional resources apart from this book, of which there are many.

Steps for Handling Arguments

The following steps for handling arguments are those identified through research to be essential toward successful conflict resolution. Although there may be slight variations in the sequence of these steps according to individual preference and context (depending on which side of the argument your child is on), the general order of these steps should be followed as closely as possible with completion of *all* of the steps. If your teen or young adult doesn't complete all of the steps described in the following, he or she is less likely to be successful at fully resolving the conflict.

1. Keep Your Cool

The first step in handling any argument or disagreement is to keep your cool. This means avoid getting upset or angry in the moment in order to avoid further upset. As you probably know too well, if your teen or young adult gets upset or angry it only makes matters worse, possibly harming the friendship irrevocably. As described in chapter 5, different people have different strategies for keeping cool. Some people mentally count to ten to help cool down, others take deep breaths, some may even need to remove themselves from the situation until they can talk calmly and rationally. Whatever strategy works best for your child, the first step in handling an argument or disagreement is to keep cool. Again, if you suspect this may be a problem for your teen or young adult, there are many good resources with useful information about emotion regulation that you might want to investigate. Detailed strategies for controlling emotional outbursts will not be covered in this book.

> *Avoid getting upset or angry in the moment in order to avoid further upset.*

2. Listen to the Other Person

The next step in handling an argument or disagreement is to listen to the other person. Although this step may seem rather simple, many people with and without social challenges have difficulty listening during an argument. For example, it's not uncommon for many people to interrupt during arguments in order to make a point, not allowing the other person a chance to finish his or her thought. If the other person is upset, people sometimes rush to explain their side, without ever hearing the details about what is so upsetting to the other person. Or some people may appear to be listening during an argument when in fact they're really just waiting for the other person to stop talking so they can make their point. Although simply pausing long enough to let the other person talk may be better than interrupting, in both cases the person may be failing to uncover what's upsetting the other person, making it extremely difficult to resolve the conflict.

Once your teen or young adult has listened and gained a good understanding of what the other person is trying to say, the next step involves showing that he or she actually listened. This part is important because until the other person feels assured that he or she has had the opportunity to speak and be heard, the argument won't be over.

> *Until the other person feels assured that he or she has had the opportunity to speak and be heard, the argument won't be over.*

3. Repeat What the Person Said

The way that your teen or young adult can show someone that he or she is listening in an argument or disagreement is to repeat what the other person said. Put in more sophisticated terminology, your child needs to be an active and empathic listener. Active listening is a communication technique that involves repeating back what the person said by paraphrasing what's been heard in your own words (not what the person said verbatim). Being an active listener is a demonstration of empathy, which involves the ability to recognize the feelings being experienced by another person. The ability to be an active and empathic listener is a confirmation that the other person has been heard and reduces the likelihood of further misunderstandings. Repeating what the person said and paraphrasing his or her thoughts also shows sincerity and concern for how he or she is feeling. The difficulty here is that teens and young adults with social difficulties often struggle with perspective taking, as we know. If identifying, labeling, and understanding emotions is a struggle for your teen or young adult, then active and empathic listening may also be a challenge. Because this can be such a common stumbling block, we've simplified this step down to what seems to be a fairly digestible strategy. If you think your teen or young adult may struggle with paraphrasing the thoughts and feelings of others in arguments (like so many), you can do what we do and teach him or her to make a simple statement starting with the sentence stem, "It sounds like . . ." For example, your child might say something like, "It sounds like you're upset" or "It sounds like you're angry" or "It sounds like you're sad." Although not terribly rich in

> The way that your teen or young adult can show someone that he or she is listening in an argument or disagreement is to repeat what the other person said.

detail, in our experience, this seems to be just enough of a dose of active and empathic listening to satisfy the other person.

It's important to understand that we use the sentence stem, "It sounds like . . ." because we want to be cautious not to prescribe any particular set of thoughts or feelings onto the other person for fear of causing greater upset if we get it wrong. In particular, avoiding sentences that begin with "You . . ." is strongly advised during arguments and disagreements. For example, "You're upset" or "You're angry" or "You're sad" are statements likely to make the other person feel defensive because people don't like to be told how they feel, particularly in the middle of an argument. This means "you" statements should be avoided altogether, and instead, "I" statements should be used. Although "you" statements in an argument are likely to result in defensiveness, "I" statements are safer for your teen or young adult because they only label his or her own thoughts and feelings. For example, "I think I upset you" or "I feel like you're angry" or "I get the feeling you're sad" are statements that sound more empathic than they do accusatory and are going to be less likely to make the other person defensive. Having said that, we're not suggesting that all teens and young adults should attempt to communicate in arguments and disagreements using "I" statements. For example, many individuals with ASD struggle with pronoun usage, making "I" statements and "you" statements rather confusing. For these teens and young adults we instead suggest the use of the sentence stem, "It sounds like . . .," which is equally nondefensive and less likely to cause confusion for those who have a tendency to mix up pronouns. You'll have to judge whether your teen or young adult would benefit from additional instruction in "I" statements versus "you" statements. Within our own program, we only teach the sentence stem, "It sounds like . . ." to keep it simple.

4. Explain Your Side

The next step in handling an argument or disagreement is to explain your side. Assuming this argument was waged by another person, if all of the steps were followed, your teen or young adult should now be familiar with the other person's side (because he or she listened), and the other person feels heard (because your child repeated what the other person said). Now it's your teen or young adult's turn to explain his or her side of the story.

We've probably all heard the old adage, "There's your side, there's my side, and the truth is somewhere in between." That's probably true for most arguments, which is why it's important that both people actually share their side. Although the more common social error in arguments is to rush to explain your side (before completing the other steps), another social error involves not explaining your side at all. So why would someone not explain his or her side? To help shed light on this social conundrum, think back to our examples of peer-rejected and socially neglected youth in chapter 2. You might recall that peer-rejected teens and adults have a tendency to be impulsive, whereas socially neglected teens and adults tend to be more passive. So which of the two is more likely to rush to explain his or her side? It's probable that the peer-rejected young person might be more likely to rush to explain his or her side in an argument. However, the socially neglected young person might be less likely to explain his or her side in an argument. So what's the problem with not explaining your side? The other person is likely to feel confused, unsure how all of this happened, and left wondering why you did or said what you did. To avoid confusion and further misunderstanding, it's important to always explain your side in an argument.

> To avoid confusion and further misunderstanding, it's important to always explain your side in an argument.

5. Apologize

After explaining your side, the next important step for resolving an argument or disagreement is to apologize. Obviously, when someone does something wrong, offends a friend, or even simply makes an innocent mistake, it's important to say you're sorry. However, it's not only in those cases alone that your teen or young adult needs to apologize; it's in every case. Even if your teen or young adult doesn't believe he or she has done anything wrong, an apology is still needed if the argument is ever going to end. That doesn't mean your child needs to accept guilt or blame; it also doesn't mean that he or she must admit to doing things not done; it simply means that he or she must say "Sorry" in some meaningful way. For example, saying, "I'm sorry that this happened" or "I'm sorry that you're upset" or "I'm sorry this left you feeling sad" are all ways of apologizing without having to accept guilt or blame when you feel you're innocent. We teach this method of apologizing in PEERS because we realize that sometimes in arguments people need to agree to disagree; yet, arguments rarely end until there's an apology. Ideally, apologies should come from both sides, including from the person who feels wronged. Even a simple, "I'm sorry this happened" goes a long way. However, it's important to point out that a simple "Sorry" alone won't get you very far. What is the natural response to a simple solitary "Sorry" with no further explanation? The most natural and common reply is, "What are you sorry for?" Help your teen or young adult to avoid that mistake by saying what he or she is sorry for without having to be asked.

> *Ideally, apologies should come from both sides, including from the person who feels wronged.*

6. Try to Solve the Problem

The final step for handling arguments and disagreements is to try to solve the problem. This step is critical to resolving conflict and moving forward but it's often forgotten. The reason this step is so crucial is that one of the consequences of an argument is that it can rupture trust, even if only for a moment. In order to repair trust during an argument, it's important to try to find a way to reassure the other person that what's just happened won't happen again. If we don't reassure the other person in this way, grudges may be held and the argument may never end. So how can your teen or young adult try to solve the problem? Here are a few suggestions:

- **Say what you'll do differently.** One of the more common ways of trying to solve problems in arguments and disagreements is to tell the person what you'll do differently either now or in the future.

For example, if a friend was upset because your teen or young adult forgot about their plans and stood him or her up, your child could offer to be more careful next time and keep better track of plans. When used in conjunction with the other steps, saying what your child will do differently will help restore the friend's faith in your child, and in time (if your child does as promised), may ultimately repair some of the broken trust.

- **Ask what the other person wants you to do.** Another way of trying to solve problems is to ask the other person what he or she wants your child to do. In the case of the friend who was accidentally stood up, your teen or young adult might ask, "What can I do to fix this?" or "What can I do to make it up to you?" When unsure how to solve a problem, friends are often perfectly willing to say how to fix it.
- **Suggest what the other person can do.** A final way to try to solve the problem is to suggest what the other person can do. This example is best used when your teen or young adult is on the other side of the grievance, perhaps feeling upset with a friend. Because not everyone knows the steps for handling an argument, your teen or young adult may need to do more of the work to bring about a resolution by trying to solve the problem by suggesting what the other person can do to fix things.

> In order to repair trust during an argument, it's important to try to find a way to reassure the other person that what's just happened won't happen again.

Social coaching tip: In some cases, it may be impossible to solve the problem. Although frustrating and disappointing, in these instances it will be important to encourage your teen or young adult to keep cool and remember that friendship is a choice. If it's a minor disagreement, your child may be able to agree to disagree. However, if your teen or young adult is unable to rebuild the broken trust and resolve the conflict, then he or she may need to reconsider if this person is a good choice for a friend.

Social coaching tip: Now that you're familiar with each of the steps necessary for handling arguments, it's critical that you and your child understand that each and every one of these steps must be followed in order to successfully resolve the conflict. In our experience at the UCLA PEERS Clinic, some teens and young adults will mistakenly believe that they can skip a step or two and it won't make a difference. So what happens if your child doesn't complete each of these steps? Have you ever found yourself in an argument that never seems to end? Bits of the disagreement play over and over like a broken record? In cases when arguments seem to go on and on, it's likely that one of these steps wasn't completed. Consider using the following examples with your teen or young adult to help illustrate the point that *all* of the steps must be followed:

- What happens if you follow all the steps for handling an argument but forget to repeat what the person said? The other person may keep telling you over and over how he or she feels, saying, "You just don't get it," because he or she hasn't felt *heard*.
- What happens if you follow all the steps but forget to explain your side? The other person may keep saying, "I just don't understand" because he or she doesn't feel *informed*.
- What happens if you follow all the steps but forget to apologize? The other person may continue to repeatedly share hurt feelings, saying, "You don't seem to care," because he or she hasn't felt your *regret*.
- What happens if you follow all the steps but forget to try to solve the problem? The other person may keep asking, "How do I know you won't do it again?" because he or she hasn't felt *reassured*.

Social coaching tip: Be sure to go over each of these steps with your child using the information in the chapter summary for teens and young adults. It's recommended that you jointly read the transcript of the corresponding social vignette and view the DVD video demonstration of dealing with arguments, discuss this example using the perspective-taking questions, and practice these steps following the suggestions outlined in the chapter exercises.

Success Story: Michael Makes Amends

Arguments among friends are not uncommon. When not too frequent or explosive, these disagreements shouldn't have to end a friendship. Yet for socially challenged teens and young adults, arguments may be more likely to result in the termination of a friendship. This is particularly true for those who have a tendency to be less flexible or think rigidly. That was the case for Michael, a twenty-one-year-old man with a history of intense social conflict. Initially described by his mother as "stubborn and inflexible," Michael had a long trail of broken friendships. "He's charismatic when he wants to be, even charming," his mother explained, "but when he gets angry with someone, forget about it. He won't budge. If you crossed him once, it was over."

Michael and his parents came to PEERS in the hopes that he might be able to learn the skills necessary to maintain close friendships. For Michael, it wasn't difficulty in making friends that was a concern—it was difficulty in keeping friends. He explained, "I've had a lot of friends over the years. I always thought the reason they didn't last was because they weren't good friends. They'd turn out to be jerks." Yet Michael did own that he might have had something to do with the problem, too. "I guess I can be kind of stubborn. That's what they tell me. But it was hard to know how to get past the fights."

Learning the steps for how to handle arguments was instrumental to Michael's success in maintaining his friendships. "At first I didn't know if he would use the steps. I mean they made perfect sense to us, but would he use them? We were skeptical," his mother explained, "but we still practiced a couple of times a week. That's what you told us to do. He would get so frustrated with us. He said he knew the steps, but we just wanted to be sure. About a week after PEERS ended, he got into this fight with his lab partner. They weren't good friends, but they had a disagreement about an assignment and they worked it out! We couldn't believe it. It was a first. He came home and told us about it. He acted like it was nothing, but we knew he was secretly proud he did it."

This was just the first of many times when Michael was able to calmly and appropriately handle a disagreement with a friend. His family also reaped the benefit of these newfound conflict resolution skills. In looking back at the two years since completing our program, Michael reflected, "I don't think I've lost one friend since then. There are some guys I don't talk to that much anymore, but that's not because of a fight or anything. We could hang out." His ability to handle disagreements even extended to making amends with former friends. As he explained, "I looked up this guy I used to know on Facebook. We were good buddies, but things went bad. Anyway, we're hanging out again. I apologized for the way I was back then. He's cool with it."

For some teens and young adults, like Michael, understanding the steps needed for handling arguments and disagreements may be the critical ingredient to maintaining lasting friendships. So if your teen or young adult struggles with conflict resolution skills, and you're feeling skeptical that he or she won't be able to overcome this obstacle, remember Michael's story. He did it and so can others.

DEALING WITH ARGUMENTS
Chapter Summary for Teens and Young Adults

> The following information is intended to be read by teens and young adults and contains a brief summary of the chapter.

Steps for Handling Arguments

Video

It's important for you to know that arguments and disagreements between friends are pretty common, and if your arguments aren't too heated or don't happen too often, they don't have to ruin your friendship. Still, every disagreement is different, so you'll have to judge (maybe with the help of your parent) whether an argument needs to end in the loss of a friend. If you're hoping to avoid some of those lost friendships, then you should know the steps for successfully handling arguments. These steps are meant to be followed closely in the order you see, without missing any steps. If you miss a step, then expect that your argument won't be over.

1. **Keep your cool.** The first step in handling any argument or disagreement is to keep your cool. This means you need to avoid getting upset or angry because that will only make things worse. Some people take deep breaths or silently count to ten to stay calm. You may even need to walk away for a bit if that helps you keep your cool.

(continued)

2. **Listen to the other person.** The next step is to listen to the other person. Interrupting to make your point will only upset the other person. Give the person a chance to say what's on his or her mind before you start sharing your side.

3. **Repeat what the person said.** The next step is to actually show the other person that you've been listening. Simply staying quiet and nodding your head isn't enough. The best way to do this is to repeat what the person said. Because it's kind of hard to summarize what someone's saying, make a simple comment starting with the sentence stem, "It sounds like . . ." For example, you could say, "It sounds like you're upset" or "It sounds like you're angry" or "It sounds like you're sad." That way the other person knows you've heard him or her.

4. **Explain your side.** After you've kept your cool, listened, and repeated what the person said, now is your chance to explain your side. A lot of people rush to do this part first. Don't make that mistake. Your friend won't want to hear what you have to say until he or she feels heard.

5. **Apologize.** No matter whether or not you think you did something wrong, an important step for handling an argument is to apologize and say you're sorry. If you made a mistake or did something you shouldn't, then you need to own up to it. But even if you think you're in the right, your friend is still waiting to hear an apology. In that case, you can say, "I'm sorry that this happened" or "I'm sorry that you're upset" or "I'm sorry this left you feeling sad." Don't make the mistake of saying, "Sorry" alone. Your friend will probably ask you, "What are you sorry for?" That's because "Sorry" by itself isn't enough. You should always say what you're sorry for.

6. **Try to solve the problem.** The last step in handling arguments is to try to solve the problem. This is the part where

you help your friend trust that this won't happen again. There are a few ways you can do this:

- Say what you'll do differently next time.
- Ask what the other person wants you to do to make it better.
- Suggest what the other person can do to make it better.

Social Vignette: Dealing with Arguments

The following social vignette is a transcript of the video demonstration from the accompanying DVD of dealing with an argument.

Yasamine: (reading a book)

Lara: (walks up, appears upset) "Yasamine, what happened Friday night? You completely stood me up!"

Yasamine: (keeping cool, not getting upset, listening)

Lara: (upset) "I mean, we had plans to go to the movies. I called you. I texted you. I mean, I stayed up until 10 PM waiting for a call back but I didn't hear anything. What happened?"

Yasamine: (calmly, showing concern) "Lara, it sounds like you're really upset."

Lara: (still upset) "Yeah, I'm really upset with you! I mean, I could have . . . I had so many other plans. I could've gone out with other friends on Friday night, but I decided to go to the movies with you because that's what we discussed. I mean I don't understand. What happened?"

Yasamine: (looks like she feels bad) "Well, here's the thing . . . you know how I have all my numbers and all my plans in my phone? I'm so reliant on it. But I left it in my locker, and so I didn't have anything to call you with. And I still don't have my phone. And I actually thought we were hanging out this weekend. So I completely misunderstood."

(continued)

Lara: (still upset) "No, we were totally sitting in the lunch room, and we talked about doing it last Friday. And, I mean, I don't need my phone, . . . I don't rely on my phone to remember when we're hanging out! I mean, it just really stinks because I wanted to go to this movie so badly with you, and I ended up sitting on my couch until 10 PM doing nothing on a Friday night!"

Yasamine: (sounding sincerely sorry) "No, you're right. I'm sorry. It must have been really awful."

Lara: (calmer) "It was awful. I mean I felt embarrassed. It's humiliating having to sit on your couch until 10 PM just waiting for a call. Not cool."

Yasamine: (sounding sorry) "I know, I know. Well, here's the thing . . . I'll really try not to depend on my phone so much. And I was really looking forward to going to the movie with you, too, so maybe if you could let me make it up to you. We could go to the movie this weekend?"

Lara: (still a little annoyed) "I don't know, I'll think about it."

Yasamine: "Okay."

Lara: "Alright."

Perspective-Taking Questions

- What was that interaction like for Lara in the end?
  Answers: Controlled, civilized, polite
- What do you think Lara thought of Yasamine in the end?
  Answers: Good listener, empathic, apologetic
- Is Lara going to want to talk to Yasamine again?
  Answer: Yes, their friendship may even be stronger moving forward.

CHAPTER EXERCISES
for Teens, Young Adults, and Parents

Teens and young adults should complete the following exercises with parents:
- Practice handling an argument using the steps outlined in this chapter with your parent.
  - Begin by reviewing the steps for handling an argument.
  - Practice following the steps for handling an argument.
  - You may want to choose a topic that's not too emotionally charged for you or your parent so you can just focus on the practice.
- Practice following the steps for handling an argument with a peer if relevant.
  - Only practice these steps if there is an actual conflict. Don't invent a problem in order to practice the steps.
  - If an argument comes up, you may want to use the FriendMaker mobile app to review the steps if possible.

10

Handling Verbal Teasing

WE'VE ALL HEARD THE OLD ADAGE, *sticks and stones may break my bones but names will never hurt me.* Tell that to typical teenagers, and they'll tell you that's just wrong. The reality is that names do hurt and are a far more familiar weapon than those medieval sticks and stones. Recent reports indicate that as many as 30 percent of middle and high school students report frequently being involved in bullying, either as the victim, perpetrator, or in some cases, both. Verbal bullying, also known as *teasing*, is perhaps the most common form of bullying among teens. Often hurtful and humiliating to the victim, this form of verbal harassment can be particularly damaging to the self-esteem of those targeted, perhaps even resulting in mental health problems.

> *Verbal bullying, also known as* teasing, *is perhaps the most common form of bullying among teens.*

Although the National Center for Educational Statistics reports that roughly 28 percent of teens in the United States are the recent victims of bullying, this number nearly doubles in size to 54 percent for teens with special needs. Prevalence rates for adolescents diagnosed with ASD are even more staggering, with 94 percent of teens experiencing some form of bullying in the previous year. Teens and young adults with other social difficulties are also not immune. So why are those with social challenges at greater risk for teasing and bullying? Teens and young adults with social challenges are often socially isolated, with very few friends, making them easier targets for teasing and bullying because they are unprotected.

Think about it. Whom do bullies like to pick on—people who are by themselves or in a group? Bullies like to pick on people who are by themselves because they're easier targets with no one to protect them. Perhaps the social awkwardness and socially odd behaviors that some kids with social challenges have also contribute to their tendency to be unfairly teased and bullied by their peers. Sadly, this is particularly true for those diagnosed with autism spectrum disorder (ASD). Yet it is the higher-functioning teens and young adults with ASD who have no intellectual disabilities who are more likely to be bullied. So why is it that those who are less outwardly impaired are more likely to be targeted by bullies? To put it bluntly, targeting the kids who appear geeky and quirky seems less sadistic to the larger peer group (who will ultimately need to condone or overlook the bullying behavior) than targeting the intellectually disabled kid.

If these words are hard to read, you're not alone. Writing them isn't that easy either. No matter how many teens and young adults we work with, we never become immune to the painful hurt caused by teasing and bullying. In many ways, it's become our own private crusade to get the word out about how to help kids handle these challenging and hurtful situations more effectively—a crusade because sadly there is so much misinformation out there. As you will soon discover, teens and young adults are constantly given the wrong advice for how to handle teasing and bullying. Yet we've seen firsthand that there is cause for tremendous hope to move beyond misinformation and sad statistics. In this chapter, we offer you help to equip your teen or young adult with the essential tools needed to navigate and manage these tough social predicaments.

One more thing, although this topic is naturally going to be emotionally charged for you (no one wants to think about his or her child being cruelly teased or bullied), you may need to resist the urge to jump in and save your child or get wound up in the emotional cyclone that often comes from thinking about your child being victimized. It's natural for you to want to try to fix these problems for your child (either by contacting his or her school or getting other parents involved), and it's also natural for you to get wrapped up in the horrible pain it causes your teen or young adult when he or she is viciously bullied. But we like to suggest parents take a different approach. We encourage parents to focus on what their teens and young adults need to know to get out of these thorny situations on their own. Empowering your child with the tools needed to independently and successfully stave off teasing and bullying will be a far greater gift than trying to emotionally or physically rescue him or her at every turn.

Strategies for Handling Verbal Teasing

Video

Sadly, the act of verbal teasing is very common, even among popular teens and young adults. In fact, all teens and young adults get teased. It's the way your child reacts to the teasing that determines how frequently or how severely he or she will be teased in the future. So what do most teens and young adults with social challenges naturally do in response to verbal teasing? Most might naturally react to verbal attacks by either getting upset, attempting to tease back, or for some with social cognition differences, providing no reaction at all because they're unaware of the teasing. Perhaps your teen or young adult has also made these mistakes.

> *Most might naturally react to verbal attacks by either getting upset, attempting to tease back, or for some with social cognition differences, providing no reaction at all because they're unaware of the teasing.*

So what's the problem with these kinds of reactions? The problem with showing upset feelings or teasing back is that these responses are actually going to make the teasing more fun for the teaser. The teaser is hoping to get a negative reaction out of his or her victims, to push their buttons and get them to put on a show, making the teaser feel more powerful because he or she is able to control the behaviors of others. In some cases, the teaser may even say to his or her friends, "Hey, watch this and see what I can make them do. . . ." So if your teen or young adult gets upset or teases back, it is making it more likely that he or she will be teased again. When upset, the teaser will take pleasure in pulling your child's strings like a marionette. When your child teases back, the teaser may enjoy the challenge of the verbal sparring. In either case, the teasing has been reinforced, making it more likely to happen again. By getting upset or teasing back, your teen or young adult may also get a bad reputation.

Although some teens and young adults provide negative reactions to teasing, others are completely unaware that they're even being teased or bullied, and consequently provide little to no reaction. Problems with social cognition or perspective taking are usually to blame for this lack of awareness. Perhaps your teen or young adult falls into this category. Although emotionally protective because what you don't know can't hurt you, the oddity of not reacting may be amusing to the teaser, making it more likely that your teen or young adult will be teased again, subsequently making it difficult for him or her to make friends.

Now that we're familiar with the common mistakes naturally made by teens and young adults with social challenges, it might be helpful to think about the unnatural mistakes made because of bad advice. What are most teens and young adults told to do to handle teasing? The three consistent answers we get at the UCLA PEERS Clinic are that teens and young adults are told to walk away, ignore the person, or tell an adult in response to teasing. Yet, when asked if these strategies work, almost invariably they say they don't work. The reason these strategies don't work is that they're not ecologically valid; they're not the strategies used by socially successful teens or young adults in response to teasing. For instance, what would happen if a teen or young adult were to walk away from a teaser? Most kids will say the teaser would follow them and continue to tease. What would happen if they ignored the teaser? The teaser would probably think they were weak and continue to tease them. What would happen if they told an adult about the teasing? They would probably be labeled a *snitch*, a *nark*, or a *tattle tale*, making the teaser want to retaliate and tease more. In all of these cases, the reaction is making it more likely that the teen or young adult will be teased again. Although well intentioned, this bad advice (walk away, ignore, or tell an adult) is an example of the poor social coaching often provided by naive adults, unfamiliar with the ecologically valid skills of socially successful teens and adults. If you've made this mistake in the past, be forgiving toward yourself. The vast majority of parents, teachers, and clinicians give this same advice. It was probably the advice given to you as a child, too. It's best to remember that everyone gets teased. Even popular kids aren't immune. Don't expect that your child won't be teased. It's going to happen, as much as we recoil at the thought. But it's how your

> *Teens and young adults are told to walk away, ignore the person, or tell an adult in response to teasing. Yet, when asked if these strategies work, almost invariably they say they don't work.*

child reacts that will determine how frequently and severely he or she is teased. So how should your teen or young adult react when confronted with verbal teasing? The answer involves concrete strategies using verbal and nonverbal comebacks, followed by disengagement from the teasing.

Short Verbal Comebacks

Research suggests that when confronted with teasing, socially savvy teens and adults simply act like what the person said didn't bother them and give the impression that the teasing remark was rather lame or stupid. How do they do this? They give a short verbal comeback that demonstrates their indifference. They might say something like, "Whatever" or "Yeah and?" or "Your point is?" or "Am I supposed to care?" or "Is that supposed to be funny?" or "Anyway . . ." The chapter summary for teens and young adults provides a list of commonly used verbal comebacks for teasing that you can review with your teen or young adult.

> *They give a short verbal comeback that demonstrates their indifference.*

Regardless who is being teased, these teasing comebacks are typically used by both genders. The biggest difference is that males tend to use verbal comebacks with greater apathy and indifference, often sounding bored. Imagine a teenage boy saying, "Whatever . . ." while shrugging his shoulders, shaking his head, and sounding bored. However, females tend to use the same verbal comebacks with more attitude and dramatic flair. Imagine a teenage girl saying, "Whatever!" while dramatically rolling her eyes and flipping her hair. Whereas gender differences may exist generally, the manner in which your teen or young adult chooses to use these verbal comebacks will vary. For example, in our experience, many socially neglected females tend to sound more bored and apathetic when using these teasing comebacks. Some peer-rejected boys may be more dramatic. You should allow your teen or young adult to choose whichever way fits his or her personality and comfort level.

> *Males tend to use verbal comebacks with greater apathy and indifference, often sounding bored. Females tend to use the same verbal comebacks with more attitude and dramatic flair.*

Social coaching tip: Although the verbal comebacks listed in the chapter summary for teens and young adults will most likely be familiar to your child, he or she will still need to practice using these comebacks. It's recommended that you have your teen or young adult choose at least three verbal comebacks from the list and practice using them with you in response to some teasing remark such as, "Your shoes are ugly." Be sure to use a teasing remark that won't be emotionally charged because this will take away from the opportunity to practice. Because the teaser will rarely give up on the first attempt, your child also needs to be equipped with at least a few teasing comebacks. Discourage your teen or young adult from making up his or her own teasing comebacks because these responses are usually less effective than the tried-and-true. See the video demonstrations from the accompanying DVD for an example of how to practice this skill with your teen or young adult.

Nonverbal Comebacks

Although verbal comebacks are critical to handling teasing, it's important to note that these teasing comebacks are also often accompanied by nonverbal behaviors such as eye-rolling, shoulder shrugging, or shaking the head in disbelief. Although these behavioral responses are quite common among socially savvy teens, it's been our experience that some teens and young adults with neurological or social differences may have trouble looking natural doing this. For example, some of our teens and young adults at the UCLA PEERS Clinic have found it difficult to appropriately roll their eyes. When asked to demonstrate what this behavior might look like, instead of naturally rolling their eyes, a good portion instead engage in a series of bizarre eye movements that involve fluttering their eyes in a strange manner, looking more like a seizure than eye-rolling. Likewise, some have also found it hard to shrug their shoulders, instead engaging in a series of rigid and peculiar shoulder movements, looking more like shoulder rolls you might do if you were stretching. Although these examples provide a funny mental image, they also offer a hint at the kind of behaviors you will want to be looking for and coaching during the practice assignments from the chapter exercises.

Social coaching tip: In order to help your teen or young adult avoid any potentially bizarre nonverbal behaviors (which would undoubtedly lead to further teasing), you might have him or her demonstrate eye-rolling, shoulder shrugging, and shaking his or her head in disbelief before suggesting these nonverbal responses to teasing in the real world.

Disengaging from Teasing

Once your teen or young adult has provided a few teasing comebacks, he or she should then disengage from the interaction by walking away or looking away. In other words, your child shouldn't stand there continuing to look at the teaser, waiting to be teased more. Instead, he or she might walk away from the teaser after providing a few verbal comebacks, or if unable to walk away, simply look away and redirect his or her attention somewhere else. What would happen if your child didn't look away or walk away but instead stood there looking at the teaser? This would look like an invitation for more teasing. But remember, your child should never walk away or disengage from the teaser without giving a teasing comeback. If he or she walked away before providing one of these responses (either verbal, nonverbal, or both), the teasing behavior will have been reinforced, making it more likely that your teen or young adult will be teased in the future.

> Once your teen or young adult has provided a few teasing comebacks, he or she should then disengage from the interaction by walking away or looking away.

The power of this strategy is that in giving the impression of not being bothered and that the teasing remark was rather lame or stupid, your teen or young adult ensures that the teasing wasn't fun for the teaser (perhaps even embarrassing), making him or her less likely to be teased again.

Expect It to Get Worse Before It Gets Better

Although in our experience this strategy is incredibly powerful and usually works rather quickly, leaving our teens and young adults feeling confident and empowered, in some cases the teasing may get worse before it gets better. If the teaser is accustomed to getting a different reaction from your child (perhaps getting upset or teasing back), the teaser is likely to try even harder to tease your child before eventually giving up.

In behavioral psychology research we call this phenomenon an *extinction burst,* which is the tendency of a particular response to increase in frequency before it ceases or comes to an end. The idea is that the teaser has to try harder to get his expected reaction. By removing the reward and no longer making the teasing fun for the teaser, your child should expect that before the teasing behavior goes away, the teaser will probably up the ante and try even harder, hoping for the usual reaction. If your teen or young adult continues to make the teasing less fun for the teaser by providing appropriate verbal comebacks (for example, "Whatever," "Anyway . . ."), eventually the teaser will give up and move on to some-one else. However, if your teen or young adult reverts to old habits and gives into the teasing by getting upset, teasing back, or putting on a show, the extinction effect will be lost and your child will have to start all over again.

> If the teaser is accustomed to getting a different reaction from your child (perhaps getting upset or teasing back), the teaser is likely to try even harder to tease your child before eventually giving up.

Expect a Recurrence of the Teasing

Occasionally in a process called *spontaneous recovery* (another technical term from behavioral psychology research), after a period of time has passed in which the teasing has gone away, the teaser will suddenly try again, attempting to draw out the desired response, even though it seemed like he or she had given up. This spontaneous recovery of the former behavior (in this case, teasing) is something that you and your teen or young adult should be prepared for, so if it happens, your child won't be taken by surprise. If your teen or young adult reverts back to old habits when the teaser suddenly tries again, he or she will probably have to start all over with the process.

When to Avoid Using Teasing Comebacks

Although highly effective for handling verbal teasing from peers, teasing comebacks (verbal and nonverbal) should not be used with bullies who have a tendency to get physically aggressive or with adults in authority. The problem with using teasing comebacks with those who have a tendency to get violent or physically aggressive is that when used appropriately, these comebacks usually embarrass the teaser. How would you expect a bully who has a tendency to get physically aggressive to react to feeling embarrassed? He or she would probably become physically aggressive. Instead, using the strategies outlined in chapter 13 would be more advisable. Finally, using teasing comebacks with those in authority such as parents,

teachers, professors, supervisors, and so on would be highly inappropriate and likely to result in some type of punishment, perhaps also giving your teen or young adult a bad reputation with the authority figure.

> *Teasing comebacks (verbal and nonverbal) should not be used with bullies who have a tendency to get physically aggressive or with adults in authority.*

Social coaching tip: Like all of the skills in this book, you should present these strategies to your child by having him or her read the chapter summary for teens and young adults and then facilitate opportunities to practice the skills using the chapter exercises. It will also be important to jointly read the social vignettes in the chapter summary, view the DVD video demonstrations of male and female examples of handling verbal teasing, and discuss these examples with your teen or young adult using the perspective-taking questions.

Strategies for Using Embarrassing Feedback—A Gift in Disguise

Sometimes when people tease, they're giving your child important feedback about how he or she is perceived by others. These embarrassing comments, though hurtful, may give your teen or young adult useful information about what others think. In PEERS, we call this information *embarrassing feedback.* Although the embarrassing feedback given during teasing is usually upsetting, it can be a gift in disguise, providing useful insight into certain elements that may be driving the ridicule and creating a wedge between your child and his or her ability to make and keep friends. This is especially true when your teen or young adult receives the same embarrassing feedback repeatedly. Although naturally hurtful and humiliating, with your help, this information can be used to help change the way people see your child in the future. If he or she considers what people are trying to say when they tease, your teen or young adult may be able to do things differently, making future teasing less likely. Of course, you and your child have to be interested in making a change, which is a very personal choice.

> *Sometimes when people tease, they're giving your child important feedback about how he or she is perceived by others.*

To illustrate how embarrassing feedback works, imagine a young man attending community college in a beach community located in a warm tropical climate. Each day he arrives to campus wearing a long military trench coat with army fatigues and combat boots, even though he has no military affiliation and the temperature outside is in the triple digits. His classmates, clad in shorts, t-shirts, and flip-flops, frequently comment on his unusual attire, many sadistically teasing him for his bizarre clothing choices. In this case, we might say the young man is engaging in atypical behavior that is provoking teasing comments and embarrassing feedback. Of course, the young man's clothing options are his own personal choice, but assuming he doesn't want to be the object of ridicule anymore, what could he do differently to make it less likely that he'll be teased? Perhaps by simply paying attention to the embarrassing feedback and changing his clothing choices, he may dramatically decrease (and possibly eliminate) the incidence of verbal teasing.

Although the decision to change physical appearance and behavior in response to embarrassing feedback is a personal choice and should not be forced on anyone, it's important for your teen or young adult to know that there may be something he or she can do to reduce or eliminate teasing if this is a problem. In our experience, many teens and young adults with social challenges don't realize the power they have in minimizing these teasing experiences. They often feel helpless, as if nothing they do will make things better. Yet, the majority of families we've worked with through the UCLA PEERS Clinic have been very successful at reducing these negative experiences simply by using teasing comebacks in the moment and using the embarrassing feedback they get to change how they're perceived.

Conversations about embarrassing feedback from peers, whether real or anticipated, can be uncomfortable—but they need to happen. To highlight how critical this point is, let me give you an example. In our clinic we often have private meetings with families to address inappropriate behaviors we observe in the group that we suspect are contributing to peer rejection outside of our group. These behaviors include habits like nose picking, passing gas, belching, and so on. Without having to investigate too much, there's usually a good chance these habits occur outside of our group and are also the focus of embarrassing feedback from peers. Apart from the obvious, the problem with these behaviors is that they often create social barriers to making and keeping friends. In fact, we often have to explain to our teens and young adults that engaging in these types of behaviors is so frowned upon that even if he or she mastered all the skills we teach, if they continue to pick their noses, pass gas, or belch around their peers, it will remain difficult for them to make and keep friends.

Perhaps your teen or young adult also receives embarrassing feedback in the form of teasing, or maybe the feedback isn't so much in the form of teasing but conveyed through questions or comments from peers. This embarrassing feedback may be related to clothing choices, grooming issues, poor hygiene, unusual behaviors or habits, or any number of things. Whatever the case may be, you and your child may have a choice about what you do with this information. You can ignore it and stick to using the teasing comebacks alone, or you can use the information you get from embarrassing feedback to also change how people perceive your teen or young adult.

Some parents (rarely teens and young adults) will struggle with this concept, stating that they want their child to be their "own person," "an individual," and "not a lemming." Of course these are perfectly reasonable statements. Every person has a right to be who he or she wants to be. But if your child's goal is to make and keep friends, then at least he or she should know that there may be something that can be done to help remove the social barrier. The reality is that whatever your teen or young adult is receiving embarrassing feedback about, it's probably creating an invisible wall between your child's desire to have friends and his or her actual ability to make and keep friends. If you suspect your teen or young adult has this problem and you want to help him or her remove this social barrier, it's worth at least having a discussion about what your child may be doing to attract embarrassing feedback. What you and your teen or young adult choose to do with this information will be up to you.

As a parent, it can be hard to come to grips with the fact that there may be something your child is doing that's making things harder socially. You want your child to be treated nicely and kindly, with respect. And you may think that it shouldn't matter if your child dresses a certain way or does certain things that other people don't like because he or she is a good person and would make a good friend. You're right. It shouldn't matter. But sadly it often does matter. The world isn't fair in that way, and the reasons people choose to be friends or not be friends can also be unfair. But the good news is that your teen or young adult may have a choice in how this turns out. If the goal is to make and keep friends, then using embarrassing feedback to change how he or she is perceived by others may be a step needed to break the invisible wall.

Social coaching tip: Table 10.1 in the chapter summary for teens and young adults provides examples of embarrassing feedback and ways in which this information might be used toward changing how your child is perceived by others. Review this table with your teen or young adult and have an honest discussion about embarrassing feedback. You will notice that many of the examples of how to use feedback will require your help. For example, changing wardrobes and using products such as deodorant, mouthwash, or dandruff shampoo are probably not things your child can do alone. So be prepared to offer some additional help in these areas. It could make a world of difference.

Success Story: Mark Manages Teasing

Knowing how to manage teasing is a skill needed by everyone. As we've discussed, it doesn't matter how popular or well liked a person is; everyone gets teased from time to time. It's how we react to that teasing that determines how often or how severely we're teased. Many teens and young adults with social challenges struggle with handling teasing appropriately. They'll get upset, lose their cool, or tease back. Sometimes they'll even tell off a teacher or another adult. This was true for Mark, a fourteen-year-old boy diagnosed with Asperger's disorder with a long history of peer rejection and teasing. "Mark has always been an amazing, bright, and talented kid," his mother explained, "but was often very socially awkward." Perhaps it was this social awkwardness that contributed to the teasing he frequently experienced from his peers. Often alone and unprotected, Mark was frequently the victim of vicious teasing—an easy target with no one there to defend him. His mother observed, "While Mark always had a lot of acquaintances, he did not have a lot of friends. He was struggling, and we didn't know how to help him."

Like many teens and young adults who've gone through PEERS, learning the tactics for how to handle teasing made all the difference for Mark. The once socially awkward victim of bullying soon escaped the vicious cycle by learning not to take the bait—to act as though what others said didn't bother him, making it less fun for the teasers. Gradually his confidence grew, feeling empowered by his new skills, and eventually he began to make friends. "Finding PEERS was an amazing gift for all of us," his mother commented. "Mark came to better understand his Asperger's and what his challenges are and the tools he could use to tackle those challenges."

Mark is now an eighteen-year-old high school senior with lots of friends and a busy social calendar. He regularly arranges get-togethers for himself and his friends, and as his younger sister put it, "he's thought of very highly by his classmates." Mark recently decided to go back east for college, no longer the socially awkward victim of teasing and bullying but a confident young adult ready to take on the world. Although his family will miss him, his mother explained, "I know he's ready to go. I am so proud of the confident, independent, bright, talented, and kind young man he has grown into."

HANDLING VERBAL TEASING
Chapter Summary for Teens and Young Adults

> The following information is intended to be read by teens and young adults and contains a brief summary of the chapter.

Video

Strategies for Handling Verbal Teasing

The next several chapters are going to focus on strategies for handling bullying. You probably already know that there are

(continued)

different kinds of bullying. The strategies that you'll learn to use will be completely different according to the kind of bullying. This chapter is focused on verbal bullying, also known as *teasing*. This is probably the most common form of bullying and pretty much affects everyone. It doesn't matter how popular you are, everyone gets teased from time to time. What does matter is how you react to it. Your reaction will determine how often and how severely you're teased. If you get upset or tease back, you're actually making the teasing fun because that's what the teaser is trying to get you to do. They want you to put on a show. If you're doing what they want and making it fun for them, then you're more likely to keep getting teased. You could also get a bad reputation if you freak out or tease back.

Adults often give advice about how to handle teasing. What do they usually tell you to do? Perhaps you've been told to walk away, ignore the person, or tell an adult. So do these strategies work? Most young people say they don't work. If you walk away, the bullies usually follow you. If you ignore them, they keep teasing you, and you end up looking weak. And if you tell an adult, you're going to make the teaser mad and want to retaliate against you. So why do adults tell you to do these things if they don't work? The truth is they probably don't know these strategies don't work, and they were probably told to do the same thing when they were your age.

Unlike other adults, we're not going to tell you to ignore, walk away, or tell an adult when you're being teased. Instead, you need to do what the most socially savvy teens and young adults do in response to teasing. They give a short verbal comeback that shows what the person said didn't bother them and, in fact, what he or she said was kind of lame or stupid. They might do something else like roll their eyes or shrug their shoulders, which shows they don't care. The following are some examples of verbal and nonverbal comebacks that are known to work well.

Verbal Comebacks

- "Whatever . . ."
- "Yeah, and?"
- "So what?"
- "Who cares?"
- "Big deal."
- "And?"
- "And your point is?"
- "Am I supposed to care?"
- "And why do I care?"
- "Is that supposed to be funny?"
- "Tell me when you get to the funny part."
- "Next . . ."
- "Anyway . . ."

Nonverbal Comebacks

- Roll your eyes
- Shrug your shoulders
- Shake your head in disbelief

When you give a short verbal comeback that shows what the bully said didn't bother you, you take the fun out of teasing. When you act like what he or she said was kind of lame or stupid, you embarrass the teaser, making it less likely that he or she will tease you again. You need to be ready, though, because they're probably not going to just tease you once and stop. You should be ready with at least three teasing comebacks in every situation. Once you've used your teasing comebacks, you shouldn't stand there and wait for more. Then you should remove yourself, either by walking away or turning away if you can't leave. But never walk away without giving some verbal comeback showing that what the person said didn't bother you.

There are a couple of groups of people you don't want to use these teasing comebacks with. You should never use them

(*continued*)

with people in authority, such as parents, teachers, professors, supervisors, and so on. That's disrespectful and a fast way to get in trouble and maybe even get a bad reputation. You also don't want to use these teasing comebacks (verbal or nonverbal) with people who have a tendency to get physically aggressive. Remember, you're probably going to embarrass the teaser. What do people who have a tendency to get aggressive do when they get embarrassed? They usually attack with physical aggression. Obviously you're not looking for a fight, so don't use these teasing comebacks with people who get aggressive. We'll talk about what you can do to handle physical bullying in chapter 13.

Social Vignette of Handling Verbal Teasing: Male Example

The following social vignette is a transcript of the video demonstration from the accompanying DVD of a male example of appropriately handling verbal teasing.

Ben: (reading a book)
Alex: (walks up to Ben) "Hey, dweeb! Reading again?"
Ben: (looks up from book, then looks right back down) "Whatever."
Alex: "Why are you reading? You're the biggest loser in school; everyone says it!"
Ben: (shrugs shoulders, shakes head, sounds bored) "Am I supposed to care?"
Alex: "Probably should, 'cuz you're a loser. Don't you want to change that?"
Ben: "Anyway . . ." (casually walks away)

Perspective-Taking Questions
- What was that interaction like for Alex?
  Answers: Frustrating, annoying (did not get the expected reaction, a little embarrassing)
- What do you think Alex thought of Ben?
  Answers: Unbothered, indifferent, apathetic

- Is Alex going to want to tease Ben again?
  Answer: Probably not, not fun

Social Vignette of Handling Verbal Teasing: Female Example

The following social vignette is a transcript of the video demonstration from the accompanying DVD of a female example of appropriately handling verbal teasing.

Lara: (reading a book)
Yasamine: (walks up to Lara) "God, Lara, your shoes are so ugly."
Lara: (looks up from book, then looks right back down) "Whatever!" (said with attitude)
Yasamine: "Whatever? Me and all the girls were making fun of them at lunch!"
Lara: (shrugs shoulders, shakes head) "Am I supposed to care?"(said with attitude)
Yasamine: "Uh, yeah, you should care. Maybe you should get some new shoes!"
Lara: "Anyway . . ." (casually walks away)

Perspective-Taking Questions

- What was that interaction like for Yasamine?
  Answers: Frustrating, annoying (did not get the expected reaction), embarrassing
- What do you think Yasamine thought of Lara?
  Answers: Unbothered, indifferent, apathetic
- Is Yasamine going to want to tease Lara again?
  Answer: Probably not, not fun

Strategies for Using Embarrassing Feedback

Sometimes when people tease you they're giving you important information about how others see you, even if it's

(*continued*)

embarrassing. We call this *embarrassing feedback,* and paying attention to your feedback can be the key to making it less likely that people will tease you. Table 10.1 gives examples of embarrassing feedback and ideas of what you could do differently if you don't want to be teased about those things anymore. Making these changes is a personal choice but if they're creating a barrier between you and your ability to make and keep friends, it might be worth using this embarrassing feedback to make a change.

Table 10.1. *Examples of Embarrassing Feedback and How to Use Feedback*

Examples of Embarrassing Feedback	Examples of How to Use Feedback
Negative comments about clothing	Consider changing your wardrobe; try to follow the clothing norms of your peer group.
Negative comments about body odor	Use deodorant; bathe regularly using soap; wash hair regularly; wear less cologne or perfume.
Negative remarks about dandruff	Use dandruff shampoo regularly.
Negative remarks about oral hygiene	Brush teeth regularly; use mouth wash; floss teeth regularly; use a tongue scraper; chew gum; use breath mints; avoid certain foods; visit the dentist regularly.
Negative comments about your sense of humor	Check your humor feedback; consider telling fewer jokes; be a little more serious when first getting to know someone.
Negative observations about unusual behaviors	Consider changing or discontinuing the behavior if possible.

CHAPTER EXERCISES
for Teens, Young Adults, and Parents

Teens and young adults should complete the following exercises with parents:

- Practice using teasing comebacks with your parent following the strategies outlined in this chapter.
  - Begin by reviewing the strategies for using teasing comebacks.
  - Practice using teasing comebacks with your parent.
    - Choose three to four teasing comebacks from the list provided to practice with.
      - Avoid coming up with your own teasing comebacks because they may not be appropriate.
    - Make sure parents use a benign teasing remark such as, "Your shoes are ugly" in order to avoid emotionally hurtful material during practice.
    - Make sure parents confirm whether eye-rolling, shoulder shrugging, and head shaking should be used in conjunction with the verbal comebacks.

- Use teasing comebacks with peers when relevant.
  - You may want to use the FriendMaker mobile app to review the teasing comebacks just before going places where teasing is likely to happen.

- Consider whether you're receiving embarrassing feedback from peers that you might use to change how other people see you and treat you. Just a few changes can make a big difference in the lives of teens and young adults.
  - Begin by reviewing the information about embarrassing feedback with your parent.

(continued)

- With the help of your parent, consider whether you're receiving embarrassing feedback from your peers.
- If motivated, begin to work with your parent to take the necessary steps to change how you're perceived by others by using this important feedback.

11

Addressing Cyber Bullying

CYBER BULLYING INVOLVES THE USE OF ELECTRONIC forms of communication such as the Internet and mobile phones to harm or harass others. Like other forms of bullying, the actions are deliberate and hostile and may even be chronic. The phenomenon of cyber bullying has become more common in the past several years, particularly among teens and young adults who frequently use the technologies associated with cyber bullying.

> Cyber bullying involves the use of electronic forms of communication such as the Internet and mobile phones to harm or harass others.

The actions of cyber bullying may include harassing, threatening, or humiliating messages or comments communicated through the use of cell phones, computers, and social networking sites. The behavior may include sending or forwarding threatening, harassing, or hurtful e-mail messages, text messages, or instant messages; spreading rumors and gossip on social networking sites; creating social networking pages to target a victim; posting photos or personal private information on the Internet without consent; or pretending to be someone else in order to humiliate someone or trick someone into revealing personal information. Researchers investigating this new phenomenon have identified six types of cyber bullying:

- **Insulting:** Posting or spreading false information, possibly causing harm to the reputation of the person targeted

- **Harassment:** Repeatedly sending malicious and harassing messages to a targeted person
- **Targeting:** Singling out a person and inviting others to attack or make fun of him or her collectively
- **Identity theft:** Pretending to be someone else to make it appear as though the targeted person said or did things he or she didn't do
- **Uploading:** Sharing e-mails or posting images of a person, particularly under embarrassing circumstances
- **Excluding:** Pressuring others to exclude the targeted person from membership or affiliation with a particular group

Because cyber bullying is often done anonymously, attacks are often even more aggressive and blatant than those committed in person. Cyber bullies may be relentless and emboldened by their anonymity, not fearing punishment or detection. Victims of cyber bullying will often feel helpless and powerless, often unsure who is even targeting them, not knowing whom they can trust and how to fight back.

Research suggests that the incidence of cyber bullying is on the rise, and although much of the research in this area has focused on describing prevalence rates and better understanding the behavior and culture of cyber bullying, a few ecologically valid social response strategies have been identified to combat this vicious form of bullying.

Strategies for Handling Cyber Bullying

The following strategies are often used by socially savvy teens and young adults confronted with cyber bullying.

Don't Feed the Trolls

Internet trolling is a term used for people who attempt to harass, upset, or disrupt another person or group of people through provocative, insulting, and confrontational messages posted online. These offensive and mean-spirited messages are often posted on social networking sites, message boards, and forums as willful attempts to upset and hurt others. The intent of *trolls*, those who post these negative comments, can only be guessed at but is probably related to negative attention seeking.

Just like in-person bullies, cyber bullies who troll the Internet posting negative comments are typically looking to get a reaction from their victims. What kind of reaction are they trying to get? They're probably hoping to upset their victims and have them put on a show or perhaps they're hoping the victims will defend themselves and engage in a fight. If your teen or young adult were to engage the troll through showing that he or she is upset or attempting to defend him- or herself, this would only reinforce and reward the behavior of the troll, making the act of trolling more fun and more likely to happen again. Consequently, a buzz phrase has developed over the Internet describing a useful tactic in dealing with these annoying trolls and their abusive and hurtful messages. *Don't feed the trolls* has become the mantra used by many victims of trolling confronted with hateful messages. The theory behind the idea is that when you engage the trolls in defense or debate, you're actually feeding them and doing exactly what they want, making it more likely you'll be cyber bullied further. However, if your teen or young adult doesn't engage them and doesn't feed the trolls, it will be less likely that the cyber bully will want to target him or her in the future. Instead, they'll probably get bored, move on, and find someone else to target.

> *When you engage the trolls in defense or debate, you're actually feeding them and doing exactly what they want, making it more likely you'll be cyber bullied further.*

Have Friends Stick Up for You

Another strategy that seems to be effective in handling cyber bullying includes the involvement of friends in providing defense and protection. The rationale behind this strategy is not so different from the underlying principle of in-person bullying, which is that bullies like to pick on people who are by themselves and appear unprotected. Bullies choose to target those who are isolated because they're easier targets, whereas teens and young adults who socialize in groups are less likely to be bullied because they have others around who might provide safety and defense. An effective safeguard against further cyber bullying is to have your teen or young adult's friends come to his or her defense. When a cyber bully posts a negative comment and then sees that others are sticking up for your child, he or she becomes a less appealing target. Although coming to your own defense is a useless tactic for handling cyber bullying (and is likely to lead to more cyber bullying), having friends stick up for you is a powerful strategy. If your teen or young adult doesn't have friends to come to his or her defense, having a sibling, cousin, or some other close relative around the same age can help. In the game of cyber bullying, no one wants to target the player who comes equipped with a strong defensive line. Consequently, having someone come to your teen or young adult's defense in response to cyber bullying may be an effective strategy in minimizing further cyber attacks.

> *Although coming to your own defense is a useless tactic for handling cyber bullying (and is likely to lead to more cyber bullying), having friends stick up for you is a powerful strategy.*

Block the Cyber Bully

A fair amount of cyber bullying is conducted over text messaging, instant messaging, e-mail, and social networking sites in which the cyber bully is identifiable and possibly even a "friend" or contact of the victim. In these cases, it's advisable to block the cyber bully by blocking their messages from delivery to your teen or young adult's phone, e-mail, or social networking page. *Blocking* is a term used to describe the action of preventing one user from sending electronic messages to another user. Most social media allow for blocking of specific contacts. For example, on social networking sites such as Facebook, a common arena for cyber bullying, blocking someone prevents that user from viewing your teen or young adult's profile and appearing in their search results or contact lists. Likewise, any connections shared between your child (the blocker) and the user being blocked will also be broken. Although blocking doesn't guarantee the prevention of all electronic communication, blocking the cyber bully is a fairly effective way of minimizing contact between your teen or young adult and the cyber bully.

> *It's advisable to block the cyber bully by blocking their messages from delivery to your teen or young adult's phone, e-mail, or social networking page.*

Lay Low Online

A lot of cyber bullying happens online, especially on social networking sites. If your child is having trouble with people cyber bullying him or her, a good strategy may be to lay low online for a while. That means your teen or young adult might consider staying off his or her social networking sites for a period of time and avoid posting comments on other people's walls or in forums. This laying low period creates distance between your teen or young adult and the cyber bullying, giving him or her a chance to let the cyber bullying die down. Sometimes it can even be helpful to have your teen or young adult close his or her social networking account for a while, if that's where the cyber bullying is happening. In this case, if the cyber bullies can't find your teen or young adult, they can't bully him or her.

> *If the cyber bullies can't find your teen or young adult, they can't bully him or her.*

Save the Evidence

In all cases of cyber bullying it's advisable to save the evidence of bullying. Cyber bullying may constitute a form of *harassment,* a term used to describe when something a person says or does makes someone fear for his or her safety or for the safety of others. For example, making threatening comments or intimidating remarks against your teen or young adult might constitute an illegal form of harassment. In certain jurisdictions this form of harassment may even be punishable by law. Cyber bullying may also constitute a form of *defamation,* a legal term used to describe behavior that causes harm to someone's reputation. For example, spreading false information about your teen or young adult on the Internet might be considered an illegal form of defamation. Cyber bullying may also create an *unsafe environment* by making your teen or young adult feel as though he or she can't go to school or work without facing some type of attack such as verbal teasing, social exclusion, or even aggressive behavior. Because schools and workplaces are held responsible for providing safe environments for their students and employees, in some cases cyber bullies may be punished by school suspension or expulsion or termination of employment, even when the cyber bullying occurs outside of school or work. Although it's not necessary for your teen or young adult to know all of these legal terms, it's helpful for you to know what you and your child's rights are. Most cases of cyber bullying never reach this level; even still, it's important to save the evidence of bullying should further action be needed.

> It's important to save the evidence of bullying should further action be needed.

Get Help from Supportive Adults When Needed

Knowing how to navigate the social challenges associated with cyber bullying is hard enough, even for socially savvy teens and young adults. So imagine what this might be like for a teen or young adult with social difficulties. Perhaps your son or daughter has been the victim of cyber bullying. If so, you know the devastation and torment it can create and the confusion and frustration felt in not knowing what to do. Consequently, involving supportive adults such as parents, teachers, clinicians, or even helpful employers may be necessary for some teens and young adults confronted with cyber bullying. Although this strategy may seem obvious, in our experience, very few teens and young adults who fall victim to cyber bullying ever think to involve these supportive adults. For some, when they do consider involving others, they may think only to involve those associated with the place where the cyber bullying originated. For example, when cyber bullied by classmates, some teens may only think to enlist support from school personnel. When cyber bullied by coworkers, they may only ask for help from those in the workplace. Involving supportive adults such as parents and other family members may be less obvious to those with social challenges because these individuals may not be affiliated with these contextual environments. Consequently, you'll want to point out the benefit and appropriateness of involving you and other trusted family members in helping to provide support in navigating these challenging social situations.

> Involving supportive adults such as parents, teachers, clinicians, or even helpful employers may be necessary for some teens and young adults confronted with cyber bullying.

Report Cyber Bullying to the Proper Authorities

In more severe or chronic cases of cyber bullying, it may be necessary to report infractions to online service providers, webmasters, schools or places of business, or even law enforcement. Because cyber bullying often violates the terms of service agreements established by Internet service providers and social networking sites, you may choose to notify these service providers so that they can take action against the users abusing the terms of the service agreement. Notifying webmasters and service providers may also result in the useful removal of defamatory statements, harassing posts, and other forms of cyber bullying. Because cyber bullying can create an unsafe environment at school or the workplace, notifying school or employment personnel may also be an effective strategy in minimizing or even eliminating cyber bullying. Many schools are required by law to address cyber bullying in their anti-bullying policies and may be swift to address the issue once raised by you. Likewise, workplace cyber bullying might easily constitute a hostile work environment, punishable by law in many jurisdictions, so employers may also be quick to assist in instances of cyber bullying in the work setting.

> In more severe or chronic cases of cyber bullying, it may be necessary to report infractions to online service providers, webmasters, schools or places of business, or even law enforcement.

Finally, in some cases, particularly those that constitute harassment, defamation, or an unsafe environment, cyber bullying may be considered a crime punishable by law. Therefore, in severe or chronic cases of cyber bullying when the strategies previously described are ineffective, contacting law enforcement may be a strategy of last resort. In less severe cases of cyber bullying, reporting the behavior to authorities may result in your teen or young adult getting a bad reputation as a *snitch* or a *nark*. You will need to carefully and cautiously judge the necessity of involving third-party protectors in these circumstances in order to help your teen or young adult avoid further unnecessary rejection.

Social coaching tip: It is recommended that you go over the strategies for handling cyber bullying in the chapter summary for teens and young adults with your child and have a discussion about the material. Sadly, no one is invulnerable to this form of social aggression, but with your help and support, if your teen or young adult should fall into this challenging situation, you will both be better equipped to handle it.

Success Story: David Doesn't Feed the Trolls

With so many teens and young adults socializing online these days, it's no wonder that even unpleasant social interactions such as bullying have pervaded this medium. Cyber bullying may be particularly widespread given the detached, sometimes even anonymous, nature of this social aggression. Sadly, many teens and young adults with social challenges fall victim to cyber bullying, often unsure how to respond effectively. This was true for David, a twenty-two-year-old socially isolated man with a history of peer rejection and emotional outbursts.

David was a self-proclaimed "loner" with a penchant for technology and a love of politics. He spent many hours of every day posting comments on blogs and forums, engaging in heated political debates. He was every troll's dream—a passionate politico who always took the bait and couldn't turn down a good fight. Within certain political forums, among the other zealots, his fervent commentary was not so unusual. But when his conservative diatribes made their way to the liberal landscape of the online forums at his university, everything changed for David.

It all began when David posted some critical comments about the upcoming presidential election on the local chapter of the Young Democrats online forum. A dyed-in-the-wool Republican venturing into the cyber land of liberals, it was no wonder that his conservative remarks were immediately attacked. He explained, "I thought I had every right to post those comments there. It's a free country. But I guess I didn't expect that kind of reaction. We got into this huge debate with all the Dems attacking me. They made it really personal, too. They called me names, like 'conservatard.' Someone even posted a picture of me in a cape with a big 'C.' And it wasn't just online. They brought it to the classroom. This girl I was friends with even stopped talking to me. I was a social pariah that quarter."

Like many teens and young adults with social challenges, David had difficulty with perspective taking. He had trouble anticipating how others might react in a given situation. In this case, it didn't occur to him that posting conservative ramblings on a liberal forum might be met with ardent resistance. "I was already having trouble making friends when I came to PEERS. This made it worse," he remarked. "It wasn't until you started talking about 'not feeding the trolls' that it kind of clicked for me. I realized that's what I was doing. I was feeding into the debate, making it worse. You told me to 'lay low' and not take the bait. So I did and eventually things calmed down."

Although it's somewhat questionable whether David was initially the troll or the one being trolled, the point is that these heated exchanges escalated into outright cyber bullying. Yet, by not continuing to feed the trolls and laying low for a period of months, he was able to successfully overcome the damage this incident had caused to his reputation. Eventually, David joined the campus chapter of the Young Republicans, finding a more appropriate venue for his political musings. Today he lives in Washington, DC, working as a political aide to a Republican congressman—enjoying healthy debates with a wide assortment of friends and colleagues.

STRATEGIES FOR HANDLING CYBER BULLYING
Chapter Summary for Teens and Young Adults

The following information is intended to be read by teens and young adults and contains a brief summary of the chapter.

This chapter is focused on cyber bullying and the strategies you can use to combat it. Cyber bullying is a type of electronic bullying that includes harassing, threatening, or humiliating messages or comments sent through cell phones, computers, or social networking sites. People who cyber bully sometimes send or forward threatening or hurtful e-mail messages, text messages, or instant messages; spread rumors and gossip on social networking sites such as Facebook; post photos or private

(continued)

information on the Internet without permission; or even pretend to be someone else in order to humiliate someone or trick that person into sharing secrets. The tricky thing about cyber bullying is that you may not even know who's doing it. Although it can be frustrating and upsetting to be targeted in this way, not knowing whom to trust or how to handle the situation, there are a few strategies that socially savvy teens and young adults use when faced with this problem. Some of the tactics are listed in this section.

Don't Feed the Trolls

You probably know that *Internet trolling* is a term used for people who bully others online by posting harassing and mean comments on social networking sites, message boards, and forums. They do this because it's fun for them, and they're trying to get a reaction out of you. What kind of reaction are they trying to get? They're probably hoping to upset you and get you to put on a show by defending yourself or engaging in a fight. They're not so different from in-person bullies, always looking for a reaction. So what happens if you put up a fight and defend yourself? You make it fun for them, ensuring that you'll continue to get bullied. Instead, don't feed the trolls. That's a buzz phrase used on the Internet that means don't confront them or try to beat them at their own game. It's a losing battle. If you don't feed the trolls, they'll probably get bored, move on, and find someone else to pick on.

Have Friends Stick Up for You

Just like in-person bullies, cyber bullies like to pick on people who are by themselves or seem unprotected. That's because when you're alone, you have no one to stick up for you or have your back. That makes you an easier target. One of the strategies for handling cyber bullying is to have a friend stick up for you. We've already talked about how it doesn't do any good for you to defend yourself. That's what the cyber bully (or troll) wants. But if other people come to your defense, such as a friend or a family member around the same age, you no longer seem unprotected. Few cyber bullies will want to play against a strong defensive line. Instead, they'll probably move on and find someone else to bully.

Block the Cyber Bully

Because some cyber bullying happens over text messaging, instant messaging, e-mail, and social networking sites where the bully is identifiable, one of the easiest ways to minimize contact is by blocking the cyber bully. That means blocking their messages from ever being delivered to your phone, e-mail, or social networking page. Blocking the cyber bully from Facebook, for example, will prevent him or her from viewing your profile, appearing in your search results or contact lists, and will break any connections shared between you and the bully. Although this strategy doesn't guarantee that the cyber bullying won't take place in other areas of the Internet, blocking the cyber bully is a fairly effective way of stopping direct contact between you and the bully.

Lay Low Online

A lot of cyber bullying happens online, especially on social networking sites. If you're being cyber bullied, a good strategy may be to lay low online for a while. That means you might consider staying off your social networking page and avoid posting comments on other people's walls or in forums, if that's where the cyber bullying is happening. This will create distance between you and the cyber bully, and let the cyber bullying have a chance to die down. Basically, if the cyber bully can't find you, he or she can't bully you.

(continued)

Save the Evidence

Another good strategy for protecting yourself from cyber bullying is to save the evidence. That means if someone sends you threatening or harassing messages or pictures, or posts harmful comments about you on the Internet, you need to save the evidence in case you need to report him or her to your school, place of work, or even a webmaster. It's best to get help from your parent or a supportive adult before you report these incidents. In some cases what the cyber bully is doing to you may even be considered illegal, so be smart and save the evidence.

Get Help from Supportive Adults When Needed

Cyber bullying can be a pretty traumatic experience for anyone. It can leave you feeling sad, frustrated, embarrassed, and even confused—not knowing whom you can trust. It's important that you remember that you don't have to deal with this on your own. Instead, you should consider getting help from a supportive adult, such as your parent, a trusted family member, a teacher, or a supervisor. You should choose someone you trust and feel comfortable talking to and who's there to support you. Parents are usually the best choice, even if they're not directly connected to the place where the cyber bullying is coming from (such as school or work). Don't feel like you have to deal with this on your own. There are people who can help!

Report Cyber Bullying to the Proper Authorities

In more severe or persistent cases, it may be necessary for you and your parent to report the cyber bullying to the proper authorities. This might include online service providers, webmasters, schools or places of business, or in the most extreme cases, law enforcement. Because knowing when and how to report cyber bullying can be confusing, you need to work with your parent on this strategy. Contacting the authorities is usually a last resort—a strategy you only use when the others aren't working—so be sure to get help from a supportive adult if you think you need this more extreme measure.

CHAPTER EXERCISES
for Teens, Young Adults, and Parents

Teens and young adults should complete the following exercises with parents:
- Review the information about strategies for handling cyber bullying outlined in this chapter with your parent.
  - Have a discussion about whether you or someone you know has ever experienced cyber bullying.
  - Identify a few strategies you or someone else you know might use to handle cyber bullying either now or in the future.
- Be sure to set privacy settings on any social networking sites you belong to. Your parents or some supportive adult may be able to help you.

12

Minimizing Rumors and Gossip

SPREADING RUMORS AND EXCHANGING GOSSIP IS ONE of the more common ways people share information, opinions, and news about the personal or private affairs of others. Rumors include opinions, stories, or statements widely circulated about others, usually without confirmation of truth or origin of source. Gossip includes idle talk about the personal and private dealings of others, usually intimate in nature and sometimes harmful in effect. People who reveal personal and private information about others and spread rumors and gossip are known as *gossips* and their reputations as people who share intimate facts and opinions about others often precede them.

Incredibly common among teens and young adults, rumors and gossip are often thought of as mean spirited, callous, and unkind. Although a type of relational bullying, rumors and gossip may also simply represent a kind of communication people use to connect and bond when socializing. So why do people spread rumors and gossip? The evolutionary origins of rumors and gossip have been debated at length. One argument is that the sharing of rumors and gossip is a way groups of people monitor the reputations of others. Research also indicates that gossiping may actually enhance social bonding in large groups as a form of shared communication. Whatever the origins are, it's important for you and your teen or young adult to understand

> *Although a type of relational bullying, rumors and gossip may also simply represent a kind of communication people use to connect and bond when socializing.*

that rumors and gossip are very common and unlikely to be eliminated from the social world in which we live.

More common among females, the spreading of rumors and gossip may be mean spirited and intended to hurt others, a type of social weapon used to retaliate against someone, get revenge on someone for something they've done, or damage the reputation of someone disliked or envied. Although some may spread gossip out of malicious intent, it's probably more likely that they're trying to get attention and feel important. Knowing secret details and facts about the personal and private lives of others is a powerful position and may even increase social standing in the larger peer group. Consequently, many young people (particularly girls) may spread rumors and gossip as a method of increasing their popularity.

> *Many young people (particularly girls) may spread rumors and gossip as a method of increasing their popularity.*

Whereas rumors and gossip are a form of relational bullying, don't forget that more often gossiping is just something people do casually when they're socializing—*water cooler* talk if you will. That doesn't mean that if the intent isn't to be mean that the effects of rumors and gossip are less damaging or hurtful. Rumors and gossip spread casually without malicious intent can still be just as harmful as when they're used as social weapons. The important point is that because gossip is so widespread, there's very little your teen or young adult can do to prevent people from gossiping. Most people engage in some degree of gossiping from time to time, usually without cruel intentions. When you skim the pages of a tabloid gossip magazine in the checkout line at the grocery store, are you doing that to be mean? You're probably just curious or bored. When you talk about the latest celebrity gossip with your friends, are you trying to be hurtful? You're probably just interested in that celebrity's life and want to talk about what you know because it's interesting and fun. It probably never occurs to you that what you're doing could be hurtful. The same is often true for teens and young adults who gossip. They don't necessarily gossip out of malicious intent. Usually they're just curious, maybe even a little nosy—interested in the lives of the people around them. Sometimes they're simply bored and looking for something to talk about. Or maybe they're hoping to get a little attention and form some connections with the people around them—maybe even increase their popularity. No matter what the reason, the bottom line is that rumors and gossip are a natural part of the social culture we live in. Even though rumors can be damaging and hurtful to their targets, the unfortunate truth is that people will always gossip, and there's very little you or your child can do about it. Before you feel discouraged, hang on. We've identified a number of strategies that work really well in minimizing the effects of gossip and even avoiding being the target altogether.

It will be helpful to learn how to help your teen or young adult avoid being the target of rumors and gossip and what to do in cases where he or she is the focus of these painful and embarrassing social weapons. Although teens and young adults with a history of social neglect are less often the target of this form of relational bullying, some with a history of peer rejection will become the targets of rumors and gossip, so you should be familiar with what to do if it comes up. The following strategies for avoiding being the target of rumors and gossip are used by socially successful teens and young adults.

Tips for Avoiding Being the Target of Rumors and Gossip

Although rumors and gossip may be an inescapable part of our social world, helping your teen or young adult avoid being the target of the rumor mill is the first step in managing rumors and gossip. The *rumor mill* refers to the communication network that spreads rumors and gossip. Helping your son or daughter become familiar with the strategies used by socially savvy teens and young adults who've been able to stave off rumors and gossip is one way for your child to avoid being the target of the rumor mill.

Avoid Being Friends with the Gossips

Remember that *gossips* are people who like to spread rumors about other people. They're usually easy to identify because their reputations often precede them. One of the strategies for avoiding being the target of rumors and gossip is to avoid being friends with the gossips. Many teens and young adults with social challenges (particularly girls) will mistakenly think that if they're friends with the gossips, they'll have protection from gossiping. The opposite is actually true. When your teen or young adult becomes friends with the gossips, he or she becomes vulnerable to them, allowing them access to personal and private information. One false move or one small disagreement with a gossip and your teen or young adult's private information and secrets may be spread through the rumor mill as a form of retaliation. What's worse is that the gossip may be more believable because the person spreading the rumor was once your teen or young adult's friend and so is more likely to know the truth of the matter. A better strategy for avoiding being the target of rumors and gossip is for your teen or young adult to steer clear of the gossips altogether.

> *Many teens and young adults with social challenges (particularly girls) will mistakenly think that if they're friends with the gossips, they'll have protection from gossiping. The opposite is actually true.*

Don't Provoke the Gossips

Just as your teen or young adult shouldn't make friends with the gossips, for fear of discord leading to retaliation, he or she also shouldn't provoke the gossips. To provoke the gossips is to get them mad or upset, causing them to want to retaliate. The same is true for upsetting or provoking friends of the gossips. If your teen or young adult were to get into a personal confrontation or conflict with a gossip or even a friend of a gossip, he or she would probably end up being the target of the rumor mill because rumor spreading is the social weapon they use. Dating the former girlfriend or boyfriend of a gossip, getting them in trouble, or saying bad things about them are all examples of how your teen or young adult might provoke a gossip, making your teen or young adult the target of the rumor mill. As before, probably the best defense against the gossips is to steer clear of them and remain as neutral as possible. Your teen or young adult shouldn't be friends or enemies with the gossips—he or she should be a casual acquaintance or have no relationship whatsoever.

> *To provoke the gossips is to get them mad or upset, causing them to want to retaliate.*

Avoid Spreading Rumors and Gossip

Another important strategy for avoiding being the target of rumors and gossip is to avoid spreading rumors and gossip. Have you ever noticed that the people who are known for spreading rumors and gossip are usually in the thick of things—often targeted by the very rumor mill they fuel? This is probably because gossips open themselves up to retaliation and revenge from those burned by their vicious rumors. Those who add fuel to the rumor mill by spreading rumors and gossip themselves are more likely to get stung by the same mechanism.

Consequently, if your teen or young adult wants to avoid being targeted by these social weapons, he or she should avoid spreading rumors and gossip about others.

> *Gossips open themselves up to retaliation and revenge from those burned by their vicious rumors.*

Strategies for Handling Rumors and Gossip

Imagine your teen or young adult is unsuccessful in avoiding the vicious rumor mill and he or she becomes the target of rumors and gossip. Although incredibly hurtful and humiliating, remember that this challenging social scenario isn't so uncommon for socially active teens and young adults. Many socially engaged teens and young adults will find themselves the target of rumors or gossip at some point. So rather than hoping this will never happen or burying his or her head in the sand when it does happens, being familiar with strategies for handling rumors and gossip will be the lifeline that your teen or young adult will need to get through it. Rumors usually take your child by surprise and can be a devastating and humiliating experience. But if your teen or young adult is familiar with the strategies used by socially savvy teens and young adults who've been successful at minimizing the impact of rumors and gossip, he or she will be better equipped to handle these challenging social situations. The following strategies have been found to be effective in decreasing the harmful impact of rumors and gossip.

Don't Try to Disprove the Rumor

One of the most frustrating things about gossip is that once rumors are out there, they're incredibly difficult to disprove (if not impossible). Once a part of the rumor mill, even blatantly false stories and accusations will be difficult to disprove. In fact, you could have a mountain of evidence that disproves a rumor, but if your teen or young adult tries to share this evidence with other people, he or she will look defensive and guilty. In fact, in the process of sharing this mountain of evidence, instead of disproving the rumor, your teen or young adult will actually add fuel to the rumor mill by adding new and interesting content to the rumor. In this case, the new rumor will be how he or she is freaking out about the gossip, running around trying to tell everyone how it isn't true. That's good new gossip! In the end, instead of killing the rumor, your teen or young adult will have only succeeded in making the rumor grow bigger and stronger.

> One of the most frustrating things about gossip is that once rumors are out there, rumors are incredibly difficult to disprove (if not impossible).

The sad truth about rumors and gossip is that there is little anyone can do to prevent the spreading of them, and once out there, it's nearly impossible to disprove them. People exposed to rumors and gossip will believe what they choose to believe, regardless of the mountains of evidence you have to share. Take celebrity tabloid gossip for example—a multimillion dollar industry. There's very little celebrities can do to prevent rumors and gossip that are being spread about them through tabloid magazines. Even when the gossip is untrue, when celebrities try to disprove these rumors they usually end up drawing more attention to the gossip and may actually make matters worse for themselves by adding fuel to the rumor mill. Think of the countless celebrities who've attempted to deny rumors and gossip. How have most of these celebrity crusades for vindication turned out? Most of the time these attempts at vindication only lead to new gossip, with the tabloids picking up on the exciting new development. "Celebrity X is denying rumor X" might be the new headline. Instead of disproving the rumor, they end up drawing more attention to it.

The same unhappy reality is true for teens and young adults who try to disprove rumors and gossip in their schools and workplaces. To illustrate this point, imagine a young teenage girl targeted by a false rumor. A former friend is spreading a rumor that the young girl has a crush on a boy in her class. Although this young girl doesn't actually have a crush on the boy, what would people say if she made it her mission to disprove the rumor—going around the school telling anyone who would listen that the rumor wasn't true? It's possible she'd look guilty and defensive. Would people believe her story (even though she's telling the truth)? It's unlikely that everyone would believe her story if she made it her personal crusade to disprove the rumor. Again, this is because you can never completely disprove a rumor or gossip. In this case, making it her mission to disprove the rumor and tell anyone who'll listen that the rumor isn't true will probably make the young girl look defensive and guilty, usually increasing the circulation of more gossip. The new gossip will be how the girl is freaking out about the rumor and telling everyone it's not true (looking very guilty and defensive in the process), leading most to believe that the rumor must be true because she's making such a big deal about it.

Don't Confront the Source of the Gossip

Let's stick with the example of the young girl who has been targeted by this embarrassing rumor. The gossip being spread about her isn't true, and everyone knows the person who is spreading the lies (including the young girl). What do you think the girl's natural instinct would be in this case? She might want to confront the person spreading the rumor (the source of the gossip), request an explanation for this unfair attack, and demand public vindication—insisting that she tell everyone it's not true. What do you think the girl would be advised to do by sympathetic adults trying to help her? Similar to the girl's natural instinct, most teens and young adults are told to confront the person spreading the rumor, tell them how you feel, and ask them to stop spreading the rumor. So how do you think that tactic will go over for the young girl? Is it realistic to think that the person spreading the gossip will suddenly apologize for his or her actions and promise to make things better by telling everyone the rumor wasn't true? What would that even sound like? Imagine the rumor spreader saying, "You know, you're right. That rumor I spread isn't true. I shouldn't have done that. I'm sorry I hurt your feelings. Let me fix it and tell everyone it's a lie." Obviously, this scenario is more than unrealistic—it's never going to happen! The act of confronting the source of the gossip is actually more likely to cause the young girl harm rather than help. Confronting the person that's spreading the rumor about her will only create more gossip and add fuel to the rumor mill. The new rumor will be how the young girl freaked out and confronted the person spreading the gossip. That's good gossip! Such a dramatic confrontation is irresistible gossip and will surely add fuel to the rumor mill in no time. Confronting the source of the gossip will also upset and anger the rumor spreader, possibly resulting in retaliation against the girl even further. Even worse, through this confrontation the young girl has now publicly solidified her rivalry with the person spreading rumors, perhaps even creating a vendetta and a stronger enemy who now feels justified for future attacks. Consequently, one of the strategies for handling rumors and gossip is that your teen or young adult should not confront the source of the gossip.

> *Confronting the source of the gossip will also upset and anger the rumor spreader, possibly resulting in retaliation.*

Avoid the Source of the Gossip

Instead of confronting the source of the gossip, a much better strategy for handling rumors and gossip is to avoid the source of the gossip. Consider the previous example. What does everyone expect the young girl to do when she discovers she is the target of this embarrassing rumor? Everyone knows who's spreading the rumor about her, so people probably expect the young girl to confront the rumor spreader. We've already addressed the problems with confronting the source of the gossip, but it's not enough for your teen or young adult to just avoid confronting the rumor spreader. He or she also needs to avoid being anywhere near that person. Going back to our example, because everyone expects a confrontation, how do you think others will react when the young girl is in close proximity to the person spreading the rumor? Imagine it's passing period at school, and the young girl is on her way to class. She has the option of two different routes to take to her next class. One route will take her past the locker of the person spreading the rumor, the other will take her down a different hallway far from this locker. Which route should she take? If she takes the route putting her in close proximity to the rumor spreader, how will this affect the rumor mill? Everyone will be expecting (perhaps even hoping for) a confrontation. They'll be looking at the young girl, then looking at the rumor spreader, then looking back at the young girl, and so on—waiting for a fight. Even if the onlookers don't see a confrontation, they'll probably invent one. For example, if the young girl passes the rumor spreader's locker without making eye contact, the new gossip will be how she couldn't even look at her! However, if she passes the locker and the two girls do make eye contact, the new gossip will be how they were looking at each other and giving each other the *evil eye!* Unfortunately, this is a no-win situation. The young girl can do very little to avoid adding fuel to the rumor mill when she's in close proximity to the rumor spreader. In either case, when she's near the source of the gossip, the young girl will create more gossip for herself. However, if the young girl were to avoid the source of the gossip and take the route that bypasses the rumor spreader's locker, she will avoid adding fuel to the rumor mill. In other words, your teen or young adult should avoid creating more attention and gossip by going near the person spreading the gossip. This doesn't include completely changing your teen or young adult's routine or not going to school or work during this time. In this case, the new rumor will be how your teen or young adult is too upset to go to school. That's also good gossip! The bottom line is that avoiding the source of the gossip in subtle ways that will prevent creating more interest and attention to the gossip should be your teen or young adult's goal.

> Avoiding the source of the gossip in subtle ways that will prevent creating more interest and attention to the gossip should be your teen or young adult's goal.

Don't Appear Upset

When trying to minimize the impact of rumors and gossip, it's important that your teen or young adult doesn't appear upset by the gossip. People will expect him or her to be upset and will be looking for any sign of distress or disturbance. If your teen or young adult appears to be upset, this will only add fuel to the rumor mill, making it more difficult to eventually kill the rumor. The new rumor will be how your teen or young adult is freaking out about the gossip. Again, that's good gossip! Even if the rumor is terribly hurtful and your child feels humiliated and mortified by what others are saying, he or she can't give the impression of being bothered if the rumor is to go away. Imagine the young girl who's being accused of having a crush on a boy she doesn't even like. Even though she may be upset and embarrassed by this false rumor, to publicly show she's upset would only draw more attention and create more gossip, making it difficult to quiet the rumor spreading. Instead, she'll need to act like she's not upset and then take a proactive approach (described in the following section) to discredit the importance and believability of the rumor, making it less amusing for people to spread.

> *If your teen or young adult appears to be upset, this will only add fuel to the rumor mill, making it more difficult to eventually kill the rumor.*

Act Amazed People Believe or Care about the Rumor

Instead of showing that your teen or young adult is upset by the rumor or gossip, he or she will need to discredit the gossip by acting amazed that people believe or care about the rumor when others bring it up. People are naturally curious and will want to know what your teen or young adult has to say about the rumor. When the rumor is brought up, if your teen or young adult acts amazed that anyone would believe the rumor, he or she is essentially discrediting its authenticity or believability. If he or she acts amazed anyone would care about the rumor, he or she is discrediting the importance of the rumor. In either case, your teen or young adult is discrediting the rumor without appearing to be defensive or guilty (like when trying to disprove the rumor). This diminishes the believability or importance of the rumor and reduces its power through casual indifference. It doesn't even matter if the rumor is true—either way the strategy is just as effective. If the rumor is true, your teen or young adult should act amazed anyone would care enough to talk about it. If the rumor is false, he or she should act amazed anyone would ever believe it.

> *If the rumor is true, your teen or young adult should act amazed anyone would care enough to talk about it. If the rumor is false, he or she should act amazed anyone would ever believe it.*

Your teen or young adult's reaction to direct mentions of the rumor will be a critical element to his or her success in killing the rumor. If others notice the indifference your child has to comments about the rumor and his or her astonishment that anyone would believe or care about it, then the importance of the rumor will be minimized, making it less likely that others will want to spread the rumor further. Using the example of the young girl, when the topic of her alleged crush is brought up in conversation, she might reflect these sentiments by saying things like, "I can't believe anyone would believe that" or "Who would believe that? People are so gullible" or "Can you believe anyone cares about that?" or "Why would anyone care about that? People need to get a life" or "People seriously need to find something better to talk about."

By acting amazed that anyone would either believe or care about the rumor, your teen or young adult is discrediting the rumor, making it seem silly for anyone else to spread the rumor further. People will be less likely to believe the rumor or think they should even care about the rumor. This means they'll be less inclined to spread the rumor, bringing your teen or young adult one step closer to killing the rumor.

Spread the Rumor about Yourself

Video

The final strategy for handling rumors and gossip involves a highly proactive approach we fondly call *spreading the rumor about yourself*. In PEERS, we use this unusual and memorable buzz phrase intentionally so that teens and young adults don't forget this important tactic. The idea that you should spread the rumor about yourself initially seems crazy and illogical. Don't most people want to get as far away from this rumor as possible? Even though your teen or young adult's instinct may be to avoid the rumor and try to get away from it, that doesn't make it go away. Instead, attacking the rumor head-on by discrediting it (without appearing defensive or guilty) is the most powerful strategy and the best way to kill the rumor. Your teen or young adult can do this by spreading the rumor about him- or herself and acting amazed anyone would believe or care about the rumor. In a way, he or she is indirectly denying the rumor's authenticity ("Who would believe that?") and importance ("Who would care about that?").

When spreading the rumor about yourself, the three key steps include acknowledging the rumor exists, making fun of the rumor, and acting amazed anyone would either believe or care about the rumor. For example, when your teen or young adult acknowledges that the rumor is out there, he or she might say something like, "Have you heard this rumor about me . . .?" Then he or she needs to make fun of the rumor by saying something like, "How lame" or "That's so stupid" or "That's too ridiculous for words" or "How stupid is that one?" Finally, your teen or young adult should act amazed anyone would either believe or care about the rumor by saying things like, "It's amazing what some people will believe" or "It's so crazy that people believe that" or "Can you believe anyone cares about that?" or "How weird that people even care about that" or "People seriously need to get a life and find something else to talk about," or "People need to get a hobby or find something interesting to talk about."

> When spreading the rumor about yourself, the three key steps include acknowledging the rumor exists, making fun of the rumor, and acting amazed anyone would either believe or care about the rumor.

When choosing to whom your teen or young adult will spread the rumor, it's important to only choose people he or she trusts and are likely to offer support. That means when your teen or young adult spreads this rumor to these trusted, supportive friends, you should expect them to agree with the absurdity of the rumor and be equally amazed that others believe or care about it.

Where and when your teen or young adult chooses to spread the rumor about him- or herself is also important. Ideally, this should happen when other people are around who will overhear the conversation. For example, good times to spread the rumor about yourself include lunchtime at a crowded lunch table, before class when others are sitting nearby, or in the break room at work when others might be listening. Whenever or wherever your teen or young adult chooses to spread the rumor, it's critical that others overhear the conversation. The key is that your teen or young adult is acknowledging the rumor to people he or she trusts in front of people who might overhear, then undermining the importance and legitimacy of the gossip. Your teen or young adult will have to be careful not to try to disprove the rumor because this rarely works and may make him or her look defensive. The differences can be subtle, but one important rule of thumb is for your teen or young adult to avoid ever saying the rumor is "not true" because this will automatically make him or her look defensive. For example, in the case of the young girl, she might do the following steps to spread the rumor about herself:

- First the young girl might acknowledge the existence of the rumor to someone she trusts who will support her while in front of others who will overhear what she is saying. She might say something like, "Did you hear this rumor about me? Apparently I have a crush on that new kid in school."
- Then she might make fun of the rumor by saying something like, "How lame. That's seriously too ridiculous for words."
- Finally, she will discredit the legitimacy and importance of the rumor by saying something like, "Can you imagine anyone would believe that? And it's kind of crazy what people talk about. People need to get a life and find something interesting to talk about."

These are the strategies most likely to minimize the negative impact of rumors and gossip. The interesting thing about these strategies is that they're rarely intuitive. In fact, when it comes to handling rumors and gossip, most people's natural instincts are wrong. Your teen or young adult's instinct to want to disprove the gossip is wrong, his or her impulse to want to confront the source of the gossip is wrong, and even showing the natural feeling of being upset is wrong when revealed to others. Instead, acting amazed anyone would believe or care about the rumor and spreading the rumor about yourself (two tactics not necessarily instinctive) will take the power out of the rumor and make others who spread it feel less important. If done properly, the new rumor will be how little your teen or young adult cares about the old rumor and how lame it was in the first place. These strategies, when used in combination, will help discredit the rumor without appearing defensive, bringing your teen or young adult one step closer to killing the rumor permanently.

> *Your teen or young adult's instinct to want to disprove the gossip is wrong, his or her impulse to want to confront the source of the gossip is wrong, and even showing the natural feeling of being upset is wrong when revealed to others.*

Social coaching tip: Present the strategies for handling rumors and gossip to your child by having him or her read the chapter summary for teens and young adults and facilitate opportunities to practice these strategies with you using the chapter exercises. It will also be important to jointly read the social vignettes in the chapter summary, view the DVD video demonstrations of inappropriately and appropriately spreading the rumor about yourself, and discuss these examples using the perspective-taking questions. The differences between inappropriate and appropriate strategies will be understated, so be prepared to have a discussion about the subtleties. The primary difference is in the attempt to disprove the rumor (inappropriate) versus acting like the rumor is kind of lame (appropriate).

Success Story: Shannon Spreads a Rumor about Herself

The spreading of rumors and gossip can be one of the more vicious forms of bullying. Often perpetrated by girls, this relational form of bullying has the capacity to ruin a reputation. Such was the case for Shannon, a seventeen-year-old girl with a long history of being targeted by rumors and gossip. Shannon came to PEERS with her parents to learn the strategies for handling relational bullying and overcome the social exclusion that resulted from being the focus of gossip.

Shannon explained, "These girls in my school decided to spread a rumor about me because one of their ex-boyfriend's liked me. The rumor wasn't even true but people believed them. I was so upset I didn't want to go to school. I begged my mom to transfer me." Instead of transferring schools, Shannon's parents brought her to PEERS. At the time she entered our program, she literally had no friends. Having been targeted by rumors and gossip in the past, Shannon had a reputation for stealing boyfriends and breaking hearts. Ironically, she had never had a real boyfriend and had only ever gone on a couple of dates. A very attractive young girl, Shannon was often the target of jealousy. Her situation when she came to PEERS was no exception.

Although Shannon desperately wanted to change schools, her parents insisted that she stick it out at her present school, which was known for its academic excellence. Her parents felt confident that if Shannon could gain the critical skills needed to handle this social challenge, she'd be better for it. "We knew she was going through a rough time," her mother reflected. "Kids can be so mean. But we didn't want her to lose her chances at getting into a good college by switching schools midstream. She only had one year left in high school, and then she could have the fresh start she was looking for." So they brought her to PEERS where she got a crash course in managing rumors and changing her reputation (chapter 14).

Shannon quickly caught on to the tactic for spreading the rumor about herself, and after several practice rehearsals she was eager to get started. She spent the next week confidently canvassing the school telling anyone she considered a potential ally how ridiculous the rumors about her were. She said things like, "Can you believe people are talking about that? Who would believe that? How stupid. People need to get a grip and find something believable to talk about." After a week of this campaign, she returned to PEERS and exclaimed, "I think it's working!" She observed that not only were people no longer staring at her and giggling, many people had come up to her and directly mentioned how unbelievable the original rumor was—sharing in the laugh.

Using the strategies she learned in PEERS, Shannon confidently stuck it out at her school. During her senior year of high school, she reconnected with several friends and even went to senior prom with her first real boyfriend. Eventually, she graduated with honors and was accepted to a prestigious university, where she is now in her sophomore year of college. She lives in her sorority house, has a large group of girlfriends, and although she admits that some girls still gossip, she now feels equipped to handle these situations with confidence and ease.

HANDLING RUMORS AND GOSSIP

Chapter Summary for Teens and Young Adults

The following information is intended to be read by teens and young adults and contains a brief summary of the chapter.

(continued)

Have you ever wondered why some people gossip? For some, spreading rumors and gossip is a way of hurting others—a type of social aggression that's meant to cause harm. People who spread rumors and gossip to be mean are considered bullies, sometimes called *gossips*. Spreading rumors and gossip may also be a way of increasing social standing and popularity. Knowing the intimate and personal details of someone's private life puts the gossiping person in a powerful position and usually gets attention and interest from others. In this case, the gossiping person may not intend to hurt anyone, although they often do. Consequently, this isn't a good way to make friends—only enemies. However, the majority of people who gossip probably do it because it's interesting to talk about what people are doing. They may be bored or curious, maybe even a little nosy, and think it's fun to talk about other people. In this case, gossiping isn't meant to cause harm (even though it still might) but is really just a form of communication used to connect and bond with other people.

You probably know the damage rumors and gossip can cause to a person's reputation and how painful and embarrassing it can feel to be the target of rumors and gossip. Maybe you've been the target yourself. If you've been targeted by this vicious sort of bullying, you probably felt pretty helpless, maybe unsure of what to do. That's how most teens and young adults feel when they're targeted by rumors and gossip. Unfortunately, your instincts don't always do you any favors when it comes to this social dilemma because most of what your gut tells you to do (like deny the rumor, confront the person spreading the rumor, or ignore the rumor) might not be the best strategy. If you've ever felt frustrated by this kind of situation, you'll be relieved to know that we've actually put together a list of tactics used by teens and young adults who've been successful at minimizing the impact of rumors and gossip. The ideas are described in the following section.

STRATEGIES FOR AVOIDING BEING THE TARGET OF RUMORS AND GOSSIP

Before we get into the strategies for handling rumors and gossip, let's talk about some ways you can avoid being the target altogether. Here are some strategies used by socially active teens and young adults who have been able to avoid being the target of rumors and gossip.

Avoid Being Friends with the Gossips

Gossips are people who like spreading rumors and gossip about other people. They think it's fun. One way for you to avoid having people spread rumors and gossip about you is to avoid being friends with the gossips. Some people make the mistake of thinking if they're friends with the gossips, then they'll be safe because friends wouldn't gossip about friends. That's not true. Actually, you're more likely to get gossiped about if you're friends with the gossips because they'll actually know things about you and won't be able to resist sharing. The worst thing is that people will be more likely to believe the gossip because your friends are the ones spreading it—and they must know. So be safe and don't try to make friends with the gossips.

Don't Provoke the Gossips

You also don't want to be enemies with the gossips. What would happen if you provoked the gossips and made them angry with you? They'd probably start spreading rumors and gossip about you as a way of retaliating, even if what they said wasn't true. You also don't want to get on the bad side of friends of the gossips because the same thing will happen. They'll want to get back at you in the way they know best. Getting them in trouble, saying bad things, or embarrassing them in some way are examples of how you could provoke the gossip and make

(continued)

yourself the target of the rumor mill. Instead, be like Switzerland and stay as neutral as possible with the gossips.

Avoid Spreading Rumors and Gossip

Have you ever noticed that people who gossip are always in the thick of things, getting targeted by the rumor mill they're always fueling? That's probably because gossips open themselves up to retaliation from people they've burned by their vicious rumors. So if you want to avoid being targeted, you shouldn't spread rumors and gossip about other people.

STRATEGIES FOR HANDLING RUMORS AND GOSSIP

Sometimes no matter how hard you try to keep your head down and stay clear of the rumor mill, you end up getting burned. Unfortunately, a lot of teens and young adults will be targeted by rumors and gossip at some point. Knowing how to handle these situations can be tough, but the good news is you've got help! The strategies described here are used by teens and young adults who have been successful at killing rumors about them. The weird thing is, very few teens and young adults know to do these things! That's because these strategies probably won't be your natural instinct. In fact, you may need to fight your urge to do other things. But if you find yourself targeted by gossip and you use these powerful tools, you'll be way more likely to get through this tricky social situation unscathed.

Don't Try to Disprove the Rumor

One of the most frustrating things about gossip is that once rumors are out there, rumors are almost impossible to disprove. Even if you have a mountain of evidence that proves the rumor isn't true, if you try to share this evidence, you'll look defensive and guilty. Even worse, you'll actually add fuel to the rumor mill by adding new and interesting details to the rumor. The new rumor will be how you're freaking out, running around trying to tell everyone how the rumor isn't true, making the rumor grow bigger and stronger. So resist the urge and don't try to disprove the rumor.

Don't Confront the Source of the Gossip

One of the natural instincts people have when they're targeted by rumors is to confront the person spreading the gossip. Bad idea! What do you think will happen if you do that? Do you think the person will say, "You know, you're right. That rumor I spread isn't true. I shouldn't have done that. I'm sorry I hurt your feelings. Let me fix it and tell everyone it's a lie." Of course not! Confronting the person and sharing how you feel will only create more gossip and add fuel to the rumor mill. The new rumor will be how you freaked out and confronted the person. That's good gossip! Plus, you're only going to antagonize the person gossiping about you, making him or her more angry and causing him to feel justified in spreading rumors about you. Don't make the mistake of starting a war with this person by being confrontational. It will only make it worse for you.

Avoid the Source of the Gossip

Instead of confronting the source of the gossip, a better plan is to avoid the source of the gossip. That means if you know who's gossiping about you, try to stay away from him or her. Don't walk down the hallway near the person's locker, don't hang out in places they like to go. Everyone is probably expecting you to confront the rumor spreader. They may even be hoping you'll confront them because that's more gossip and good drama! Even if you don't confront the rumor spreader but you end up somewhere near each other, people will create more gossip. For example, let's say you walk by the person's locker during passing period. If you don't make eye contact, the new gossip will be how you couldn't even

(continued)

look at that person. If you do make eye contact, the new gossip will be how you were giving each other the evil eye. Unfortunately, this is a no-win situation for you, so instead of adding fuel to the rumor mill, just try to avoid the source of the gossip. That doesn't mean stop going to school or work—that will also create more gossip. Just do what you can to stay out of that person's way until the gossip dies down.

Don't Appear Upset

It's only natural that being the target of rumors and gossip will be hurtful and embarrassing. People will be expecting you to be upset, and they'll be looking for signs that you are. Even though it's going to be really hard, you've got to act like you're not upset. The reason is, if you show that you're upset, you're going to be adding fuel to the rumor mill and giving people more to talk about. The new rumor will be how you're freaking out because of the gossip, making your situation even worse. Instead, don't appear upset when people are around and privately get help from supportive friends and family you trust who won't tell others how upset you're feeling.

Act Amazed People Believe or Care about the Rumor

One of the most important tactics you'll use to kill the rumor is to discredit it by acting amazed that people believe or care about the rumor when they bring it up to you. When you act amazed that anyone would believe the rumor, you're discrediting the truth of it without appearing to be defensive or guilty. When you act amazed that anyone would *care* about the rumor, you're diminishing the importance of the rumor and reducing its power. It doesn't even matter if the rumor is true. If the rumor is true, act amazed anyone would care enough to talk about it. If the rumor is false, act amazed anyone would ever believe it. When you're the target of a rumor or gossip, people will naturally approach you to find out whether it's true. This is your opportunity to act amazed anyone would care or believe the rumor by saying something like the following:

- "I can't believe anyone would believe that."
- "Who would believe that? People are so gullible."
- "Can you believe anyone cares about that?"
- "Why would anyone care about that? People need to get a life."
- "People seriously need to find something better to talk about."

When you act amazed, people will be less likely to believe the rumor or think they should even care about the rumor. This means they'll be less likely to spread the rumor, which is what you want.

Spread the Rumor about Yourself

Video

The final strategy for handling rumors and gossip is the most powerful, so you'll want to use it! It involves spreading the rumor about yourself. That sounds crazy, right? Actually it's really clever and not something most people would even think to do. This is how it works. You're going to start by acknowledging the rumor is out there by mentioning it to someone you trust and you know has your back. You're going to do this when other people are around and will overhear what you're saying. During lunchtime, before class begins, during a break, or when people are sitting around talking are all good times to spread the rumor about yourself. The next step is to make fun of the rumor. This shows that you're not upset and that the rumor isn't a big deal—in fact, it's kind of stupid. The final step is to act amazed anyone would believe the rumor or care about the rumor. This indirectly discredits the rumor and makes the people listening less likely to want to spread the original rumor. The new rumor may actually become how stupid the old rumor was. This strategy is very

(continued)

effective in killing the rumor, without making you look upset, guilty, or defensive. But you can't just do this once. You're going to want to spread the rumor about yourself several times—always to people you trust in places where others will overhear. The steps are listed here with some examples of what you can say.

1. **Acknowledge that the rumor exists.**
   - "Have you heard this rumor about me . . .?"
2. **Make fun of the rumor.**
   - "How lame."
   - "That's so stupid."
   - "That's too ridiculous for words."
   - "How stupid is that one?"
3. **Act amazed anyone would believe or care about the rumor.**
   - "It's amazing what some people will believe."
   - "It's so crazy that people believe that."
   - "Can you believe anyone cares about that?"
   - "How weird that people even care about that."
   - "People seriously need to get a life and find something else to talk about."
   - "People need to get a hobby or find something interesting to talk about."

Social Vignette of Spreading the Rumor about Yourself: Bad Example

The following social vignette is a transcript of the video demonstration from the accompanying DVD of inappropriately spreading the rumor about yourself.

Yasamine: (sounding upset) "Oh, my God, Lara, did you hear that rumor that I totally have a crush on Ben?"

Lara: "Yeah, I did hear that."

Yasamine: (sounding defensive) "Oh, my God. So not true! I mean, you know me . . . Ben is not my type. I like, you know, blonde, tall, and Ben is not that, right?! I mean we don't even have anything in common. "

Lara: (unsure of the truth) "I guess. If you say so."

Yasamine: (sounding defensive, guilty, a little hysterical) "Yeah, I mean it's totally crazy. Who would believe that? It's just . . . it's just crazy."

Lara: (uncertain) "Yeah, that is kind of crazy."

Yasamine: (sounding worried, panicked) "Yeah."

Perspective-Taking Questions

- What was that interaction like for Lara?
  Answers: Uncomfortable, awkward
- What do you think Lara thought of Yasamine?
  Answers: Defensive, guilty, trying too hard to disprove the rumor
- Is Lara or anyone listening going to believe the rumor?
  Answer: They might believe the rumor is true; Yasamine appears upset, defensive, and guilty.

Social Vignette of Spreading the Rumor about Yourself: Good Example

The following social vignette is a transcript of the video demonstration from the accompanying DVD of appropriately spreading the rumor about yourself.

Yasamine: (calmly) "Oh, my God, Lara. Did you hear that rumor that I have a crush on Ben?"

Lara: "I totally heard that!"

Yasamine: (casually) "Who would believe that?"

Lara: "I don't know who'd believe it. It's ridiculous."

Yasamine: (sounding amazed) "It's so ridiculous. I mean, why would anyone care?"

Lara: (agreeing) "I don't know. Who would care?"

(continued)

Yasamine: (sounding indifferent) "It's so lame. People need to find something better to talk about."

Lara: "Absolutely.

Yasamine: (sounding amazed) "So stupid."

Lara: (agreeing) "So!"

Perspective-Taking Questions

- What was that interaction like for Lara?
  Answers: Fine, interesting
- What do you think Lara thought of Yasamine?
  Answers: Normal, ordinary, nondefensive, guilt-free
- Is Lara or anyone listening going to believe the rumor?
  Answer: They probably won't believe the rumor or want to spread the original rumor.

CHAPTER EXERCISES
for Teens, Young Adults, and Parents

Teens and young adults should complete the following exercises with parents:

- Practice with your parent acting amazed that people believe or care about the rumor using the tactics outlined in this chapter.
  - Begin by reviewing the strategies for handling rumors and gossip.
  - Practice acting amazed people believe or care about the rumor.
- When relevant, practice acting amazed with peers (this may occur rarely) that people believe or care about the rumor.
  - You may want to use the FriendMaker mobile app to review how to use this strategy when it comes up.

- Practice with your parent spreading the rumor about yourself using the steps outlined in this chapter.
  - Begin by reviewing the strategies for handling rumors and gossip.
  - Practice following the steps for spreading the rumor about yourself.
- When relevant, practice with peers you trust when others might overhear (this may occur rarely) following the steps for spreading the rumor about yourself.
  - You may want to use the FriendMaker mobile app to review how to use this strategy when it comes up.

13

Avoiding Physical Bullying

IN OUR WORK WITH PARENTS at the UCLA PEERS Clinic, there is no topic more emotionally charged than bullying, particularly physical bullying. Understandably, parents visibly cringe and turn apprehensive when we raise the topic. This is of course because one of the most important roles you have as a parent is to make sure your child is safe and protected. No good parent wants to stand by and allow his or her child to be the victim of a tormentor.

Perhaps your teen or young adult has been bullied, too. If so, you've probably felt frustrated and helpless at times, as though your hands were tied, unable to help your child out of these painful and frightening circumstances. Parents often report to us that they feel angry and incensed, unable to understand how such behavior can be tolerated. They often feel heartbroken and sad, imagining the pain and the fear that their child must face. Many have gone to the school, demanded that the administration do something about the problem, only to be met with empty promises that things will change. Some have even changed schools, started homeschooling, and any number of alternative choices because they wanted their child to be safe, to have the security and protection he or she needs to live a happy and healthy life without fear or trepidation. We want that, too. We want that for your child and for all teens and young adults. That's the purpose of this chapter and, more broadly, this book.

With the high occurrence of bullying rates among adolescents, it's no wonder that the media has picked up on the epidemic. News outlets flood us with stories about bullying in our schools, reminding us of the emotional impact it can have on our kids. Symptoms of depression or anxiety, feelings of loneliness or low self-esteem, and even increased substance abuse or poor academic performance are all possible consequences of bullying. Suicidal thoughts and even attempts, every parent's worst nightmare and the most frightening and cruelest cost, have also been linked to bullying among teens and young adults.

Given the staggering number of young people victimized by bullying in our schools and knowing the horrifying consequences of these cruel acts, many schools have been swift to respond. Anti-bullying campaigns abound, preaching tolerance via a no-hate movement. Although these bully-prevention crusades certainly send a positive message to students and may even be helpful in promoting tolerance and acceptance, the notion that we can completely abolish bullying is unrealistic (a tough pill to swallow). Although much of the focus on bullying spotlights the perpetrators and the movement to eradicate bullying from our schools, less attention is actually paid to the victims and how these innocents might reduce the impact of bullying.

As we continue to strive to create bully-free zones in our schools, it's equally important to equip teens and young adults with useful strategies for handling bullying. Part 3 of this book has attempted to provide strategies for handling peer rejection, using skills with ecological validity—tactics that have been supported by research and are used by teens and young adults who have successfully staved off rejection from their peers. Our strategies so far have focused on tactics for handling teasing (verbal bullying), cyber bullying (electronic bullying), and rumors and gossip (relational bullying). It's important for you and your teen or young adult to understand the differences among physical bullying, verbal teasing, cyber bullying, and rumors and gossip because the strategies for handling each of these types of bullying are completely different. This chapter will focus on strategies for handling the fourth type: physical bullying—possibly the most severe form of social aggression.

By definition, physical bullying includes any kind of behavior that involves intent to hurt someone's body or damage someone's possessions. It could include a range of behaviors from throwing

Physical bullying includes any kind of behavior that involves intent to hurt someone's body or damage someone's possessions.

bits of paper at someone in class, tripping someone in the hall, or shoving them into a locker, to more severe forms of physical violence such as kicking, hitting, pushing, or even punching. Physical bullying also includes behaviors such as stealing, defacing personal effects, or destroying someone's property.

As with previous chapters, the following skills don't represent run-of-the-mill approaches to handling physical bullying. Instead, they include effective strategies used by socially savvy teens and young adults who've been able to minimize the impact of physical bullying.

Strategies for Handling Physical Bullying

Consider what most teens and young adults are told to do in response to physical bullying. According to the teens and young adults we've seen in our clinic, when confronted with physical bullying they're told to either tell an older adult or fight back. Although telling a supportive adult or authority figure may be a useful strategy if your teen or young adult is in danger, under physical threat, or is experiencing chronic bullying, telling on a bully for more minor offenses such as throwing pieces of paper, tripping, or shoving may be less effective in avoiding future incidents. What might happen if your teen or young adult were to tell on a bully for throwing paper at him or her? The result may be that the bully gets in trouble, which may make him or her want to retaliate against your teen or young adult even further, thus worsening the situation. The issue with fighting back, of course, is that this tactic could result in injury, get your teen or young adult in trouble, or even give him or her a bad reputation among peers and authority figures. Instead, when facing less severe forms of physical bullying, your teen or young adult may want to consider trying some of the following strategies shown to be effective in either minimizing or eliminating this type of social aggression.

Avoid the Bully

One of the most effective strategies for handling physical bullying is to avoid the bully. That means to stay out of reach of the bully and try to avoid being in the same place as the bully at the same time. For example, if your teen or young adult knows the bully hangs out in a certain area of the lunchroom, avoid that area. If he or she knows the bully has a locker in a certain hallway, avoid walking down that hall. Or if he or she knows the bully likes to hang out in a certain part of campus, avoid going to that part of campus when possible. By staying out of reach of the bully and avoiding the places frequented by the bully, your teen or young adult may be able to successfully avoid being the target. In other words, if the bully can't find your child, he can't bully him or her.

> If the bully can't find your child, he can't bully him or her.

Lay Low When the Bully Is Around

One of the common social errors often committed by peer-rejected teens and young adults is that they draw attention to themselves when the bully is around. They might make jokes or act silly when the bully is near, reminding the bully of their presence and making the bully want to target them. Instead of drawing attention, one useful strategy for handling physical bullying is to advise your teen to lay low when the bully is around. If your teen or young adult can keep a low profile and try to fly under the radar when the bully is near, he or she will be less likely to be targeted by the bully. In other words, if the bully doesn't notice your child, he's less likely to bully him or her.

> If the bully doesn't notice your child, he's less likely to bully him or her.

Don't Provoke the Bully

Your teen or young adult should also avoid provoking the bully at all times. Of course, this means not teasing or making fun of the bully or causing the bully any form of annoyance or embarrassment. When bullies become annoyed or embarrassed, they feel provoked and will often retaliate with violence. That means your teen or young adult should avoid any provocation that could result in the bully feeling agitated or embarrassed, including using the teasing comebacks described in chapter 10. The strategies used for handling teasing such as saying, "Whatever" or "Yeah and?" or "Your point is?" often cause embarrassment to the person they're directed toward. Therefore, your teen or young adult should refrain from using teasing comebacks with physical bullies (even those who tease with words) to avoid further upset and aggression. Instead, help your teen to use the strategies outlined in this chapter for handling physical bullying.

> *Refrain from using teasing comebacks with physical bullies (even those who tease with words) to avoid further upset and aggression.*

Don't Police the Bully

Some teens and young adults with social difficulties have a tendency to point out rule violations and mistakes made by others, a behavior described in chapter 3 that we call *policing*. Apart from the peer rejection that often accompanies this social error, policing a bully who has a tendency to get physically aggressive may result in a physical attack. So obviously telling on bullies (or the friends of bullies) for minor offenses is highly discouraged. This means if the bully is passing notes in class and this behavior is not permitted, it's not your teen or young adult's job to point this out to the teacher. If the bully is cheating on an exam, it's not his or her business to point this out to the professor. Or if the bully is late for work, it's not his or her responsibility to tell the supervisor. Pointing out the offenses of classmates, coworkers, and peers is not your teen or young adult's responsibility or business. Aside from giving him or her a bad reputation among the larger peer group, when directed toward the wrong individual, this behavior may result in physical bullying.

> *Policing a bully who has a tendency to get physically aggressive may result in a physical attack.*

One obvious exception to the no policing rule is if the bully brings a weapon to school or work or is threatening physical harm to someone. In that case, your teen or young adult should tell someone in authority immediately, such as a teacher, professor, or supervisor. But it's very important that he or she do this discreetly without telling peers or coworkers because you don't want the bully to find out your teen or young adult was the one who got him or her in trouble. That will make the bully want to retaliate against your child, landing him or her in hot water.

Don't Try to Make Friends with the Bully

Another common social error committed by teens and young adults with social challenges is to try to make friends with the bully. This strategy is highly ineffective because it rarely works, and instead draws attention to the victim and enables further persecution. Yet many peer-rejected teens and young adults will make futile attempts to befriend those who bully them, perhaps thinking they can win them over with their wit and charm or dazzle them with their brilliant intellect. In the end, many become further exploited and victimized. For some, this behavior draws attention to their differences, putting them in the spotlight, leading to more bullying. Others may be exploited by the perpetrator, perhaps leading to the belief that they've befriended the bully, but then are taken advantage of in some unkind way. Exploitation can manifest itself in many forms including financial exploitation (taking money), material exploitation (taking possessions), behavioral exploitation (getting the victim to engage in certain behaviors), emotional exploitation (playing mind games and tricks), or even, frighteningly, sexual exploitation (demanding sexual favors). Obviously, your first priority is to protect your teen or young adult from these types of exploitation. One powerful way to do that is to make sure he or she doesn't try to make friends with bullies.

> Many peer-rejected teens and young adults will make futile attempts to befriend those who bully them.

Social coaching tip: Although some teens and young adults with social difficulties may recognize the manipulative and exploitative behavior often associated with new "friendships" with bullies, others may be resistant to suggestions that the bully's intentions are impure. If your teen or young adult tends to be more trusting and socially naive than is safe, mistaking exploitation for friendship, you may want to return to the discussion in chapter 2 outlining the characteristics of a good friend and how you can tell when you're accepted as a friend by another person. Through that discussion, your teen or young adult may discover characteristics such as equality, commitment, and loyalty are lacking in that exploitative friendship. Although this revelation can be painful, you should gently remind your teen or young adult that friendship is a choice; there are good choices and bad choices in friendships. Your teen or young adult doesn't need to be friends with everyone, and everyone doesn't need to be friends with him or her. This person may be a bad choice, but there will be other (better) choices.

Hang Out with Other People

In an earlier chapter we asked the question, "Whom do bullies like to pick on, people who are by themselves or in a group?" The answer, of course, is that bullies like to pick on people who are by themselves because they're easier targets. Remember that when your teen or young adult is alone, he or she is unprotected, with no one there to defend or back him or her up. Bullies are keenly aware of the vulnerability of being alone, and often choose to pick on loners or those who are socially isolated. Consequently, one of the most effective strategies for handling physical bullying is to simply hang out with other people. That means your teen or young adult should never eat lunch alone, walk to class alone, or travel to and from school alone if there's a history of physical bullying. Instead, eating lunch with a friend (or even an acquaintance), walking to class with a peer, and traveling to and from school with a classmate or sibling will be useful strategies for staving off physical bullying because bullies are less likely to target your teen or young adult if there are people around who could potentially offer protection.

> *One of the most effective strategies for handling physical bullying is to simply hang out with other people.*

Stay Near Authority Figures When the Bully Is Around

Another useful strategy for avoiding physical bullying is to stay near adults or authority figures when the bully is around. This tactic is effective because very few bullies are so brash as to physically bully others in front of authority figures who might discipline or reprimand them. Consequently, even standing or sitting in the general vicinity of an adult or authority figure may keep the bully at bay temporarily. That doesn't mean your teen or young adult needs to go up

> *Very few bullies are so brash as to physically bully others in front of authority figures who might discipline or reprimand them.*

and start a conversation with the lunch monitor or walk to class every day with the campus security guard. He or she simply needs to stay near authority figures when the bully is around to prevent physical attacks in the moment.

Get Help from a Supportive Adult When in Danger

Finally, in instances when the threat of physical harm or danger is imminent, it's always important to get help from a supportive adult. This is also true in cases when the bullying is chronic and pervasive and the strategies outlined previously haven't been effective. Enlisting the help of parents and family members as well as school or work personnel may be the necessary step needed to put an end to physical bullying or any other form of bullying that your teen or young adult may be experiencing. It's never acceptable for others to harass or bully, and when equipped with effective strategies for handling these challenging social situations, in combination with assistance from you and others, your teen or young adult may be better able to minimize and even eliminate the occurrence of these difficult and often frightening experiences.

> In instances when the threat of physical harm or danger is imminent, it's always important to get help from a supportive adult.

Social coaching tip: These are the strategies for handling physical bullying used by teens and young adults who've been able to effectively diminish and even eliminate this type of social aggression. You may have noticed as you went through the chapter that there was less emphasis on the emotional consequences of bullying and greater focus placed on what you and your teen or young adult can do in these situations to make it less likely that he or she will be bullied in the future. We approach most social challenges in this way in PEERS. Although we empathize with the emotionally painful aspects of bullying, we know that we can't do much to help you and your teen or young adult escape these problems by simply sharing your pain and reminding you that you're not alone. The truth is that we do share your pain and you're absolutely not alone, but instead we encourage you to take a proactive approach to this problem and channel your energy into helping your teen or young adult gain the skills needed to overcome these social hurdles. Think of yourself as not only a protector but as a cheerleader, reassuring and cheering your teen or young adult on to greater empowerment and liberation from victimization.

Success Story: Larry Lays Low

Of all the different types of peer rejection, physical bullying, which in its worst form includes physical threats and violence, is perhaps the most concerning. No person should have to fear for his or her safety—and yet countless socially challenged teens and young adults do. Larry, a sixteen-year-old boy diagnosed with autism spectrum disorder (ASD) with a long record of peer victimization was sadly no exception.

Prior to coming to PEERS, Larry was mainstreamed in a small private school—his parents sought the structure of a small class size. Although he excelled academically in this setting, Larry was not socially success-ful. According to his parents, the benefits of a small class also had a downside—it made his differences stand out much more. "There was no place for him to blend in," his mom explained. "On a daily basis he would get bullied, threatened, and at times, physically punched and abused because he just had no idea how to fit in. We moved him to dif-ferent schools, trying to find the right fit." Even with the physical threats and the other social challenges, Larry miraculously managed to stay posi-tive. "At this point, his optimism was his greatest gift," she explained. "As bad as his days at school were, he got up each morning happy and forgiv-ing of everything that had gone on the previous day, and ready to start fresh." But Larry's optimism had its limits. "Eventually he became more and more tied to his computer," his mother reflected. "He didn't like to leave the house, he didn't play sports, he wasn't involved in school activi-ties, and he had no friends. He said he didn't care about his lack of friend-ships but we knew he did. He just needed incentive and the right tools to give him some much-needed successes, no matter how small they were." This was the point when they brought him to PEERS.

Larry was an eager pupil, soaking in every new strategy like a sponge. A model for his fellow group members, he took the program very seriously and expected others to do the same. The lessons on bullying he listened to with intense curiosity and quiet reflection. You could metaphorically see the wheels turning in his mind. Each week he reported back the exquisite details of his practice attempts to use the skills. He was the model PEERS participant—always completing his practice assignments with enthusiasm and optimism. Not surprisingly, he excelled at learning the skills.

Now no longer the target of physical bullying and armed with a plethora of friends, Larry is a true success story. In thinking of the man he's become, his mother commented, "He's barely recognizable now as the child I just described. All that remains is that beautiful optimism that he has somehow held onto throughout all the adversity of his 'previous' life. He knows what it's like to persevere through the hard times, and that is also something helping him cope with living away from home right now." Larry is now nineteen years old, attending college far from home, and happily flourishing in his freshman year—the ghosts of his former life a thing of the past. With pride his mother shared, "He laughed after his first semester of college ended when he said 'Mom, I'm the kid who never even went to camp for a few days, and now I'm living three thousand miles away at college.' He's proud of himself. And he should be!"

Larry's story is like countless others. No longer the innocent victim of bullying, this socially challenged teen blossomed into a confident young man, ready to face the world on his own. If your teen or young adult has also fallen victim to the frightening and lonely world of bullying, and you fear that he or she may never escape, think of Larry's inspirational story of hope and perseverance.

STRATEGIES FOR HANDLING PHYSICAL BULLYING
Chapter Summary for Teens and Young Adults

> The following information is intended to be read by teens and young adults and contains a brief summary of the chapter.

Over the last several chapters, we've talked about different kinds of bullying such as teasing, cyber bullying, and rumors and gossip. In this chapter, we focused on physical bullying, which includes anything from someone throwing bits of paper at you, to tripping you in the hall, to stealing or damaging your personal items, to even more violent things such as shoving, kicking, hitting, pushing, or even fighting. It's important for you to understand the differences between physical bullying and other kinds of bullying because the strategies you'll need to use will be completely different.

We know that this topic can be pretty upsetting to talk about and we know that lots of teens and young adults have been tormented by bullying. Maybe you're one of them. Like so many of the things we've talked about here, you're not alone. Countless teens and young adults have been the innocent victims of bullying, often feeling defenseless and unprotected. That's not okay and that's why we're here to help. Although we know how miserable it can feel to be pushed around and taken advantage of, we're actually not going to talk about what it feels like to be bullied. Instead, we're going to focus on what you can do to make it less likely that you get bullied in the future. If you feel like you need to talk about what these experiences have been like for you, talking to your parent or some other supportive adult might be a good start.

Before we talk about the specific tactics you can use to handle physical bullying, let's think about what you've been told to do in the past. What do most older adults tell teens and young adults to do in response to physical bullying? You're usually told to either tell someone (such as a teacher) or fight back. Although telling someone that can help is always a good option if you're in danger or the bullying is too difficult to manage on your own—what could be the problem with telling an adult if someone were simply throwing bits of paper at you in class? Although that's mean and certainly not okay, if you told a teacher or some other adult, the bully would probably get in trouble and want to retaliate against you. Now you've made your situation even worse. What if you were to fight back? Someone could get hurt,

(continued)

you could get in trouble, and you may even get a bad reputation. So instead of doing those things, we're going to share some ideas that teens and young adults who've been successful at decreasing or eliminating physical bullying have done.

Avoid the Bully

One of the best strategies for handling physical bullying is to avoid the bully. That means you need to stay out of reach of the bully. For example, if the bully hangs out in a certain area of the lunchroom, avoid that area. If the bully has a locker in a certain hallway, avoid walking down that hall. Or if the bully likes to hang out in a certain part of campus, avoid that part of campus when you can. If the bully can't find you, he can't bully you.

Lay Low When the Bully Is Around

One of the mistakes some teens and young adults make is they draw attention to themselves when the bully is around. They make jokes or act silly when the bully is near, putting them in the spotlight and reminding the bully of their presence. Instead of drawing attention to yourself, you need to keep a low profile and try to fly under the radar when the bully is around. If the bully doesn't notice you, he's less likely to bully you.

Don't Provoke the Bully

You also want to make sure you don't provoke the bully. That means you shouldn't tease or make fun of the bully and you should avoid annoying or embarrassing the bully in any way. When bullies become annoyed or embarrassed they feel provoked and will often retaliate with violence. So the strategies you learned for handling verbal teasing such as saying, "Whatever" or "Yeah and?" or "Your point is?" shouldn't be used with anyone who has a tendency to get violent because they'll embarrass the bully, and you could end up getting hurt.

Don't Police the Bully

Another mistake teens and young adults sometimes make is that they police the bully. Remember that policing is when you point out mistakes that other people make. No one likes it when you police, especially not bullies. You're more likely to be the target of bullying and physical attacks if you police others, so don't point out minor mistakes or offenses. That means if the bully is passing notes in class, cheating on an exam, or shows up late for work, it's not your job to tell on him or her. It's none of your business and will only cause you problems because the bully will want to get back at you. However, if the bully brings a weapon to school or work or is threatening physical violence—that's a different story. Then you should tell someone in authority such as a teacher or a supervisor but never let the bully find out you told or you could be in danger of retaliation.

Don't Try to Make Friends with the Bully

Another common mistake is trying to make friends with the bully. This is a horrible strategy because it usually only draws attention to you and opens you up to being taken advantage of and exploited by the bully. Some bullies will pretend to be your friend but really they're just trying to manipulate you or get something out of you. Bullies are rarely good friends anyway—so don't make the mistake of trying to become buddies. It doesn't work and will probably just make things worse for you. Plus, you could get a bad reputation for just hanging out with the bully.

Hang Out with Other People

Remember when we talked about cyber bullying and we asked the question, "Whom do bullies like to pick on, people who are by themselves or in a group?" The answer was, of course, that bullies like to pick on people who are by themselves because they're easier targets. When you're alone, you look unprotected

(continued)

and weak, so you're more likely to be bullied. However, if you hang out with other people, you're less likely to be bullied because there are people who could have your back and stick up for you. So if you want to avoid being bullied, make sure you eat lunch with a friend (or even an acquaintance), walk to class with a peer, travel to and from school with a classmate or a sibling, and so on. Hanging out with other people is one of the most powerful strategies for avoiding physical bullying.

Stay Near Authority Figures When the Bully Is Around

Another great tactic for avoiding physical bullying is to stay near adults or authority figures when the bully is around. This is a good strategy because most bullies wouldn't pull any tricks when there's someone near that could punish them. Even just standing or sitting near an adult or authority figure will probably keep the bully away for the time being. That doesn't mean you should go up and start talking to the lunch monitor or walk to class with the campus security guard. You should just stay near authority figures when the bully is around to prevent physical attacks in the moment.

Get Help from a Supportive Adult When in Danger

Our final strategy for handling physical bullying is to get help from a supportive adult when you're in danger or when the other strategies aren't working for you. That means if you feel physically threatened, you should talk to your parent, teacher, professor, supervisor, or some supportive adult whom you trust. Or if the physical bullying feels never-ending and the strategies we've described previously don't seem to be working, that's also a good time to get some additional help. You shouldn't feel embarrassed about asking for help. We all need help from time to time. So if you feel threatened, like you could be in danger, or you need help stopping the bullying because nothing seems to be working, you shouldn't wait. Get help right away and remember you're not alone in this!

CHAPTER EXERCISES
for Teens, Young Adults, and Parents

Teens and young adults should complete the following exercises with parents:

- Review the information about strategies for handling physical bullying outlined in this chapter with your parent.
  - Have a discussion with your parent about whether you or someone you know has ever experienced physical bullying.
  - Identify a few strategies you or someone you know might use to effectively handle physical bullying now or in the future.

14

Changing a Bad Reputation

MANY TEENS AND YOUNG ADULTS with a history of peer rejection are besieged by bad reputations, which may make it difficult for them to make and keep friends. In our experience through the UCLA PEERS Clinic, some parents take offense to the use of the word *reputation* because they associate it with things like doing drugs or being sexually promiscuous. Although that association may have been true when the parents we work with were themselves teenagers, the term *reputation* is now used more broadly by teens to include a general opinion or impression about a person held by the larger peer group. It involves specific characteristics, traits, habits, or abilities that are attributed to the person. Reputations can be good or bad. For those with a history of peer rejection, their reputation is often bad. For those with a history of social neglect, their reputation may be nonexistent.

The thorny issue about reputations is that teens and young adults typically get their reputations based on whom they hang out with. So when someone has a bad reputation, very few people want to be friends with him or her for fear of getting a bad reputation by association. This means that if your teen or young adult is struggling with a bad reputation, it may be harder for him or her to make and keep friends until this reputation has died down.

> *If your teen or young adult is struggling with a bad reputation, it may be harder for him or her to make and keep friends until this reputation has died down.*

Knowing how to help your teen or young adult escape a bad reputation can feel like an impossible challenge. Wanting to help him or her flee or get a fresh start are common reactions. So what do you think most parents do to help their child break away from a bad reputation? Many well-intentioned parents will try to help by changing schools. Perhaps you've done the same. The idea is that with a new school comes the opportunity for a new beginning. Sadly, the problem with this strategy is that the bad reputation often follows the person. Perhaps the teen or young adult lives in a community where students from the new school know students from the old school. In this case, the reputation follows him or her through the metaphorical grapevine, where rumors and gossip are spread by word of mouth. Another explanation is that the teen or young adult continues to engage in the behaviors that caused the bad reputation in the first place. Maybe he or she has a bad habit of policing or being a conversation hog. Perhaps your teen or young adult has a reputation for doing something similar. The problem then is that what gives your teen or young adult a reputation in one place is likely to give him or her the same reputation in another place if it goes unaddressed. In this case, simply changing schools or places of work are not always effective ways for overcoming your teen or young adult's reputation. Changing the behaviors associated with the reputation is the first step. That's what we've been working on for the last thirteen chapters. Finding an accepting source of friends with common interests is another step. That's what we worked on all the way back in chapter 2. Our next step will be to work on changing your teen or young adult's reputation in the current social setting, which is the focus of this chapter.

> *Simply changing schools or places of work are not always effective ways for overcoming your teen or young adult's reputation.*

To begin with, we need to figure out what your teen or young adult's reputation is. Most teens and young adults (if they're not experiencing significant social neglect) have some type of a reputation with their peers. Even shy or withdrawn teens and young adults will at least be known for being shy and withdrawn, which doesn't constitute a bad reputation. It's those experiencing peer rejection who often have the bad reputations, usually preventing them from making and keeping friends within their social surroundings. If your teen or young adult is one of the many struggling with a bad reputation, it will be critical to help him or her find a source of friends outside the unaccepting social network, at least until his or her reputation dies down. We hope this is something you've been working on since reading chapter 2, but if you're still struggling to figure out if your teen or young adult has a bad reputation, you may want to revisit the questions outlined in chapter 2 in the section called "Understanding and Determining Your Child's Reputation."

If after careful thought, you've determined that your teen or young adult seems to be struggling with a bad reputation, don't despair. There are things you can do to help. Sharing the ecologically valid steps followed by teens and young adults who've been able to successfully change their reputation will be a big part of that help. Changing a bad reputation is a lengthy process, requiring time and patience. So in the meantime, you'll also need to help identify an appropriate source of friends outside of the setting where your teen or young adult is struggling, at least until his or her reputation calms down. Remember that chapter 2 provides a comprehensive plan for finding sources of friends through extracurricular activities and social hobbies. When a bad reputation is involved, the source of friends will probably be found in the community, far from where your teen or young adult is already known.

Now that you generally know what you've got to do, before we talk about how to do it, let's take a moment to decompress. Similar to our discussions about peer rejection and bullying, the topic of bad reputations can be understandably emotional for parents. No one wants to imagine his or her child feeling ostracized or disliked. You want your teen or young adult to feel accepted and valued, just like he or she deserves. You want others to see the wonderful and special qualities he or she possesses, to appreciate his or her differences rather than reject them. You want people to care for your son or daughter the way you do. We want that, too. The focus of this chapter is on helping you and your teen or young adult overcome one of the greatest social barriers he or she may face: a bad reputation. If that sounds daunting, believe it or not, it doesn't have to be. It's never easy to change a bad reputation and it's never quick—but it can be done. We've seen it happen countless times in our work with families through our clinic. Like Michael, who had a bad reputation for policing, whose mother encouraged him to join the debate team (the one place he was allowed to police), where he made several new friends, and whose love for politics and debate eventually led him to run for student council where he won a seat as a class representative! Or Michelle, who had a bad reputation for being a conversation hog, but whose parents helped her enroll in an anime club where she made several new friends who were very happy to trade information about her favorite interest, and whose love for comic books and anime has not only led to a successful career as a graphic design illustrator but has opened up a new social world of comic book conventions with other self-proclaimed anime geeks! These are just two quick snapshots of what's possible.

Steps for Changing a Bad Reputation

The following steps have been used by teens and young adults who've been successful at changing their reputations.

1. Lay Low

The first step in changing a reputation is to lay low. This means your teen or young adult will need to fly under the radar for a bit, not drawing attention to him- or herself. Consider laying low a cooling-off period, when your teen or young adult is giving his or her reputation the opportunity to die down. In this step, the order of business is staying out of sight for a while—not doing anything that will put the focus of attention on him or her. If done correctly, your teen or young adult's peers will slowly and gradually forget all about his or her bad reputation during this step.

> Consider laying low a cooling-off period, when your teen or young adult is giving his or her reputation the opportunity to die down.

Although this step may sound rather simple, the laying-low period can be relatively challenging for certain teens and young adults. Many who struggle with a bad reputation engage (either knowingly or unknowingly) in unusual behaviors found unacceptable by the larger peer group. These behaviors might involve talking incessantly (being a conversation hog), being intrusive when joining group conversations, using inappropriate humor, or engaging in other strange or socially unacceptable behavior.

If your teen or young adult is attempting to change his or her reputation, it will be important to stop this kind of behavior immediately and keep a low profile for a period of time—an adjustment that may be difficult for some. The length of time needed to lay low will vary from person to person, but it's usually no less than a few months. Summer break from school can be a good time to lay low because there are usually fewer social interactions with the larger peer group during that time. During the school year, a semester term might be enough time, but the length of the laying-low period will be directly related to the severity of the reputation, with more negative reputations requiring more cooling-off time.

Although some may find it difficult to alter certain behaviors or habits during the laying-low period, if your teen or young adult's goal is to make and keep friends, then he or she will need to be motivated to try. Whereas some of the behaviors associated with social differences may make it difficult for teens and young adults to avoid drawing attention to themselves, using the social skills described in this book will help in this process.

2. Follow the Crowd

During the period of time when your teen or young adult is laying low, he or she will also need to follow the crowd. The buzz phrase, *"follow the crowd,"* refers to following the social norms established by the larger peer group rather than trying to go against them. When your teen or young adult is following the crowd, he or she is just trying to fit in and not stand out in any unusual way. If you suspect your teen or young adult is doing anything outwardly that is attracting negative attention, this behavior will need to be stopped if he or she is going to fit in and follow the crowd. To highlight this point, consider the following three examples:

- Imagine a teenage boy who isn't mandated to wear a school uniform, yet he wears the same clothes to school every day, attracting negative attention and embarrassing feedback from his peers. This pattern of unusual behavior will have to stop if his reputation is going to change. It's hard to lay low if people are commenting on your clothes every day.
- Picture a teenage girl who has a tendency to repeat lines or jokes from her favorite TV show, with no apparent reason or context.

Her behavior, which is chastised by her peers, will also have to stop in order to change her reputation. Attracting negative attention is no way to keep a low profile.

- Visualize a young man who has issues with hygiene. He doesn't bathe regularly, doesn't wear deodorant, and constantly smells of body odor. His behavior, rebuked by his peers, will also need to be altered during this cooling-off period if he's to successfully change his reputation.

> *When your teen or young adult is following the crowd, he or she is just trying to fit in and not stand out in any unusual way.*

Social coaching tip: Similar to laying low, this particular step may be difficult for certain teens and young adults with social differences. In the event that your teen or young adult is unable to change certain behaviors, which seem to be contributing to a bad reputation, you may need to consider helping him or her find an alternative source of friends separate from the place where the negative reputation exists. But if these behaviors are within your teen or young adult's control, then it will be important to follow the crowd and fit in as much as possible if changing his or her reputation is the goal.

Social coaching tip: If your teen or young adult isn't interested in changing the behaviors associated with his or her bad reputation or doesn't really care what others think, then there's nothing you can do to force him or her to follow these steps. As frustrating as that may be, your teen or young adult's motivation to change how people see him or her will be the key to making all of this work.

3. Change Your Look

After going through a period of laying low, following the crowd, and stopping any unusual behaviors that may have been contributing to a bad reputation, the next step is for your teen or young adult to alter his or her look in some dramatic way that demonstrates a change. This step—which should not be attempted until you're confident that your teen or young adult's reputation has died down—involves doing something dramatic to get the attention back on him or her.

Changing your look is somewhat akin to a makeover, which is a way of changing one's appearance to reflect a new image. In our experience through the UCLA PEERS Clinic, teens and young adults who've been successful at changing their reputations have done a variety of things to change their look including getting new haircuts, wearing different clothes, getting new eyeglasses or contact lenses, wearing cosmetics for girls, and even losing weight or becoming more fit. This step usually requires assistance from parents and family members, so you'll need to consider how to best support your teen or young adult and think of some good ways to change his or her look to draw positive attention. However, if your teen or young adult chooses to change his or her look, be sure that the new look fits the social norms of his or her school or workplace. The idea is still to fit in and not stand out in some unusual way.

> *Changing your look is somewhat akin to a makeover, which is a way of changing one's appearance to reflect a new image.*

The reason this step is so important is that after a period of cooling down (when you hope people have forgotten all about your teen or young adult's bad reputation), something dramatic and positive has to happen to get the attention back. Getting this attention back is critical because it creates an opportunity to show people that your teen or young adult is different. Changing your look on the outside gives the impression that something has changed on the inside—that the negative impressions others used to hold are no longer valid because they no longer exist. Your teen or young adult's new look will essentially be a physical representation of his or her new self.

> *Changing your look on the outside gives the impression that something has changed on the inside—that the negative impressions others used to hold are no longer valid because they no longer exist.*

To underscore the importance of changing your look to change your reputation, think of the three examples from the previous discussion. Imagine these three young people had successfully laid low for a period of months. During that time, they each followed the crowd either by not wearing the same outfit every day, no longer reciting dialogue from a favorite TV show, or improving hygiene by bathing regularly and using deodorant. Now each wants to change his or her look in some dramatic way to get the attention back and show others that they're different. Perhaps each gets a new hairstyle, replaces old glasses with new, cooler frames, and wears new clothes, presumably reflecting a new sense of self. What do you think their peers will do when they notice this change? Most socially engaged teens and young adults are interested in their surroundings and will notice when someone or something has changed. So when they notice that someone has changed his or her look, more inquisitive members are likely to approach and comment on these changes. They do this because they're naturally curious and want to be in-the-know—to have inside information about something others are noticing and talking about. So what will they say when they approach? They'll most likely begin by commenting on the new look. If the job was done correctly, these comments should be flattering. At this point, they're also likely to point out whatever negative reputation used to exist. For example, they might say something like the following:

- "Hey, you got some new clothes. I remember you used to wear the same thing every day. That was kinda weird, but this new look is working for you."
- "I like this new look. You seem different, like you've changed or something. Remember how you used to quote bits from *Family Guy* all the time? You were a trip."
- "Look at you. You cleaned yourself up. Looks like you washed your hair and stuff. You seriously used to reek but you look good now."

Although these kinds of compliments are all clearly backhanded and could easily make anyone feel defensive and self-protective, your teen or young adult's reaction to the mention of his or her previous reputation will literally make or break success in changing that reputation. Therefore, the next step is particularly vital.

4. Own Up to Your Previous Reputation

Once your teen or young adult has brought about some positive attention by changing his or her look, it will be critical to own up to any mention of his or her previous reputation. Backhanded compliments, which are essentially insults disguised as compliments (sometimes intentional and sometimes inadvertent), are usually pretty common around this time. It's essential that when confronted with references to his or her bad reputation (even in the form of backhanded compliments), your teen or young adult own up to these interpretations. That doesn't mean he or she needs to agree with negative comments from others. Instead, simply acknowledge that these perceptions existed but point out that things are different now. This might be communicated by saying things like the following:

- "Yeah, I know I used to do that but not anymore."
- "I know that's what people thought about me, but I'm kind of different now."
- "Yeah, I've heard that before, but things are kind of different now."

Owning up to a previous reputation will show others that your teen or young adult may in fact be different. To illustrate this point, imagine that our three young people went in the opposite direction, and instead of owning up to their previous reputations, said something like, "No, I wasn't really like that. You just didn't know me." What would the other people think? They would probably think that nothing has changed at all—that these are in fact the same people, just cleaned up a bit. When people try to deny or disprove their previous reputation, they look defensive and unchanged. However, by simply acknowledging that this reputation existed but that he or she is now different, your teen or young adult will have more credibility in the pursuit of a new image and ultimately a new reputation.

> *Owning up to a previous reputation will show others that your teen or young adult may in fact be different.*

5. Find an Accepting Social Group

Once through the lengthy process of laying low, following the crowd, changing your look, and owning up to your previous reputation, the next step is to find an accepting social group. This doesn't mean that your teen or young adult gets to be friends with the most popular kids in school or the coolest people at work—it just means that now there's a better chance of finding a social group that will accept him or her. Remember, when someone has a bad reputation, very few people will want to be friends with that person for fear that they'll also get that reputation. Now that your teen or young adult has successfully escaped the previous reputation, as long as he or she continues to engage in socially accepted behaviors and avoids doing the things that contributed to the previous reputation, he or she is more likely to find a source of accepting friends. Of course, the most appropriate and accepting social group will probably be a group of people with common interests. For a refresher on choosing appropriate friends, chapter 2 provides comprehensive suggestions for finding a social group.

> *Of course, the most appropriate and accepting social group will probably be a group of people with common interests.*

Social coaching tip: Now that you know the steps for changing a bad reputation, you can begin to work with your teen or young adult on the long process of working toward that goal, if relevant. It will be critical for you to provide assistance during this transformation. Changing a reputation is rarely an individual endeavor for teens and young adults with social difficulties and will definitely require additional support. Families who've gone through the UCLA PEERS Clinic have sometimes enlisted extra help from siblings, cousins, family friends, and even personal shoppers (whose services are sometimes free at major department stores).

What about Individuality?

It's probably worth mentioning that in our experience most families are grateful for the information provided in this chapter and are eager to begin the process of helping their teen or young adult change his or her reputation. Yet some families are less receptive to this information. One criticism of this strategy (more often communicated by parents rather than teens or young adults) relates to the steps "following the crowd" and "changing your look" and their relevance to the concept of individuality.

Technically speaking, individuality is a state of being independent and separate from others while possessing your own interests, goals, and self-expression. Although individuality is certainly an important characteristic of personality, contributing to a sense of self, if this individuality is causing harm by creating an inability to make and keep friends, a difficult choice might have to be made. If your teen or young adult's first priority is to make and keep friends, then he or she may be more willing to make the changes prescribed in this chapter. However, if your teen or young adult's first priority is to maintain individuality, then he or she may be less inclined to make these changes. Either way, the steps involved in changing a bad reputation are an individual choice—not to be forced on anyone. Regardless of your personal preferences or what you believe to be good for your teen or young adult, the choice to use these steps will be in the hands of your son or daughter, just as is true for all of the skills taught in this book.

Regardless of your personal preferences or what you believe to be good for your teen or young adult, the choice to use these steps will be in the hands of your son or daughter, just as is true for all of the skills taught in this book.

Be Patient: This May Take Some Time

Although the steps outlined in the current chapter may suggest a certain degree of simplicity, there's nothing simple or easy about changing a reputation. It's a long process that requires a great deal of effort. That means you and your teen or young adult need to be prepared to be patient. You also need to be ready to work hard because many of the changes require a lot of extra effort. However, if your teen or young adult follows the steps provided in this chapter and uses the other skills taught in this book, he or she has a far greater chance of changing how others perceive him or her and ultimately finding a source of meaningful friendships.

Success Story: Chandra Changes Her Reputation

Many teens and young adults with social challenges struggle with bad reputations—often the direct result of the social errors they make. They may police others, hog conversations, or use humor inappropriately. They may enter conversations in an intrusive manner or perseverate on topics of personal interest. Whatever the causes of these bad reputations, many find it difficult to escape them once fully formed. This was true for twelve-year-old Chandra, who struggled with making friends. Diagnosed with social anxiety disorder prior to coming to PEERS, according to her mother, "Chandra couldn't talk on the phone, order a meal in a restaurant, or hold a conversation with someone outside of the family. Her constant struggle to fit in was heartbreaking." Apart from her social anxiety, Chandra also struggled with a bad reputation. Known for her social awkwardness, sadly few of her classmates wanted to be her friend. This concern was what brought her and her family to PEERS.

"Throughout the program," her mother explained, "she was forced to talk to kids on the phone and learn to have conversations. I never realized that to many kids, learning to have a conversation is like learning a foreign language. Chandra went through the program and took the lessons and experiences she had there to heart." Although Chandra improved her social skills over time, she still struggled to break free from her reputation. It was like a shadow that followed her wherever she went—an invisible barrier to making new friends. So with the help of her mother, "Chandra decided to reinvent herself and enter her first year of high school as a different person. A lesson she learned from PEERS." Her mother explained, "She changed her hairstyle, bought new clothes, and started joining clubs, including varsity golf, the swim team, and the color guard." She recalled proudly, "Chandra had lots of opportunities to 'trade information' with the new kids she met at band camp, a requirement for color guard. She actually used that language when she told me about it. Another PEERS lesson that she remembered." Three years after going through PEERS, Chandra has turned a corner and escaped her previous reputation. Her mother reflected, "Chandra has made a wonderful transformation in high school. She has made lots of friends and has an active social life. Her whole life has changed."

Success stories like these are possible because of the hard work and dedication of devoted parents like Chandra's mother. Learning the skills needed to make friends and handle rejection is the first step. Putting those skills into practice is the next step. Without dedicated parents like you, transformations like Chandra's would more likely be a wish rather than a reality. If you, too, are concerned about your teen or young adult's reputation, we hope you will follow the steps outlined in this chapter and more broadly in this book so that you, too, can revel in your own success story.

STEPS FOR CHANGING A BAD REPUTATION
Chapter Summary for Teens and Young Adults

The following information is intended to be read by teens and young adults and contains a brief summary of the chapter.

One of the biggest social barriers you can face in the pursuit of friendships is having a bad reputation. Having a reputation means that people know about you before they even meet you. Sometimes your reputation isn't a good reflection of who you truly are, which can be really frustrating—especially because that can make it hard for you to make and keep friends. When that happens, you might need to take steps for changing your reputation. That's what this chapter is all about.

Before we get into the steps for changing your reputation, you first need to think about whether you feel accepted by your classmates or your coworkers. If you're not sure, you might want to go back and take a look at table 2.2 in chapter 2, which goes over the signs of acceptance and lack of acceptance from social groups. If you're not feeling that accepted by the people you're trying to make friends with, try not to worry. We know it feels bad when you don't feel a part of the group (especially when you feel like you're not getting a fair shot), maybe because your reputation isn't the greatest. The good news is that if you're interested in trying to change how people see you in the future, we've uncovered the steps that teens and young adults who've been successful at changing their reputations have used. Following these steps takes time and you're going to need some help from your parent or some supportive adult, but if you're patient and work at it using the other strategies you've learned in this book, you have a good shot at a fresh start! If you're interested, the steps are listed in this section. Make sure you follow them in the order listed.

(continued)

1. Lay Low

The first step in changing your reputation is to lay low. This means you're going to need to fly under the radar and not draw a lot of attention to yourself for a while. This is like a cooling-off period when you're letting your reputation die down. If you do this step right, people are supposed to forget all about you for a bit. This step usually take several months, sometimes as long as a semester, maybe even longer. Summer break from school can be a good time to lay low. Lots of people come back from summer break completely transformed, like a fresh start. Whenever you choose to lay low, it's important that you don't completely give up on trying to make friends and be social. Instead, you might try making friends with people outside of the place where you're concerned about your reputation. Maybe join a club or social activity in the community where people don't know or care about your reputation.

2. Follow the Crowd

While you're laying low, you're also going to need to follow the crowd. This means you don't want to stand out from everyone else in some unusual way if you can help it. Instead, you want to try to fit in with everyone else as much as you can. For example, if you've been paying attention to your embarrassing feedback and you're discovering that there are certain things that people are making fun of you about, that might be something you need to work on to follow the crowd. Of course, it's totally up to you whether you do this or not. The way you choose to act, dress, or present yourself to other people is a personal choice and completely your decision. So don't feel like you're being forced into anything. We're just sharing the steps that teens and young adults have used to change their reputations. Like everything else in this book, it's up to you what you do with this information.

3. Change Your Look

After going through a long period of laying low, while following the crowd and stopping any unusual behaviors that might have been hurting your reputation, the next step is to alter your look in some dramatic way that shows you've changed. Changing your look is more than a makeover—it's your way of showing people that you're different. When you change your appearance in some specific way, it alerts people that something about you is different. They start to notice you again and pay attention. Teens and young adults we've worked with have done things such as getting new haircuts, wearing different clothes, getting new eyeglasses or contact lenses, wearing makeup for girls, and even losing weight or becoming more fit. This step will probably require help from your parent, so it's good he or she is working with you on these strategies. Changing your look is an important step in the process of transforming how people see you. However you decide to change your look, you need to be sure that it still fits in with the group you're trying to change your reputation with. Otherwise, this step wouldn't make much sense and would only make you stand out it some odd way, not really changing your reputation in a good way in the end.

4. Own Up to Your Previous Reputation

One of the things that will happen really soon after you change your look is that your classmates or your coworkers are going to notice this change and start to check you out. The more curious ones will actually come up to you and start commenting on your new look, asking you questions to figure out what's different about you. They do this because they like to be in-the-know. Lots of teens and young adults like to know things that people are noticing and talking about. It gives them

(continued)

a kind of power to be in-the-know. So when you show up one day looking different, they're going to approach you and want to figure you out. They'll probably comment on whatever is different about you, but they're also likely to mention something about your reputation from before. This can sound like a backhanded compliment. That's when someone gives you a compliment sort of wrapped in an insult. For example, they might say, "Hey, you got some new clothes. I remember you used to wear the same thing every day. That was kind of weird but you look good now." Even though comments like that can be upsetting, the way you react to them is the critical ingredient to making this work. Instead of getting defensive and trying to prove that the person is wrong, you need to own up to your previous reputation. That doesn't mean you need to agree with them. It only means that you need to admit that people thought that about you but you're different now. In response, you might say something like, "Yeah, I know I used to do that but not anymore." Or more generally you might say something like, "Yeah, I know people used to say that about me but I'm different now." By not getting defensive and instead owning up to what people thought of you, they're more likely to think you've changed. If you say something like, "I didn't do that!" or "You just didn't know me!" they're going to think it's the same old you with a new haircut or the same old you with some new clothes—and then you've lost your opportunity to change your reputation. Instead, just own up to your previous reputation and show them that you're different from what they thought.

5. Find an Accepting Social Group

Once you've gone through the lengthy process of laying low, following the crowd, changing your look, and owning up to your previous reputation, the last step is to find an accepting social group. This doesn't mean you get to be friends with the most popular people at school or work; it just means that now you've got a better shot at making friends with people you have common interests with. If you're not sure which social groups to try to join, go back and take a look at the chapter exercises from chapter 2 to identify some good sources of friends.

CHAPTER EXERCISES
for Teens, Young Adults, and Parents

Teens and young adults should complete the following exercises with parents:

- Discuss the steps for changing a reputation outlined in this chapter with your parent.
  - Decide whether you're interested in changing your reputation.
  - If you decide to change your reputation, with the help of your parent, begin to follow the steps outlined in this chapter.
    - It's highly recommended that during the laying-low period you find a source of friends unaware or unconcerned with your reputation and use the skills you've learned in this book with that new group of people. Your parent can help!

EPILOGUE
Moving Forward

Friendship is the best medicine.

AS WE REACH OUR FINAL PAGES, I am reminded of a quote a parent once shared with me. It was the end of a PEERS training and the mother of a teenage boy who had struggled his whole life with making and keeping friends shared this story. She said that her son had been medicated through-out much of his life for anxiety and depression. He had gone through a long list of psychotropic medications, yet none had worked very well for him. For years he lived in social isolation, wishing he could be like the other kids, wanting to have friends but just not sure how to go about it. Blaming his social challenges on his anxiety and depression, he had nearly given up. Then at last—he had success! He managed to make some friends. Suddenly his anxiety and depression didn't feel so insurmount-able. In the end, her son declared, "Friendship is the best medicine!" We happen to agree.

Is the Program Working For You?

By now you and your child have become familiar with the contents of this book by reading the chapter summaries for teens and young adults; you have practiced the strategies by following the chapter exercises; and you have allowed sufficient time for the seeds of friendship to grow.

For those who have followed the guidelines outlined in this book, many of you will find that your son or daughter is well on the way to developing meaningful relationships. We have seen hundreds of teens, young adults, and their families benefit from this program. We hope you are one of them.

For those of you who've followed the guidelines in this book but have been less successful at helping your teen or young adult make and keep friends, let's consider what potential barriers might be getting in the way.

Potential Barriers to Social Success

Although there may be many reasons why someone may still be struggling, in our experience working with families through the UCLA PEERS Clinic, the most common obstacles to making and keeping friends after going through this training relate to one or more of the following: negative reputation among peers, inability to find a source of friends, or lack of social motivation.

Negative Reputation among Peers

Recall the behavioral signs for peer rejection identified in chapter 2. If you suspect that your teen or young adult has a bad reputation among his or her peers but has been attempting to engage these same peers using the skills outlined in this book, this choice in potential friends might explain the lack of success with the program. If you're concerned that your teen or young adult may have a bad reputation, you'll need to become familiar with the ecologically valid steps for changing a reputation outlined in chapter 14. Although changing a reputation is a lengthy process, requiring time and patience, if your teen or young adult is going to be socially successful, you will need to fully engage in this transformation and help him or her find a new source of friends in the interim.

Inability to Find a Source of Friends

Lack of social success at this point might also be explained by an inability to find a source of friends. Consider whether your teen or young adult has identified and engaged an accepting social group with common interests at school or work. Also consider whether your teen or young adult is currently enrolled in an extracurricular activity or social hobby that meets regularly (at least once a week) and includes peers that do the following:

- Are accepting of your teen or young adult
- Are similar in age
- Are similar in developmental level
- Share common interests
- Are not familiar with your teen or young adult's bad reputation (if he or she has one)

If not, you might consider going back to chapter 2, reviewing the strategies for finding and choosing appropriate friends and try helping your teen or young adult find an appropriate source of potential friends. For those also struggling with a bad reputation, this source of friends will likely be found in the community, far from the place where he or she has a negative reputation.

Lack of Social Motivation

Lack of motivation to use the tools in this book on the part of your teen or young adult may be another barrier to social success. As mentioned in the preface to this book, motivated teens and young adults interested in learning the skills necessary to make and keep friends are those who are most likely to benefit from what this book has to offer, whereas less motivated teens and young adults aren't as likely to profit from our tools. Unfortunately, regardless of your eagerness to help, without the buy-in of your teen or young adult, helping him or her to make and keep friends may feel like a painful uphill battle. We see in working with families of teens and young adults reluctant to learn and practice the skills we teach, that the experience can be extremely frustrating for parents. You want to do right by your kids, you want to see them flourish, and you worry for their futures. You know how important it is to have friends and close relationships and maybe you worry that your teen or young adult will never have those kinds of relationships. As frustrating as all of that may feel, it's also important to remember that friendship is a choice— you don't get to be friends with everyone, and everyone doesn't get to be friends with you. An extension of this saying is, *you don't have to be friends with anyone if you choose because friendship is a choice all the way around.* It's a tough pill to swallow, but what that means is if your teen or young adult isn't motivated to make and keep friends or doesn't want to use the skills in this book, ultimately that's his or her choice.

As hard as that choice may be to face, remember that your role in this process was to provide relevant information and opportunities for practice around the skills needed for making and keeping friends for your son or daughter. Teens and young adults were given the freedom to choose what to do with the information and whether to follow these guidelines. The information contained in this book is conveyed in the same spirit. We're simply providing readers with information based on scientific evidence of what works and what doesn't work socially. You get to decide what to do with it if anything.

If you or your teen or young adult have been struggling to get motivated to put these skills to work, at the very least remember that knowledge is power. You may not have hit the ground running, but when you do take those first steps, standing on your own may be easier with the knowledge and support of these helpful tools.

Will My Child Change His or Her Mind about Making Friends?

At the UCLA PEERS Clinic we often follow our clients for months and years after they receive training. In our long-term, follow-up studies with these teens and young adults, we've found that the vast majority not only get better after going through our program but also continue to improve months and even years after treatment. Although continued social success is the norm in PEERS (most likely because of continued parent involvement in making sure the skills are used), some families don't completely benefit immediately following training. Yet, among those who were initially less successful with the program (typically no more than 10 percent of our families), many eventually adopted the strategies taught in PEERS and began to come out of their shells. We fondly call this group of teens and young adults our *late bloomers* and they probably make up about 5 percent of the families we work with. These are the clients who don't begin to benefit from our program until after the intervention is over.

In the event that your teen or young adult isn't interested in learning or using these skills at this time, we recommend that you save the tools and strategies contained in this book for a later time when things may change and the seeds of friendship are ready to sprout. When that time comes (we hope in the near future), you'll be prepared to offer the same social coaching, with lots of support, so your late bloomer can blossom like so many before.

MOVING FORWARD
for Teens, Young Adults, and Parents

The following information is intended to be read by teens and young adults and includes some final thoughts for moving forward.

As the old adage goes, there is no greater gift than friendship. Yet many teens and young adults with social difficulties struggle with making and keeping friends. Throughout this book, we've become familiar with the major components essential toward developing and maintaining meaningful relationships. It's important to remember that friendship is a choice, that we don't need to be friends with everyone, and everyone doesn't need to be friends with us. Among other things, we've learned the following:

- We know that friendships are based on common interests. These shared interests are the things we talk about and the things we do together.
- We now know that in order to make and keep friends, we need to find common interests, and the way we do that is by trading information.
- We've learned that trading information is a way of describing the act of having a good conversation, which includes verbal and nonverbal forms of communication.
- We've learned the steps for starting individual conversations and entering group conversations, assessing when we're accepted, and knowing how to exit conversations when we need to.

(continued)

- We understand the components of being a good sport and having successful get-togethers, as well as how to use electronic communication for developing closer friendships.
- We've also learned how to handle conflict and rejection, critical coping skills needed for friendship protection and social survival.

As this book draws to a close, we find ourselves feeling like a friend at the end of a journey who has to say good-bye but who hopes to always stay in touch. We hope that you've learned these strategies for making and keeping friends and for having lasting social success. Although not everyone is guaranteed to receive the full benefit of the skills we offer, if you have followed the guidelines closely, received the recommended social coaching, and have been a willing pupil, then you should be well on the way to developing some potentially meaningful relationships. Assuming these skills continue to be used well into the future (we hope with continued support and social coaching), you can expect greater social success. This is what we've found in our research through the UCLA PEERS Clinic. Families who've gone through our program one to five years before not only continue to do well with making and keeping friends but also in many cases improve even further. We attribute this social success to the powerful combination of the parent and teen or young adult duo. So don't underestimate the work that you've done with your parent, and above all else, don't give up working just because this book is coming to a close.

Although our final chapter has come to an end, the book shouldn't close on making and keeping friends. Moving forward into the next chapter of your lives, you're now equipped with a new set of tools to navigate the social world. These tools are offered from scientists but think of us also as your partners and friends. Our ideas are based on scientific study uncovering the fundamental elements needed for developing and maintaining friendships. Using your new scientifically supported, ecologically valid social skills, you're closing the book on any antiquated notions that social behavior is an abstract art form, turning the page to a new chapter of social development—based on the science of making and keeping friends. We hope you will take us, our research, and our support with you wherever your journey takes you.

System Requirements

PC with Microsoft Windows 2003 or later
Mac with Apple OS version 10.1 or later

Using the DVD with Windows

To view the items located on the DVD, insert the DVD into your computer's DVD drive or your DVD player.

If you do not have autorun enabled on your computer, or if the autorun window does not appear, follow these steps to access the DVD:

1. Click Start ⟶ Run.
2. In the dialog box that appears, type d:\start.exe, where d is the letter of your DVD drive. This brings up the autorun window.
3. Choose the desired option from the menu.

In Case of Trouble

If you experience difficulty using the DVD, please follow these steps:

1. Make sure your hardware and systems configurations conform to the systems requirements noted under "System Requirements" above.
2. Review the installation procedure for your type of hardware and operating system. It is possible to reinstall the software if necessary.

To speak with someone in Product Technical Support, call 800-762-2974 or 317-572-3994 Monday through Friday from 8:30 a.m. to 5:00 p.m. EST. You can also contact Product Technical Support and get support information through our website at www.wiley.com/techsupport.

Before calling or writing, please have the following information available:

- Type of computer and operating system.
- Any error messages displayed.
- Complete description of the problem.

BIBLIOGRAPHY

Altman, I., & Taylor, D. (1973). *Social penetration: The development of interpersonal relationships.* New York: Holt, Rinehart & Winston.

Anckarsäter, H., Stahlberg, O., Larson, T., Hakansson, C., Jutblad, S. B., Niklasson, L., & Rastam, M. (2006). The impact of ADHD and autism spectrum disorders on temperament, character, and personality development. *American Journal of Psychiatry, 163,* 1239-1244.

Attwood, T. (2000). Strategies for improving the social integration of children with Asperger syndrome. *Autism, 4,* 85-100.

Attwood, T. (2003). Frameworks for behavioral interventions. *Child and Adolescent Psychiatric Clinics of North America, 12,* 65-86.

Azmitia, M. (2002). Self, self-esteem, conflicts, and best friendships in early adolescence. In T. M. Brinthaupt (Ed.), *Understanding early adolescent self and identity: Applications and interventions* (pp. 167-192). Albany: State University of New York Press.

Barnhill, G. P. (2007). Outcomes in adults with Asperger syndrome. *Focus on Autism and Other Developmental Disabilities, 22,* 116-126.

Barnhill, G. P., Cook, K. T., Tebbenkanmp, K., & Myles, B. S. (2002). The effectiveness of social skills intervention targeting nonverbal communication for adolescents with Asperger syndrome and related pervasive developmental delays. *Focus on Autism and Other Developmental Disabilities, 17,* 112-118.

Baron-Cohen, S. (1995). *Mindblindness: An essay on autism and theory of mind.* Cambridge, MA: MIT Press.

Baron-Cohen, S., Leslie, A., & Frith, U. (1985). Does the autistic child have a "theory of mind"? *Cognition, 21,* 37-46.

Barry, C. M., Madsen, S. D., Nelson, L. J., Carroll, J. S., & Badger, S. (2009). Friendship and romantic relationship qualities in emerging adulthood: Differential associations with identity development and achieved adulthood criteria. *Journal of Adult Development, 16,* 209-222.

Barry, T. D., Klinger, L. G., Lee, J. M., Palardy, N., Gilmore, T., & Bodin, S. D. (2003). Examining the effectiveness of an outpatient clinic-based social skills group for high-functioning children with autism. *Journal of Autism and Developmental Disorders, 33,* 685-701.

Baumeister, R. F., Zhang, L., & Vohs, K. D. (2004). Gossip as cultural learning. *Review of General Psychology, 8,* 111–121.

Bauminger, N., & Kasari, C. (2000). Loneliness and friendship in high-functioning children with autism. *Child Development, 71,* 447–456.

Bauminger, N., Shulman, C., & Agam, G. (2003). Peer interaction and loneliness in high-functioning children with autism. *Journal of Autism and Developmental Disorders, 33,* 489–507.

Bauminger, N., Solomon, M., Aciezer, A., Heung, K., Gazit, L., Brown, J., & Rogers, S. J. (2008). Children with autism and their friends: A multidimensional study in high functioning autism spectrum disorders. *Journal of Abnormal Child Psychology, 36,* 135– 150.

Baxter, A. (1997). The power of friendship. *Journal on Developmental Disabilities, 5*(2), 112–117.

Beaumont, R., & Sofronoff, K. (2008). A multi-component social skills intervention for children with Asperger syndrome: The Junior Detective Training Program. *Journal of Child Psychology and Psychiatry, 49,* 743–753.

Berndt, T. J., Hawkins, J. A., & Jiao, Z. (1999). Influences of friends and friendships on adjustment to junior high school. *Merrill-Palmer Quarterly, 45,* 13–41.

Bock, M. A. (2007). The impact of social-behavioral learning strategy training on the social interaction skills of four students with Asperger syndrome. *Focus on Autism and Other Developmental Disabilities, 22,* 88–95.

Bordia, P., DiFonzo, N., Haines, R., & Chaseling, E. (2005). Rumors denials as persuasive messages: Effects of personal relevance, source, and message characteristics. *Journal of Applied Social Psychology, 35,* 1301–1331.

Boulton, M. J., & Underwood, K. (1992). Bully/victim problems among middle school children. *British Journal of Educational Psychology, 62,* 73–87.

Bowler, D. M., Gaigg, S. B., & Gardiner, J. M. (2008). Subjective organization in the free recall learning of adults with Asperger's syndrome. *Journal of Autism and Developmental Disorders, 38,* 104–113.

Brown, B. B., & Lohr, M. J. (1987). Peer-group affiliation and adolescent self-esteem: An integration of ego-identity and symbolic-interaction theories. *Journal of Personality and Social Psychology, 52,* 47–55.

Buhrmester, D. (1990). Intimacy of friendship, interpersonal competence, and adjustment during preadolescence and adolescence. *Child Development, 61,* 1101–1111.

Buhrmester, D., & Furman, W. (1987). The development of companionship and intimacy. *Child Development, 58,* 1101–1113.

Bukowski, W. M., Hoza, B., & Boivin, M. (1993). Popularity, friendship, and emotional adjustment during early adolescence. In B. Laursen (Vol. Ed.), *New directions for child development: Close friendships in adolescence,* no. 60 (pp. 23–37). San Francisco: Jossey-Bass.

Bukowski, W. M., Hoza, B., & Boivin, M. (1994). Measuring friendship quality during pre- and early adolescence: The development and psychometric properties of the Friendship Qualities Scale. *Journal of Social and Personal Relationships, 11*(3), 471–484.

Burack, J. A., Root, R., & Zigler, E. (1997). Inclusive education for students with autism: Reviewing ideological, empirical, and community considerations. In D. J. Cohen & F. Volkmar (Eds.), *Handbook of autism and pervasive developmental disorders* (pp. 796–807). Hoboken, NJ: John Wiley & Sons.

Capps, L., Sigman, M., & Yirmija, N. (1996). Self-competence and emotional understanding in high-functioning children with autism. In M. E. Hertzig & E. A Farber (Vol. Eds.), *Annual Progress in Child Psychiatry & Child Development,* (pp. 260–279).

Carter, A. S., Davis, N. O., Klin, A., & Volkmar, F. R. (2005). Social development in autism. In F. R. Volkmar, R. Paul, A. Klin, & D. Cohen (Eds.), *Handbook of autism and pervasive developmental disorders* (pp. 312–334). Hoboken, NJ: John Wiley & Sons.

Castorina, L. L., & Negri, L. M. (2011). The inclusion of siblings in social skills training groups for boys with Asperger syndrome. *Journal of Autism and Developmental Disorders, 41,* 73–81.

Cederlund, M., Hagberg, B., & Gillberg, C. (2010). Asperger syndrome in adolescent and young adult males. Interview, self- and parent assessment of social, emotional, and cognitive problems. *Research in Developmental Disabilities, 31,* 287–298.

Chang, Y. C., Laugeson, E. A., Gantman, A., Dillon, A. R., Ellingsen, R., & Frankel, F. (in press). Predicting treatment success in social skills training for adolescents with autism spectrum disorders: The UCLA PEERS program. *Autism: The International Journal of Research and Practice.*

Church, C., Alisanski, S., & Amanullah, S. (2000). The social, behavioral, and academic experiences of children with Asperger syndrome. *Focus on Autism and Other Developmental Disabilities, 15,* 12–20.

Coie, J. D., Dodge, K. A., & Kupersmidt, J. B. (1990). Peer group behavior and social status. In S. R. Asher & J. D. Coie (Eds.), *Peer rejection in childhood* (pp. 17–59). New York: Cambridge University Press.

Coie, J. D., & Kupersmidt, J. B. (1983). A behavioral analysis of emerging social status. *Child Development, 54,* 1400–1416.

Coie, J., Terry, R., Lenox, K., Lochman, J., & Hyman, C. (1995). Childhood peer rejection and aggression as predictors of stable patterns of adolescent disorder. *Development and Psychopathology, 7,* 697–713.

Collins, W. A., & Madsen, S. D. (2006). Personal relationships in adolescence and early adulthood. In A. L. Vangelisti & D. Perlman (Eds.), *The Cambridge handbook of personal relationships* (pp. 191–209). New York: Cambridge University Press.

Constantino, J. N., & Todd, R. D. (2005). Intergenerational transmission of subthreshold autistic traits in the general population. *Biological Psychiatry, 57,* 655–660.

Crick, N. R., & Grotpeter, J. K. (1996). Children's treatment by peers: Victims of relational and overt aggression. *Development and Psychopathology, 8,* 367–380.

Crick, N. R., & Ladd, G. W. (1990). Children's perceptions of the outcomes of social strategies: Do the ends justify being mean? *Developmental Psychology, 26,* 612–620.

Croen, L. A., Grether, J. K., Hoogstrate, J., & Selvin, S. (2002). The changing prevalence of autism in California. *Journal of Autism and Developmental Disorders, 32,* 207–215.

DeRosier, M. E., & Marcus, S. R. (2005). Building friendships and combating bullying: Effectiveness of S. S.GRIN at one-year follow-up. *Journal of Clinical Child and Adolescent Psychology, 24,* 140–150.

Dodge, K. A., Schlundt, D. C., Schocken, I., & Delugach, J. D. (1983). Social competence and children's sociometric status: The role of peer group entry strategies. *Merrill-Palmer Quarterly, 29,* 309–336.

Elder, L. M., Caterino, L. C., Chao, J., Shacknai, D., & De Simone, G. (2006). The efficacy of social skills treatment for children with Asperger syndrome. *Education & Treatment of Children, 29,* 635–663.

Emerich, D. M., Creaghead, N. A., Grether, S. M., Murray, D., & Grasha, C. (2003). The comprehension of humorous materials by adolescents with high-functioning autism and Asperger's syndrome. *Journal of Autism and Developmental Disorders, 33,* 253–257.

Fraley, R., & Davis, K. E. (1997). Attachment formation and transfer in young adults' close friendships and romantic relationships. *Personal Relationships, 4,* 131–144.

Frankel, F. (1996). *Good friends are hard to find: Help your child find, make, and keep friends.* Los Angeles: Perspective Publishing.

Frankel, F., & Myatt, R. (2003). *Children's friendship training.* New York: Brunner-Routledge.

Frankel, F., Myatt, R., Whitham, C., Gorospe, C., & Laugeson, E. A. (2010). A controlled study of parent-assisted children's friendship training with children having autism spectrum disorders. *Journal of Autism and Developmental Disorders, 40,* 827–842.

Frith, U. (2004). Emanuel Miller lecture: Confusions and controversies about Asperger syndrome. *Journal of Child Psychology and Psychiatry, 45,* 672–686.

Gantman, A., Kapp, S. K., Orenski, K., & Laugeson, E. A. (2011). Social skills training for young adults with high-functioning autism spectrum disorders: A randomized controlled pilot study. *Journal of Autism and Developmental Disorders, 42*(6), 1094–1103.

Gauze, C., Bukowski, W. M., Aquan-Assee, J., & Sippola, L. K. (1996). Interactions between family environment and friendship and associations with self-perceived well-being during early adolescence. *Child Development, 67,* 2201–2216.

George, T. P., & Hartmann, D. P. (1996). Friendship networks of unpopular, average, and popular children. *Child Development, 67,* 2301–2316.

Gerhardt, P. F. & Lainer, I. (2011). Addressing the needs of adolescents and adults with autism: A crisis on the horizon. *Journal of Contemporary Psychotherapy, 41,* 37–45.

Goldstein, A. P., & McGinnis, E. (2000). *Skill streaming the adolescent: New strategies and perspectives for teaching prosocial skills.* Champaign, IL: Research Press.

Gralinski, J. H., & Kopp, C. (1993). Everyday rules for behavior: Mother's requests to young children. *Developmental Psychology, 29,* 573–584.

Gresham, F. M., Sugai, G., & Horner, R. H. (2001). Interpreting outcomes of social skills training for students with high-incidence disabilities. *Exceptional Children, 67,* 331–345.

Griffin, H. C., Griffin, L. W., Fitch, C. W., Albera, V., & Gingras, H. G. (2006). Educational interventions for individuals with Asperger syndrome. *Intervention in School and Clinic, 41,* 150–155.

Hartup, W. W. (1993). Adolescents and their friends. In B. Laursen (Ed.), *New directions for child development: Close friendships in adolescence,* no. 60 (pp. 3–22). San Francisco: Jossey-Bass.

Hill, E. L. (2004). Executive dysfunction in autism. *Trends in Cognitive Sciences, 8,* 26–32.

Hillier, A., Fish, T., Coppert, P., & Beversdorf, D. Q. (2007). Outcomes of a social and vocational skills support group for adolescents and young adults on the autism spectrum. *Focus on Autism and Other Developmental Disabilities, 22,* 107–115.

Hodgdon, L. Q. (1995). Solving social-behavioral problems through the use of visually supported communication. In K. A. Quill (Ed.), *Teaching children with autism: Strategies to enhance communication and socialization* (pp. 265–286). New York: Delmar.

Hodges, E., Boivin, M., Vitaro, F., & Bukowski, W. M. (1999). The power of friendship: Protection against an escalating cycle of peer victimization. *Developmental Psychology, 35,* 94–101.

Hodges, E., Malone, M. J., & Perry, D. G. (1997). Individual risk and social risk as interacting determinants of victimization in the peer group. *Developmental Psychology, 33,* 1032–1039.

Hodges, E.V.E., & Perry, D. G. (1999). Personal and interpersonal antecedents and consequences of victimization by peers. *Journal of Personality & Social Psychology, 76,* 677–685.

Hollingshead, A. B. (1975). *Four factor index of social status.* (Available from P.O. Box 1965, Yale Station, New Haven, CT 06520, USA.)

Howlin, P. (2000). Outcome in adult life for more able individuals with autism or Asperger syndrome. *Autism, 4,* 63–83.

Howlin, P., & Goode, S. (1998). Outcome in adult life for people with autism, Asperger syndrome. In F. R. Volkmar (Ed.), *Autism and pervasive developmental disorders* (pp. 209–241). New York: Cambridge University Press.

Hume, K., Loftin, R., & Lantz, J. (2009). Increasing independence in autism spectrum disorders: A review of three focused interventions. *Journal of Autism and Developmental Disorders, 39,* 1329–1338.

Humphrey, N., & Symes, W. (2010). Perceptions of social support and experience of bullying among pupils with autistic spectrum disorders in mainstream secondary schools. *European Journal of Special Needs Education, 25,* 77–91.

Jennes-Coussens, M., Magill-Evans, J., & Koning, C. (2006). The quality of life of young men with Asperger syndrome: A brief report. *Autism, 10,* 511–524.

Johnson, S. A., Blaha, L. M., Houpt, J. W., & Townsend, J. T. (2010). Systems factorial technology provides new insights on global-local information processing in autism spectrum disorders. *Journal of Mathematical Psychology, 54,* 53–72.

Kapp, S. K., Gantman, A., & Laugeson, E. A. (2011). Transition to adulthood for high-functioning individuals with autism spectrum disorders. In M. R. Mohammadi (Ed.), *A comprehensive book on autism spectrum disorders* (pp. 451–488). Rijeka, Croatia: InTech. Available at www.zums.ac.ir/files/research/site/medical/Mental%20and%20 Behavioural%20Disorders%20and%20Diseases%20of%20the%20Nervous%20System/ A_Comprehensive_Book_on_Autism_Spectrum_Disorders.pdf

Kasari, C., & Locke, J. (2011). Social skills interventions for children with autism spectrum disorders. In D. G. Amaral, G. Dawson, & D. H. Geschwind (Eds.), *Autism spectrum disorders* (pp. 1156–1166). New York: Oxford University Press.

Kerbel, D., & Grunwell, P. (1998a). A study of idiom comprehension in children with semantic-pragmatic difficulties. Part I: Task effects on the assessment of idiom comprehension in children. *International Journal of Language & Communication Disorders, 33*(1), 1–22.

Kerbel, D., & Grunwell, P. (1998b). A study of idiom comprehension in children with semantic-pragmatic difficulties. Part II: Between-groups results and discussion. *International Journal of Language and Communication Disorders 33*(1), 23–44.

Klin, A. (2011). From Asperger to modern day. In D. G. Amaral, G. Dawson, & D. H. Geschwind (Eds.), *Autism spectrum disorders* (pp. 44–59). New York: Oxford University Press.

Klin, A., & Volkmar, F. R. (2003). Asperger syndrome: Diagnosis and external validity. *Child and Adolescent Psychiatric Clinics of North America, 12,* 1–13.

Klin, A., Volkmar, F. R., & Sparrow, S. S. (2000). *Asperger syndrome.* New York: Guilford Press.

Koegel, L. K., Koegel, R. L., Hurley, C., & Frea, W. D. (1992). Improving social skills and disruptive behavior in children with autism through self-management. *Journal of Applied Behavior Analysis, 25,* 341–353.

Koning, C., & Magill-Evans, J. (2001). Social and language skills in adolescent boys with Asperger syndrome. *Autism, 5,* 23–36.

Krasny, L., Williams, B. J., Provencal, S., & Ozonoff, S. (2003). Social skills interventions for the autism spectrum: Essential ingredients and a model curriculum. *Child and Adolescent Psychiatry Clinics of North America, 12,* 107–122.

Larson, R., & Richards, M. H. (1991). Daily companionship in late childhood and early adolescence: Changing developmental contexts. *Child Development, 62,* 284–300.

Lasgaard, M., Nielsen, A., Eriksen, M. E., & Goossens, L. (2009). Loneliness and social support in adolescent boys with autism spectrum disorders. *Journal of Autism and Developmental Disorders, 40,* 218–226.

Laugeson, E. A., Ellingsen, R., Sanderson, J., Tucci, L., & Bates, S. (2012). The ABC's of teaching social skills to adolescents with autism spectrum disorders in the classroom: The UCLA PEERS program. Manuscript submitted for publication.

Laugeson, E. A., & Frankel, F. (2010). *Social skills for teenagers with developmental and autism spectrum disorders: The PEERS treatment manual.* New York: Routledge.

Laugeson, E. A., Frankel, F., Gantman, A., Dillon, A. R., & Mogil, C. (2012). Evidence-based social skills training for adolescents with autism spectrum disorders: The UCLA PEERS program. *Journal of Autism and Developmental Disorders, 42*(6), 1025–1036.

Laugeson, E. A., Frankel, F., Mogil, C., & Dillon, A. R. (2009). Parent-assisted social skills training to improve friendships in teens with autism spectrum disorders. *Journal of Autism and Developmental Disorders, 39,* 596–606.

Laugeson, E. A., Paley, B., Frankel, F., & O'Connor, M. (2011). *Project Good Buddies trainer workbook.* Atlanta: US Department of Health and Human Services, Centers for Disease Control and Prevention.

Laugeson, E. A., Paley, B., Schonfeld, A., Frankel, F., Carpenter, E. M., & O'Connor, M. (2007). Adaptation of the Children's Friendship Training program for children with fetal alcohol spectrum disorders. *Child & Family Behavior Therapy, 29*(3), 57–69.

Laursen, B., & Koplas, A. L. (1995). What's important about important conflicts? Adolescents' perceptions of daily disagreements. *Merrill-Palmer Quarterly, 41,* 536–553.

Little, L. (2001). Peer victimization of children with Asperger spectrum disorders. *Journal of the American Academy of Child & Adolescent Psychiatry, 40,* 995.

Mandelberg, J., Frankel, F., Gorospe, C., Cunningham, T. D., & Laugeson, E. A. (in press). Long-term outcomes of parent-assisted Children's Friendship Training for children with autism spectrum disorders. *Journal of Mental Health Research in Intellectual Disabilities.*

Mandelberg, J., Laugeson, E. A., Cunningham, T. D., Ellingsen, R., Bates, S., & Frankel, F. (in press). Long-term treatment outcomes for parent-assisted social skills training for adolescents with autism spectrum disorders: The UCLA PEERS program. *Autism: The International Journal of Research and Practice, Special Issue on Evidence-Based Treatments for Autism Spectrum Disorders.*

Marriage, K. J., Gordon, V., & Brand, L. (1995). A social skills group for boys with Asperger's syndrome. *Australian & New Zealand Journal of Psychiatry, 29,* 58–62.

Matson, J. L. (2007). Determining treatment outcome in early intervention programs for autism spectrum disorders: A critical analysis of measurement issues in learning-based interventions. *Research in Developmental Disabilities, 28,* 207-218.

Matson, J. L., Matson, M. L., & Rivet, T. T. (2007). Social-skills treatments for children with autism spectrum disorders: An overview. *Behavior Modification, 31,* 682-707.

McGuire, K. D., & Weisz, J. R. (1982). Social cognition and behavior correlates of preadolescent chumship. *Child Development, 53,* 1478-1484.

McKenzie, R., Evans, J. S., & Handley, S. J. (2010). Conditional reasoning in autism: Activation and integration of knowledge and belief. *Developmental Psychology, 46,* 391-403.

Mehzabin, P., & Stokes, M. A. (2011). Self-assessed sexuality in young adults with high-functioning autism. *Research in Autism Spectrum Disorders, 5,* 614-621.

Mesibov, G. B. (1984). Social skills training with verbal autistic adolescents and adults: A program model. *Journal of Autism and Developmental Disorders, 14,* 395-404.

Mesibov, G. B., & Stephens, J. (1990). Perceptions of popularity among a group of high-functioning adults with autism. *Journal of Autism and Developmental Disorders, 20,* 33-43.

Miller, P. M., & Ingham, J. G. (1976). Friends, confidants and symptoms. *Social Psychiatry, 11,* 51-58.

Morrison, L., Kamps, D., Garcia, J., & Parker, D. (2001). Peer mediation and monitoring strategies to improve initiations and social skills for students with autism. *Journal of Positive Behavior Interventions, 3,* 237-250.

Müller, E., Schuler, A., & Yates, G. B. (2008). Social challenges and supports from the perspective of individuals with Asperger syndrome and other autism spectrum disabilities. *Autism, 12,* 173-190.

Murray, D. S., Ruble, L. A., Willis, H., & Molloy, C. A. (2009). Parent and teacher report of social skills in children with autism spectrum disorders. *Language, Speech and Hearing Services in Schools, 40,* 109-115.

Nelson, J., & Aboud, F. E. (1985). The resolution of social conflict between friends. *Child Development 56,* 1009-1017.

Newcomb, A. F., & Bagwell, C. L. (1995). Children's friendship relations: A meta-analytic review. *Psychological Bulletin, 117,* 306-347.

Newcomb, A. F., Bukowski, W. M., & Pattee, L. (1993). Children's peer relations: A meta-analytic review of popular, rejected, neglected, controversial, and average sociometric status. *Psychological Bulletin, 113,* 99-128.

Newman, B., Reinecke, D. R., & Meinberg, D. L. (2000). Self-management of varied responding in three students with autism. *Behavioral Interventions, 15,* 145-151.

O'Connor, A. B., & Healy, O. (2010). Long-term post-intensive behavioral intervention outcomes for five children with autism spectrum disorder. *Research in Autism Spectrum Disorders, 4,* 594-604.

O'Connor, M. J., Frankel, F., Paley, B., Schonfeld, A. M., Carpenter, E., Laugeson, E., & Marquardt, R. (2006). A controlled social skills training for children with fetal alcohol spectrum disorders. *Journal of Consulting and Clinical Psychology, 74*(4), 639-648.

O'Connor, M., Laugeson, E. A., Mogil, C., Lowe, E., Welch-Torres, K., Keil, V., & Paley, B. (2012). Translation of an evidence-based social skills intervention for children with prenatal alcohol exposure in a community mental health setting. *Alcoholism: Clinical and Experimental Research, 36*(1), 141-152.

Olweus, D. (1993). Bullies on the playground: The role of victimization. In C. H. Hart (Ed.), *Children on playgrounds* (pp. 45–128). Albany: State University of New York Press.

Orsmond, G. L., Krauss, M. W., & Selzter, M. M. (2004). Peer relationships and social and recreational activities among adolescents and adults with autism. *Journal of Autism and Developmental Disorders, 34,* 245–256.

Ozonoff, S., & Miller, J. N. (1995). Teaching theory of mind: A new approach to social skills training for individuals with autism. *Journal of Autism and Developmental Disorders, 25,* 415–433.

Parker, J. G., & Asher, S. R. (1993). Friendship and friendship quality in middle childhood: Links with peer group acceptance and feelings of loneliness and social dissatisfaction. *Developmental Psychology, 29,* 611–621.

Parker, J., Rubin, K., Price, J., & de Rosier, M. (1995). Peer relationships, child development, and adjustment. In D. Cicchetti & D. Cohen (Eds.), *Developmental psychopathology: Risk, disorder, and adaptation* (Vol. 2, pp. 96–161). Hoboken, NJ: John Wiley & Sons.

Perry, D. G., Kusel, S. J., & Perry, L. C. (1988). Victims of aggression. *Developmental Psychology, 24,* 807–814.

Perry, D. G., Williard, J. C., & Perry, L. C. (1990). Peer perceptions of the consequences that victimized children provide aggressors. *Child Development, 61,* 1310–1325.

Phillips, C. A., Rolls, S., Rouse, A., & Griffiths, M. D. (1995). Home video game playing in schoolchildren: A study of incidence and patterns of play. *Journal of Adolescence, 18,* 687–691.

Putallaz, M., & Gottman, J. M. (1981). An interactional model of children's entry into peer groups. *Child Development, 52,* 986–994.

Rao, P. A., Beidel, D. C., & Murray, M. J. (2008). Social skills interventions for children with Asperger's syndrome or high-functioning autism: A review and recommendations. *Journal of Autism and Developmental Disorders, 38,* 353–361.

Rapin, I. (1999). Appropriate investigations for clinical care versus research in children with autism. *Brain & Development, 21,* 152–156.

Reichow, B., & Volkmar, F. R. (2010). Social skills interventions for individuals with autism: Evaluation for evidence-based practices within a best evidence synthesis framework. *Journal of Autism and Developmental Disorders, 40,* 149–166.

Remington, A., Swettenham, J., Campbell, R., & Coleman, M. (2009). Selective attention and perceptual load in autism spectrum disorder. *Psychological Science, 20,* 1388–1393.

Riggio, R. (1989). Assessment of basic social skills. *Journal of Personality and Social Psychology, 51,* 649–660.

Rubin, Z., & Sloman, J. (1984). How parents influence their children's friendships. In M. Lewis (Ed.), *Beyond the dyad* (pp. 223–250). New York: Plenum.

Sansosti, F. J., & Powell-Smith, K. A. (2006). Using social stories to improve the social behavior of children with Asperger syndrome. *Journal of Positive Behavior Interventions, 8,* 43–57.

Schopler, E., Mesibov, G. B., & Kunce, L. J. (1998). *Asperger's syndrome or high-functioning autism?* New York: Plenum Press.

Shantz, D. W. (1986). Conflict, aggression and peer status: An observational study. *Child Development, 57,* 1322–1332.

Shattuck, P., Seltzer, M., Greenberg, M. M., Orsmond, G. I., Bolt, D., Kring, S., et al. (2007). Change in autism symptoms and maladaptive behaviors in adolescents and adults with an autism spectrum disorder. *Journal of Autism and Developmental Disorders, 37,* 1735–1747.

Shtayermann, O. (2007). Peer victimization in adolescents and young adults diagnosed with Asperger's syndrome: A link to depressive symptomatology, anxiety symptomatology and suicidal ideation. *Issues in Comprehensive Pediatric Nursing, 30,* 87–107.

Sigman, M., & Ruskin, E. (1999). Continuity and change in the social competence of children with autism, Down syndrome, and developmental delays. *Monographs of the Society for Research in Child Development, 64,* 114.

Smith, T., Scahill, L., Dawson, G., Guthrie, D., Lord, C., Odom, S., et al. (2007). Designing research studies on psychosocial interventions in autism. *Journal of Autism and Developmental Disorders, 37,* 354–366.

Solomon, M., Goodlin-Jones, B., & Anders, T. F. (2004). A social adjustment enhancement intervention for high-functioning autism, Asperger's syndrome, and pervasive developmental disorder NOS. *Journal of Autism & Developmental Disabilities, 34*(6), 649–668.

Spek, A. A., Scholte, E. M., & Van Berckelaer-Onnes, I. A. (2010). Theory of mind in adults with HFA and Asperger syndrome. *Journal of Autism and Developmental Disorders, 40,* 280–289.

Starr, E., Szatmari, P., Bryson, S., & Zwaigenbaum, L. (2003). Stability and change among high-functioning children with pervasive developmental disorders: A 2-year outcome study. *Journal of Autism and Developmental Disorders, 33,* 15–22.

Sterling, L., Dawson, G., Estes, A., & Greenson, J. (2008). Characteristics associated with presence of depressive symptoms in adults with autism spectrum disorders. *Journal of Autism and Developmental Disorders, 38,* 1011–1018.

Stokes, M., Newton, N., & Kaur, A. (2007). Stalking, and social and romantic functioning among adolescents and adults with autism spectrum disorders. *Journal of Autism and Developmental Disorders, 37,* 1969–1986.

Sullivan, A., & Caterino, L. C. (2008). Addressing the sexuality and sex education of individuals with autism spectrum disorders. *Education and Treatment of Children, 31,* 381–394.

Tantam, D. (2003). The challenge of adolescents and adults with Asperger syndrome. *Child and Adolescent Psychiatric Clinics of North America, 12,* 143–163.

Taylor, J. L., & Seltzner, M. M. (2010). Changes in autism behavioral phenotype during the transition to adulthood. *Journal of Autism and Developmental Disorders, 40,* 1431–1446.

Thurlow, C., & McKay, S. (2003). Profiling "new" communication technologies in adolescence. *Journal of Language and Social Psychology, 22,* 94–103.

Travis, L. L., & Sigman, M. (1998). Social deficits and interpersonal relationships in autism. *Mental Retardation and Developmental Disabilities Research Reviews, 4,* 65–72.

Tse, J., Strulovitch, J., Tagalakis, V., Meng, L., & Fombonne, E. (2007). Social skills training for adolescents with Asperger syndrome and high-functioning autism. *Journal of Autism and Developmental Disorders, 37,* 1960–1968.

Turner-Brown, L. M., Perry, T. D., Dichter, G. S., Bodfish, J. W., & Penn, D. L. (2008). Brief report: Feasibility of social cognition and interaction training for adults with high functioning autism. *Journal of Autism and Developmental Disorders, 38,* 1777–1784.

Van Bourgondien, M. E., & Mesibov, G. B. (1987). Humor in high-functioning autistic adults. *Journal of Autism and Developmental Disorders, 17,* 417–424.

Volkmar, F. R., & Klin, A. (1998). Asperger syndrome and nonverbal learning disabilities. In E. Schopler, G. B. Mesibov, & L. J. Kunce (Eds.), *Asperger syndrome or high-functioning autism?* (pp. 107–121). New York: Plenum Press.

Warm, T. R. (1997). The role of teasing in development and vice versa. *Journal of Developmental & Behavioral Pediatrics, 18,* 97–101.

Webb, B. J., Miller, S. P., Pierce, T. B., Strawser, S., & Jones, P. (2004). Effects of social skills instruction for high-functioning adolescents with autism spectrum disorders. *Focus on Autism and Other Developmental Disabilities, 19,* 53–62.

Weiss, M. J., & Harris, S. L. (2001). Teaching social skills to people with autism. *Behavior Modification, 25*(5), 785–802.

Wentzel, K. R., Barry, C. M., & Caldwell, K. A. (2004). Friendships in middle school: Influences on motivation and school adjustment. *Journal of Educational Psychology, 96,* 195–203.

White, S. W. (2011). *Social skills training for children with Asperger syndrome and high-functioning autism.* New York: Guilford Press.

White, S. W., Keonig, K., & Scahill, L. (2007). Social skills development in children with autism spectrum disorders: A review of the intervention research. *Journal of Autism and Developmental Disorders, 37,* 1858–1868.

White, S. W., Koenig, K., & Scahill, L. (2010). Group social skills instruction for adolescents with high-functioning autism spectrum disorders. *Focus on Autism and Other Developmental Disabilities, 25,* 209–219.

White, S. W., & Robertson-Nay, R. (2009). Anxiety, social deficits, and loneliness in youth with autism spectrum disorders. *Journal of Autism and Developmental Disorders, 39,* 1006–1013.

Whitehouse, A. J., Durkin, K., Jaquet, E., & Ziatas, K. (2009). Friendship, loneliness and depression in adolescents with Asperger's syndrome. *Journal of Adolescence, 32,* 309–322.

Wing, L. (1983). Social and interpersonal needs. In E. Schopler & G. Mesibov (Eds.), *Autism in adolescents and adults* (pp. 337–354). New York: Plenum Press.

Winter, M. (2003). *Asperger syndrome: What teachers need to know.* London: Jessica Kingsley.

Wood, J. J., Drahota, A., Sze, K., Har, K., Chiu, A., & Langer, D. A. (2009). Cognitive behavioral therapy for anxiety in children with autism spectrum disorders: A randomized, controlled trial. *Journal of Child Psychology and Psychiatry, 50,* 224–234.

Wood, J. J., Drahota, A., Sze, K., Van Dyke, M., Decker, K., Fujii, C., Bahng, C., Renno, P., Hwang, W., & Spiker, M. (2009). Effects of cognitive behavioral therapy on parent-reported autism symptoms in school-aged children with high-functioning autism. *Journal of Autism & Developmental Disabilities, 39,* 1608–1612.

Woodward, L. J., & Fergusson, D. M. (2000). Childhood peer relationship problems and later risks of educational under-achievement and unemployment. *Journal of Child Psychology and Psychiatry, 41,* 191–201.

INDEX